JN300526

Legal Cultures in Human Society

Legal Cultures in Human Society
――A Collection of Articles and Essays――

Masaji Chiba

2002

SHINZANSHA International
TOKYO JAPAN

© Masaji Chiba, 2002. For copyright of individual chapters refer to the Acknowledgements. All rights reserved. No part of this publication may be reproduced, stored in a retrieval system, or transmitted in any form or by any means, electric, mechanical, photocopying, recording, or otherwise without the prior permission of the author and publisher.

Shinzansha International, TOKYO JAPAN
6-2-9-102 Hongo, Bunkyo-ku
2002. 7 first impression
Takashi Sodeyama (issue)
printed in japan
ISBN 4-7972-3083-5 C3332
NDC 321.301

Preface

This book, a collection of my articles and essays published in the years 1989-2000, concludes my pursuit of working legal cultures from a non-Western perspective.

The pursuit began during World War II applying sociological methods to the study of Japanese customary law in village communities. Among others, this research included studies of school district systems and community shrines resulting in Chiba 1962 and 1970 in Japanese. The research then broadened to non-Western traditional law in Asia, Africa, and other continents and islands, using anthropological methods, as partially represented by Chiba 1986 in English. It finally developed to include indigenous law throughout the world, non-Western as well as Western, guided by the orientation outlined in Chiba 1989 and 1993 in English as well as in Capeller & Kitamura 1998 in French. The results of these pursuits make it clear that non-Western law and human indigenous law are usually formed on cultural foundations too subtle to be conceptualized by jurisprudential methodologies. Their pursuit requires a new method adequate to conceptualize cultural factors in law. The chapters in this book were each originally produced on my way to explore the variations of legal cultures among different peoples or cultural regions, using a methodology I believed might be appropriate for the task. They may present, I hope, interested readers some aspects of human legal cultures at work viewed from the perspective of a fledgling research method, while I know that much is left to be done by cooperative and comparative studies. This book may thus suggest some of the ground still to be covered by volitional legal scientists, including non-Western scholars, to advance the scientific study of human legal culture, both Western and non-Western.

I would like to add two comments on apparent defects in the formal structure of this collection, which keen readers may discover. One is the lack of proper stylistic coordination of scholarly format such as foot notes, citations, etc. through out the chapters. However, I wished to preserve important cultural features in the publication style of each chapter as it originally appeared in English, French or American books and journals, while still giving all the chapters a degree of coordination based on international practice. The other apparent defect is my difficult, or rather erroneous English. While the French in two of the chapters was rewritten by my friends who are native specialists in legal science, the English in the other thirteen chapters was polished by different native speakers who, except one, are non-specialists in law. It is for this reason that the book resulted in a lack of coordination in linguistic style. However, I express my responsibility for all the defects still left, together with deep thankfulness to them all and the readers who were so generous toward my inadequate proficiency in foreign languages. In addition, I would like also to express that Western scholars might be similarly generous toward other non-Western scholars struggling to write under unfavorable conditions.

Beyond the generosity I have encountered, I have also enjoyed immeasurable benefits from many foreign friends through their personal and organizational activities related to various international, European, and American associations. Some of their names appear as formal Editors or Organizers in "Acknowledgements." In addition, I want to acknowledge the informal but valuable contribution made by many other friends. At this opportunity, I express my deep gratitude to them all for their favors to me, as well as Japanese circumstances that enabled me to pursue my research throughout the years, including the unfailing encouragement given by my wife, Mieko.

Masaji Chiba
January, 2002

CONTENTS

Preface
The Original of the Chapters
Acknowledgements

INTRODUCTION
Chapter 1. Appealing for the Study of Non-Western Law *1*

PART I : ASIAN LAW
Chapter 2. Legal Pluralism in Japanese History and Society *11*
Chapter 3. Legal Pluralism in Sri Lankan Society:
Toward a General Theory of Non-Western Law *63*
Chapter 4. Islamic Law transplanted in Asian Countries *79*

PART II : NON-WESTERN LAW
Chapter 5. Droit non-occidental *91*
Chapter 6. A Horizon of Legal Anthropology *99*
Chapter 7. Une conclusion d'identité culturelles juridiques
non-occidentales *103*

PART III : HUMAN LAW
Chapter 8. Folk Law in Human History and Society *141*
Chapter 9. Legal Culture of Sports *149*
Chapter 10. Legal Pluralism in Mind *167*
Chapter 11. Other Phases of Legal Pluralism in the Contemporary
World *179*
Chapter 12. World Peace through What Law ? *199*

PART IV: EXPLORING METHODOLOGY
Chapter 13. The Intermediate Variable of Human Rights *209*

Chapter 14. The Intermediate Variable of Legal Concept 217

Chapter 15. An Operational Definition of Legal Culture 231

Appendix 1. Survey Research on Crime, Criminal Law and
   Criminal Justice in Japan (1973) 245

Appendix 2. A Comparative Analysis of Attitudes toward
   Individual Rights among Westerners, Africans and
   Japanese (1975) 259

References 275

Subject Index 285

Name Index 289

The Original of the Chapters

Each chapter contained in this book was originally published as follows:

Chapter 1. "Toward a Truly International Sociology of Law through the Study of the Legal Pluralism Existing in the World," in *Legal Culture and Everyday Life*, Oñati Proceedings 1, ed. by André-Jean Arnaud, Oñati: International Institute for the Sociology of Law, 1989, pp. 129-136;

Chapter 2. "Japan," in *Asian Legal Systems: Law, Society and Pluralism in East Asia*, ed. by Poh-Ling Tan, Sydney: Butterworths, 1997, pp. 82-123;

Chapter 3. "Legal Pluralism in Sri Lankan Society: Toward a General Theory of Non-Western Law," *Journal of Legal Pluralism and Unofficial Law* (33), 1993, pp. 197-212;

Chapter 4. "Book review: *Islamic Law Transplanted in Asian Countries* (in Japanese)," *Newsletter* (32), *IUAES Commission on Folk Law and Legal Pluralism*, 1999, pp. 41-46;

Chapter 5. "Droit non-occidental," in *Une introduction aux cultures juridiques non occidentales: autour de Masaji Chiba*, ed. by Wanda Capeller & Takanori Kitamura, Bruxelles: Bruylant, 1998, pp. 37-44;

Chapter 6. "Book review: *A Horizon of Legal Anthropology: In Commemoration of 70th Birthday of Professor Masaji Chiba* (in Japanese)," *Droit et Cultures* (30), 1995, pp. 264-268;

Chapter 7. "Ce qui est en remis en question dans la culture juridique non-occidentale," in *Une introduction aux cultures juridiques non occidentles: autour de Masaji Chiba*, ed. by Wanda Capeller & Takanori Kitamura, Bruxelles: Bruylant, 1998, pp. 235-271;

Chapter 8. "Book review: *Folk Law: Essays in the Theory and Practice of Lex Non Scripta*, 2 vols, ed. by Alison D. Renteln & Alan Dundes," *Asian Folklore Studies* 65 (2), 1995, pp. 319-322;

Chapter 9. "Sports Law as a Sub-Culture and a Supra-Culture," Tokai University *Journal of Behavioral and Social Sciences*, Vol. 1994 (3), pp. 225-241;

Chapter 10. "Legal Pluralism in Mind: A Non-Western View," in *Legal Polycentricity: Consequences of Pluralism in Law*, ed. by Hanne Petersen & Henrik Zahle, Aldershot: Dartmouth, 1995, pp. 71-83;

Chapter 11. "Other Phases of Legal Pluralism in the Contemporary World," *Ratio Juris* 11 (3), 1998, pp. 228-245;

Chapter 12. "World Peace through What Law?," *The International Journal of Humanities and Peace* 11 (2), 1995-96, pp. 77-79;

Chapter 13. "Seeking for the Intermediate Variable of Human Rights," *The International Journal of Humanities and Peace* 16 (1), 2000, pp. 94-95;

Chapter 14. "The Intermediate Variable of Legal Concepts," *Journal of Legal Pluralism and Unofficial Law* (41), 1998, pp. 131–143;

Chapter 15. "An Operational Definitin of Legal Culture in View of both Western and Non-Western," in *Changing Legal Cultures*, Oñati Pre-Publications, ed. by Johannes Feest & Erhard Blankenburg, Oñati: International Institute for the Sociology of Law, 1997, pp. 93–107.

Acknowledgements

The author and publisher of this book express many thanks to the following publishers and editors for their permission to use copyright material:

International Institute for the Sociology of Law directed by Bill Felstiner, and André-Jean Arnaud, Johannes Feest and Erthard Blankenburg, for Chapters 1 and 15;

Butterworths and Poh-Ling Tan, for Chapter 2;

Journal of Legal Pluralism and Unofficial Law edited by Gordon Woodman, and Carol Geenhouse, Fons Strijbosch and André-Jean Arnaud, for Chapters 3 and 14;

Newsletter, IUAES Commission on Folk Law and Legal Pluralism edited by Fons Strijbosch, and Malanie G. Wiber, for Chapter 4;

Etablissements Emile Bruylant, S.A., and Wanda Capeller, Takanori Kitamura, André-Jean Arnaud, for Chapters 5 and 7;

Centre Droit et Cultures and Norbert Rouland for Chapter 6;

Asian Folklore Studies of Nanzan University and Peter Knecht for Chapter 8;

Tokai University *Journal of Behavioral and Social Sciences* direted by Rei Shiratori for Chapter 9;

Ashgate Publishing Limited, and Hanne Petersen and Henrik Zahle, for Chapter 10;

Blackwell Publishers, and Enrico Pattaro, Alessandra Facchi and Gianfrancesco Zanetti, for Chapter 11;

The International Journal of Humanities and Peace edited by Vasant V. Merchant for Chapters 12 and 13.

Thanks are also extended to:

Norbert Rouland, André-Jean Arnaud, and David Engel for their polishing/rewriting author's foreign languages in Chapters 5, 7, and Preface respectively;

Japan Society for the Promotion of Sciences for their Grant-in-Aid for Scientific. Research (Grant-in-Aid for Publication of Scientific Research Results) in 2002.

INTRODUCTION

Chapter 1. Appealing for the Study of Non-Western Law*

This ceremony is to inaugurate the Oñati International Institute for the Sociology of Law, which was created through an official agreement between the Basque Government and the ISA Research Committee on Sociology of Law. To begin my lecture today, I would like to ask you to allow me first to recall my personal memories related to the Research Committee and this Institute in fulfilling this honorable role of speaking to you on this memorable occasion.

There is a popular saying in Japan, literally translated, "to doubt one's ears," when something beyond all expectations happens to a person. I doubted my ears when I received a telephone call from Professor André-Jean Arnaud, Director of this Institute, inviting me to give the inauguration lecture, because I had never imagined such an important role to be played by myself. The reason for that thought stemmed from a fixed idea and reluctance of mine.

The fixed idea was an expectation which has become molded in my mind since I started my studies at a graduate school in Japan forty-six years ago, and which has been reinforced since I joined the international circle of the sociology of law on the occasion of the annual meeting of the Research Committee in Evian in 1966. The expectation was that all the leading roles in this discipline are to be filled by Western scholars. This expectation is founded on confirmed facts which are evident in the development of the discipline. The sociology of law came into existence through the achievements of Western forerunners, as is duly represented by Eugen Ehrlich. The Research Committee, the first international organization for the sociology of law, was created by Western scholars and has been operated under their leadership. And the epoch-making creation of this Institute was made possible by their prompt decision to accept the favorable, or rather utopian, offer of the Basque Government. As a matter of course in this connection, I expected Western scholars at work to assume all the formal roles in this inauguration ceremony as well.

My reluctance was in immediately accepting Professor Arnaud's personal initiative to nominate me to deliver the inauguration lecture on the focus of non-Western law. Truly, I am convinced of the significance of the topic in the contemporary sociology of law, and was pleased by his appreciation of the topic and my achievements on it. But, for a moment I was not convinced of my qualification to accept his invitation.

However, after a moment during the telephone conversation with him, both the fixed idea and the reluctance began to shift when two facts among many othres in relation to the Research Committee became particularly vivid in my memory from the past.

One was its annual meeting for 1975 under the presidency of Professor Jan Glastra van Loon, which was held at a beautiful mountain site at the foot of Mt. Fuji in Japan. The Secretary of the Research Committee, to whose assistance I owed much in organizing the meeting, was the present President, Professor Jean van Houtte. In consideration that the meeting was the first one which was held outside of Western countries, we Japanese organizers proposed an idea to add a session to discuss "Law in Developing Countries".

Much to our happiness, we succeeded in receiving a quick, positive acceptance of our proposal from the Board of the Research Committee, and also, a favorable decision from UNESCO to provide the traveling expenses for the four specialists from Asian and African countries whom we had planned to invite. In this way, the first appearance of the topic on non-Western law in the Research Committee activities and the first participation of scholars from Third World countries were realized. The memory of this meeting succeedingly reminded me of a session that I organized on "Modern Law vs. Traditional Law" at the annual meeting of the Research Committee in Uppsala in 1978. Those memories began to urge me to feel my responsibility to present my idea of non-Western law at this occasion more than ten years after the Uppsala meeting.

The other was what I heard several years ago from Professor William M. Evan who happened to visit Tokyo, when I asked him why such a sociologist like him had thought of organizing in early 1960's the ISA Research Committee on Sociology of Law in agreement with another sociologist, Professor Adam Podgorecki. I was strongly impressed by his answer having suggested the admirable outcome of their personal initiative. In fact, they did not think at first of organizing an international association. but they simply wanted to have another meeting with other interested scholars when they had a chance in the U.S.A. to discuss the common problems of law. Soon after, they consulted with a senior law professor about their idea; and the ISA Research Committee on Sociology of Law was eventually organized as the manifestation of their efforts with the presidency of that law professor, Professor Renato Treves, sitting in the Chair of this inauguration with Professor Jean Carbonnier. This memory urged me to take the more account of the personal initiative[1].

As a result of these recollections, I moved to feel obliged to accept the invitation of Professor Arnaud.

Now returning to the main issue of my lecture, I would like, first of all, to express my profound admiration for the benefit of the Western culture, which has been created and developed by the wisdom of Western people. During my years of childhood and youth, I was both mentally and intellectually immersed in the traditional Japanese culture, a typical non-Western one. Still, my aspiration for human and social ideals, like most of the other youths', mainly directed toward the models which Western culture had achieved in art and literature, philosophy and science, human personality, social morality, and means of social control. When I started the learning of the Japanese legal system, it was taught by the teachers as received from Western countries.

My aspiration toward Western models was accelerated when I chose my special orientation to the sociology of law. Firstly because the sociology of law should be international beyond Japanese national boundaries due to its nature as a social science, while it may be developed to tackle the particular problems attributed to particular national societies. Secondly because its models had been mostly supplied by Western scholars. Because of this aspiration, I never forget the joy I felt when I was allowed to be a regular member of the Research Committee, which was still a small closed group at that time, after its annual meeting in Varna in 1970. Shortly after, the Research Committee was reorganized into an open association devoted to every volunteer in the World, and thus offered me a broader forum for my orientation.

To my regret, however, I am not sure whether I have made best use of this association, for I have been limited in my capacity for proficient foreign languages and enough traveling expenses. Still, the benefit which has been conferred upon me by the Research Committee is in fact enormous in the scientific stimuli through its activities and my communication with its members. The Research Committee has truly performed an admirable role in promoting the new social science called the sociology of law in the world through the leadership of Western scholars.

On the other hand, I feel its circumstances shifting in recent years, nearly a generation after its birth.

Firstly, many new associations have internationally been organized with the purposes apparently similar to that of the Research Committee. When it was first organized for the sociology of law, there was no other international organization with similar purposes. There were two national associations: one, the Japanese of a closed character for their particular cultural backgrounds and another, the Law and Society Association in the U.S.A. open to abroad; but each had independent activities, although their attitudes were cooperative with the Research Committee. Today, in contrast, in addition to many national associations organized afterwards, there are numerous international or regional associations which have been organized to promote advanced studies on various specific problems which can partially be found in the domain of the sociology of law as a whole. Furthermore, some general problems which the Research Committee had developed or suggested have begun to cross or parallel those which are treated by some established international associations for the philosophy of law, comparative law and the anthropology of law. In the face of those shifting circumstances, the international sociology of law represented by the Research Committee may be forced to reconfirm its sound *raison d'être* among those fellow associations.

Secondly, It would almost be a desperate attempt to inclusively collect various forms of overflowing publications related to the sociology of law; even to collect information on them all seems to be impossible except for a limited number of the specialists priviledged to utilize best-furnished institutions or libraries. Without any effective measure to collect the related information wholly or make reasonable selections among them to serve interested scholars, the sociology of law would be difficult to achieve its sound development deserving to be called "international". Such a measure is among others vital to the intended activities of non-Western scholars, who are, in general, prevented from enjoying existing information due to their technical incoveniences in communication and lack of sufficient financial resoruces.[2]

By way of the mention of non-Western situations, I would point out, thirdly, the growing importance of furthering the study of non-Western law systematically. I never intend to insist that it is the most important task of the contemporary sociologists of law. However, I do want to advocate it firstly because it has been my main target of study among many others in the sociology of law, and secondly because it has been too often treated unduly for its nature and importance in reality in the Western study of law prevailing in the contemporary world. It is my intention to give the study of non-Western law a due position in the catalogue of the sociology of law.

In search of the starting point of my argument for that purpose, I think of an established premise of the orthodox jurisprudence prevalent among not only Western scholars but also most of non-Western scholars. By this premise, the existing non-Western law has been deprived of its nature of law as being not authentic. Theoretically, the law which is approved as authentic should be confined to the state law of the modern nation alone. Practically at the same time, the modern state succeeded in unifying customary laws within its jurisdiction and further regarded international law outside of its jurisdiction as valid for the reason of its own acceptance. The non-Western countries have tried with no exception to become such modern states. Grounded on such a theory and a fact, "state law monism" prevailed in the entire world.

The legal monism in non-Western countries is thus living as transplanted from Western models, whether by involuntary imposition or voluntary reception, or else whether from capitalist countries or socialist countries. Faithfully to this premise, new nations endeavored in the period soon after their independence from colonial status to unify their indigenous law into the transplanted system of official law.

Before long, however, the transplanted law was found to be never working without being supplemented or, on the contrary, undermined by indigenous law. Truly, the non-Western peoples have each cherished their indigenous law as integral part of their cultural heritage. During their long histories their laws have, on occasions, encountered foreign laws, and these encounters have sometimes led to peaceful assimilation but other times to destructive struggle between indigenous law and transplanted law. The indigenous law may have sometimes failed to maintain itself, while at other times it may have succeeded either by rejecting the encountered law or by adapting itself to preserve its cultural identity. Contemporary non-Western law is thus seen as one, in a current state, in a ongoing process of self-developing indigenous law, whether successfully or not. This state of law has been known to Western people as an exception to the premise of legal monism, but hardly had been taken seriously.(cf. Chiba 1986: v)

However, some Western scholars freed from the Western bias began to pay attention to these kinds of facts and conceptualized the term "legal pluralism" as consisting of transplanted law and indigenous law in non-Western countries. I would like to thank them for two reasons. Firstly, as I am a native Japanese, they stirred up much attention to scientific exploration in behalf of non-Western scholars, who are originally obliged, as I believe, to raise such a problem of their own before the foreground of international social sciences for the accurate observation of the circumstances. And secondly, as I am a sociologist of law, because they provided a stimulus to the international sociology of law that legal pluralism be an indispensable topic of the discipline as long as it is a sociological fact of law in non-Western countries which, in reality, are larger in territorial size and population than Western countries.

I appreciate their conceptualization of legal pluralism. Still, I am hesitant in accepting its concept just like they adopted. Because the concept is limited to denote the plural structure of law in correlation between transplated law and indigenous law, in other words, state law and living law, in non-Western countries. It is my last point to investigate the actual circumstances of the legal pluralism working in the contemporary worlds, both non-Western and Western.

The term, legal pluralism, may be used to denote various types of pluralism of law insofar as its lexicographical difinition allows. In fact, some use it for the federal structure of state laws as is well-known in Western countries. I think of further two types of legal pluralism to be recognized as urgent problems in the contemporary sociology of law. One is the pluralism of another two levels of law: symbolically expressing, one of state law and international law. There are no scholars of law who would deny the valid function of internationl law in the existence and working of state law. The two levels of laws can and should be reformulated as a form of legal pluralism. The other is the legal pluralism in Western countries. Western scholars, as seen from non-Western eyes, tend not to mention the legal puralism actually existing in their countries, while we non-Westerners have much interest in it on the analogy of our own circumstances. In fact, I have often heard Western scholars discussing what is to be conceptualized as legal pluralism. For instance, living law existing and working in correlation with state law was found by Ehrlich on the basis of Western practices; contemporary European legal pluralists use the term "folk law" to be applicable to both non-Western and Western societies; and some American scholars identify indigenous law or organizational law in their society.[3]

It may be safely assumed, as a result, that legal pluralism is not limited to a particular area of human society but a universal phenomenon covering both Western and non-Western societies, and, at the same time, appearing in not only the dual structure of state law and minor customary law but also the triple of customary law, national law and international law. This is a rough idea of mine, symbolically expressed without detailed demonstration. But, I never doubt of the importance of the study of all forms of legal pluralism existing in the contemporary world. Because the sociology of law will be sure to be developed into the truly international one by advancing such a study of legal pluralism.

In conciusion, the sociology of law is required to reform itself to meet the emerging circumstantial needs for its *raison d'être*. At this very timing, the Oñati International Institute for the Sociology of Law was created by the ISA Research Committee on Sociology of Law which has just stepped into its new generation. The activities which are expected to this Institute for the benefit of the sociologists of law in the world are too many and variant to enumerate here exactly. I firmly believe, however, that the study of legal pluralism will be sure to be counted among them. Because this Institute is directed by Professor André-Jean Arnaud who edited a dictionary of the sociology and theory of law collecting Western achievements with an unprecented broad perspective, and who still self-criticizes it stating in its Introduction that "in the final analysis, this Dictionary showes itself to be terribly western, definitively western".

Notes

(*) This chapter was originally the inauguration lecture which I delivered at the International Institute for the Sociology of Law, instituted by the ISA Research Committee on Sociology of Law at Oñati, Spain, on May 24, 1989.

(1) Cf. IISL 1991 for the accurate history of the ISA RCSL.

(2) The utilization of computer which today has prevailed among almost all active scientists was limited to a small number of legal scholars at that time of this lecture.

(3) See Chapter 11 for still other phases of legal pluralism.

Part I

ASIAN LAW

Chapter 2. Legal Pluralism in Japanese History and Society

1. Introduction——Japan in the world and Asia

[1. 1]

In the past, Japan has often been regarded by the West as a country strangely characterised by the coexistence of pairs of contrasting features. For example, it has a dense population in a small geographical area and social cohesion combined with occasional individual activities. Other such dichotomies have included Japan's economic prosperity despite its poor natural resources and the national coexistence of tradition and modernity, as exemplified by the transplanting of a modern Western legal system into a traditional culture. This pattern of contrasting features can even be seen in the cultural symbols of the chrysanthemum and the sword. However, after World War II, Western scholars began to recognise some unifying characteristics in Japanese society. For example, the homogeneity of the people, the collective principle of *wa* (harmony), the emphasis on a vertical hierarchy, a sense of *amae* (indulgent dependence), a tendency to imitate rather than create and a readiness to accommodate contradictory principles and philosophies.

From an East Asian perspective, this kind of analysis is superficial and lacks real insight into the people and the culture. In ancient times, Japan's relation to surrounding countries was limited, its only contact with other civilisations consisting of the one-sided introduction of Chinese and Indian cultures. Then, in premodern times, Japanese merchants, emigrants, warriors and intellectuals visited neighbouring countries, such as Thailand and Korea, to engage in both peaceful and aggressive activities.[1] Modern Japan's policy of 'catching up' with Western civilisation succeeded to the extent that it gave Japan the reputation of being the forerunner in westernisation among the Asian countries; however, it failed to the extent that it resulted in the imitation of Western colonialism in the Asian region,

12 Chapter 2. Legal Pluralism in Japanese History and Society

leading ultimately to the extension of World War II to Asia. After the war, Japan was, and is, considered to have achieved the most advanced economic growth amongst the East Asian countries, but it still fails to give serious consideration to its neighbouring peoples. As a result, the attitude of these neighbouring countries to Japan is ambivalent. The aim of this chapter, by analysing the internal structure of the Japanese legal system, is to clarify some of the perceptions which may have contributed to this ambivalence.[2]

2. Methodoloical comments[3]

Legal pluralism

[2. 1]

Legal pluralism is an appealing, productive approach to the study of contemporary legal systems in the world. However, its value as a scientific methodology is still heuristic, and it is at the frontier of post-modern jurisprudence. Thus, there are some issues which require clarification in order for it to be an effective scientific approach.

The concept of 'legal pluralism' is generally used to denote the 'situation in which two or more legal systems coexist in the same social field'.[4] This pluralism is often taken to mean major state law being transplanted from Western countries to non-Western countries and coexisting with traditional minor indigenous law: in other words, the existence of a dual structure. The concept of this dual structure raises problems of interpretation and in fact has limitations in its application. It tends to disregard, first, the dual structure existing in Western countries, second, plural structures existing within both the state law and minor law and, third, legal pluralism existing across plural countries. These issues may not be important from a Western perspective, but they are of vital significance from the non-Western one. Advocates of the non-Western perspective are rare in the world of legal science, raising the question of who observes whose law. My scheme of legal pluralism, which may allow non-Westerners to observe their own law, requires these questions to be answered.

[2. 2]

The significance of state law for legal pluralism should be reexamined, for, in reality, it does not form a single structure as is the premise of the established doctrine of state law monism. The state law of a country coexists normally with various other systems of law, thus exhibiting a form of legal pluralism. For instance, it often horizontally coexists with other forms of law ofiicially authorised by state law, such as religious law (Canon law, Protestant church laws. Islamic law, etc.) and military law. Then vertically, state law officially authorises different levels of sub-systems, ranging from local self-governing bodies which exist in most countries to autonomous governments existing in federated states such as Russia, USA and Australia. Other forms of legal pluralism surrounding state law are also found in extraordinary circumstances such as a national govemment encountering opposing revolutionary governments and their laws. This was, and is, the situation often seen in Third World countries, and in mainland China and Taiwan as well as North Korea and South Korea. The concept of legal pluralism must be reformulated so that it can correctly represent these facts.

Unofficial law, customary law, native law, tribal law, people's law and folk law have all been included by scholars in the category of minor law (another component of the alleged dual structure) to the extent that they work to regulate people's daily lives and social organisations even when not officially authorised by state law. However, studies have not been sufficiently balanced, having focused mainly on Africa and North America. More attention needs to be paid to European (and to other Western) countries, as Western scholars have tended to neglect observing their own circumstances. In addition, little interest has been shown in the existence of minor laws in areas such as Latin America, Oceania, Scandinavia, Siberia and Central Asia.

When reference is made to state law, its sociological unit is not usually considered. This is because of the doctrine of state law monism. which limits the concept of law, as a special form of social norm, to state law alone and further limits the sociological unit of the law to the sovereign state.[5] In contrast, the respective sociological units of the various forms of minor law need to be discerned accurately. There are various different kinds of sociological units: for instance, local units in small or large communities, extended families or clans, ethnic units in tribes or nations, religious units of different doctrines or denominations, stratified units in classes or professions, and voluntary associations with a sociological meaning. These shall be referred to as 'socio-legal entities', due to their special relevance to law.[6] In summary, the investigation of legal pluralism is not to be limited to the jurisdiction of state law, as is ordinarily the case, but is to be extended first to each socio-legal entity within the national boundary.

[2. 3]

For this reason, the socio-legal entities which extend across and beyond national boundaries must next be investigated.[7] This idea is not recognised in the prevailing perception of legal pluralism, undoubtedly as a result of the identification of legal pluralism as a dual structure. However, the word 'plural' means not only two, but two or more. Also, 'international law', which is indispensable in the total system of human law, exists outside the jurisdiction of state law. The dual structure concept, therefore, should at least be revised into that of a triple structure, to include this third form of law which exists across and beyond plural state laws.

The term 'international law', however, is set within a framework of the established concepts of state law monism and Western law universalism. The term 'international law'[8] may tentatively be replaced by the term 'world law'. 'World law' includes every form of law validly prevailing across and beyond national boundaries, such as international custom,[9] social norms,[10] humanity law[11] and various unofficial but formal agreements between private organisations and persons from different countries. World law can then be further classified into regional law, law which is valid within a number of national boundaries in a certain region, and universal law, law which is valid across and beyond every national boundary.

The topic of legal pluralism can therefore schematically be explored as a triple structure of minor law, state law and world law, each of which is maintained by different levels of socio-legal entities. One task may be to reformulate the legal pluralism maintained by a particular socio-legal entity in the form of its whole working structure and function.[12] With research in all three levels, each legal pluralism, both horizontal and vertical, of the socio-legal entity will reveal a particular cultural feature. This is because the particular combination of various laws in the legal pluralism of a socio-legal entity is nothing but the manifestation of the legal culture of that socio-legal entity.

Legal culture

[2. 4]

Interest in legal culture emerged earlier than interest in legal pluralism, and was stimulated by discussions on political culture by political scientists. But in the past 20 years or so, legal culture and legal pluralism have developed some correlation because both topics have the common aim of searching for legal factors other than state law. However, the focus and results of each topic have been rather different. Legal culture has been studied by scholars from every field of legal theory, including comparative law as well as philosophy, sociology, anthropology and history of law, whereas legal pluralism has been studied by scholars focusing mainly on anthropological and/or sociological studies. The main objective of legal culture is to identify cultural factors underlying the structure and function of state law, in other words, 'legal tradition',[13] while the main objective of legal pluralism is to identify another system of law coexisting with state law. Accordingly, studies of legal culture have encompassed both Western and non-Western countries,[14] whereas legal pluralism was mainly focused on non-Western countries.

There is no generally approved definition of the term 'legal culture'. Concepts such as consciousness of law, attitudes towards law, values and ideology of law, have been useful in finding important cultural traits in the law. However, few of these concepts are formulated elaborately enough to be used as scientific tools. A rare example is Blankenburg's idea that law is composed of four variables: law in action channeled by the institutional infrastructure of the legal system, patterns of legally relevant behaviour, law in books, and legal consciousness.[15] However, these definitions are useful only for Western legal systems. Their defects include, first, that they are based on the established belief of state law monism which is not applicable to non-Western circumstances. Second, the scientific value of these definitions remains on a heuristic level with no definitive operational definition provided, thus making it impossible for other scholars to verify or nullify them. Third, there has been no effective cooperation with anthropologists, thus preventing any scientific reformulation of the concept from the perspective of anthropologists and other social scientists.

[2. 5]

My definition of legal culture as a 'cultural configuration in law' [16] attempts to correct these defects. Two key concepts in this definition may require explanation. The first, 'law', includes legal pluralism in its broader meaning and will be elaborated upon in the next numbered paragraph. The second, 'cultural configuration', is derived from the established anthropological concept of Ruth Benedict, who defined it as 'a more or less consistent pattern of thought and action' of a 'significant sociological unit'.[17] However, I admit some defects still remaining in this anthropological definition: for instance, that it is not yet operationalised.

The concept of law will now be analysed, for it is pivotal in understanding the three key terms of this chapter: that is, socio-legal entity, legal pluralism and legal culture. The definition below enables observation and analysis of a certain legal culture as a whole, whereas prevailing heuristic definitions of legal culture tend to regard legal culture as the reaction of an individual person to his or her state law, that is, in the form of psychology, thought or action of individual persons. Thus, an operational definition of legal culture needs to be developed to produce a useful scientific tool.[18]

Operational definition of law

The definitions of scientific terms were methodologically divided into two categories by Kant: theological definitions, which are verified deductively on the presupposed truth as in theology or aesthetics, and philosophical definitions, which are verified inductively on inferential findings as in the social sciences or natural sciences. Established jurisprudence regards the definition of law as belonging to the former category, for it presupposes that the legitimacy of the legal system is supported by the doctrine of state law monism, connected with Western law universalism. Legal history and comparative law are aimed at searching for exceptional forms of law within that definition. The fields of sociology and anthropology of law are aimed at establishing a definition of law based on empirical data which is consistent with Kant's philosophical definition. Thus, the both concepts of legal pluralism and legal culture, which require observation of how law is received and practised, fall within Kant's philosophical definition.

The very nature of a philosophical definition requires definition to be an operational one. Some attempts have been made at developing an operational definition of law, but few of them have paid serious attention to non-Western circumstances.

This chapter ventures to define 'law' as a kind of social norm, which designates the specified qualification for entitled behaviour patterns as right, and the corresponding responsibility for obliged behaviour patterns as duty, being supported by a particular set of values and ideas on the one hand, and by the legitimate authority of a certain socio-legal entity on the other. The key components are still not fully operationalised but, with concerned efforts from interested scholars,[19] this may be the starting point in eventually obtaining a workable operational definition, which I call 'three dichotomies of law under the identity postulate' as follows.

[2. 7]

Various systems of law comprising a whole working structure maintained by socio-legal entities are classified on the basis of the source of authority of each system. There are two categories within the working structure. First, there is 'official law', which includes both 'state law' and other systems officially authorised by the state law, such as military law in many countries and religious law in Christian and Islamic countries and many others. Second, there is 'unofficial law', which prevails amongst a certain circle of people without official authorisation by the state law but which distinctly influences the effect of the official law.

The significance of this classification is that the interaction between both forms of law, whether harmonious or conflicting, can be observed. The interaction may be identified by examining how official law treats the unofficial law. For example, does the former accept or reject the latter, or is it indifferent to the latter? If there is its acceptance of the unofficial law, is this by informal toleration or formal adoption? If there is formal adoption, is this partial or whole, or has there been some modification of the original unofficial law? The findings will assist in the representation of legal pluralism in its whole structure and function. For instance, the results will show the different combinations of various systems of official law and unofficial law within a whole structure (the reasons for this difference being based on the sociological nature of the socio-legal entities concerned) and ultimately enable the comparison of the features of different legal pluralisms, that is, the legal cultures maintained by the socio-legal entities.

Plural systems of law of a socio-legal entity can also be classified on the basis of their cultural origin, being either 'indigenous law' or 'transplanted law'. There are several issues raised by this classification. First, transplantation is a general term, which means not only intentional importation and exportation but also, as I want to add, unintentional diffusion. Another term reception is rejected so as to avoid any Western bias implied by the term; that is, the Western tendency to regard dissemination of Roman law or modern Western law to other regions as the typical examples of reception, while disregarding other non-Western examples. Second, transplantation of law raises many issues relating to the existing indigenous law, such as its reaction to the transplanted law. Does the indigenous law assimilate or oppose the transplanted law, and does it do so immediately or gradually, or else latently or manifestly? Third, transplanted law may be subclassified into voluntarily received law and involuntarily imposed law.[20] This classification of a transplanted law occurs in the initial stage of transplantation, but the acculturation processes which follow may alter the character of the transplanted law so that an indigenised law is yielded. Alternatively, if the acculturation process fails, a rejected law results. The combination, or interaction, in the acculturation process and its results represent a feature of legal pluralism, or legal culture, maintained by each socio-legal entity.

The legal pluralism, or legal culture, of a socio-legal entity may be observed and analysed in its whole working structure through the above four tool concepts classified into two dichotomies. There is a third dichotomy based on 'legal

Chapter 2. Legal Pluralism in Japanese History and Society *19*

rules' or 'legal postulates' which may be useful. Although this classification may appear less important to modem law and jurisprudence,[21] it is more important, or rather vital, to the other systems of law. For example, each formalised religious law system, such as Canon law, Christian Church laws, Islamic law, seems to be well formalized. However, these systems profess to work under the imperative legal postulates derived from its religious docrines,while many other systems of religious law and a variety of secular customary laws are used to work with less formalised, perhaps not even verbalised, legal rules under the efficient control of legal postulates. The structure of each of these legal systems may appear immature or confusing, but the dichotomy of legal rules and legal postulates is a useful tool to let us accurately observe the legal system. This dichotomy allows analytical observation of the structure of such laws by assessing the degree of formalisation or verbalisation of legal rules and by confirming the function of legal postulates.

[2. 8]

By applying the above three dichotomies of tool concepts, the whole working structure of the law of a socio-legal entity, and how it is composed of various forms of legal systems, can accurately be observed. A theoretical question then arises: that is, how can those different forms of law be combined into a whole structure? Generally, a whole structure should fundamentally be integrated in its existence and function with all minor negative factors contained. It is presupposed that an integrating postulate will form the structure into an ordered whole by accepting harmonious factors and rejecting contradictory ones. This postulate is the 'identity postulate' of a legal culture. Legal postulates in a dichotomy work to orientate, or correct, legal rules within a system of law. In contrast, the identity postulate works to afford the whole structure a form of integration, although with different efficacies for different socio-legal entities. It thus represents a feature of the legal pluralism, or legal culture, of a socio-legal entity. The term identity postulate and its theoretical framework is unprecedented, but its conception can be found in leading principles of different systems of law. It is often labelled as the 'reasonableness' of Common law, the systematic coordination of state laws in continental law, Allah's precepts of Islamic law, the *Tien* principle of Chinese law, and Dharma of Indian law.

There are two conclusions resulting from the above discussion on tool concepts. First, legal pluralism may accurately be observed and analysed as a whole working structure comprising various systems of law maintained by a socio-legal entity. Second, legal culture may be represented by the cultural traits existing in the various combinations of the three dichotomies under the identity postulate. The legal system of Japan will now be described in a way which attempts to verify the above tool concepts.

3. Historical developments[22]

Original indigenous law

[3.1]

Little is known about Japanese law prior to the seventh century. Before Chinese characters were transplanted and adopted by the Japanese, the Japanese had no alphabet of their own with which to record their history. Chinese characters were known to the Japanese in earlier centuries, but the process of assimilation of these characters into their indigenous language system took place in the third century. The assimilation took place not only in language, but in almost all areas of Japanese life. This was due to the eagerness of the Japanese to transplant the culture of advanced continental civilisations, which was achieved mainly via adjacent countries in the Korean Peninsula rather than directly from the Chinese mainland.[23]

Two of the greatest systems of human philosophy and religion, Confucianism and Buddhism, were officially transplanted in 284-5 and 552 AD respectively, and became deeply acculturated into indigenous Japanese thought and ethics. In addition, various advanced arts and techniques in every field of production, such as agriculture, weaving, pottery-making, building construction, medicine and tanning, were brought to Japan by immigrants from the Peninsula. The sweeping influence of these immigrants is evidenced by the many Japanese names of Korean origin still existing in family names, place names and names of Shinto shrines in the western half of Japan.

The massive flow of immigrants was accelerated by both internal and external circumstances. The external factors were the continuing political instability and turmoil in the Peninsula, as well as the struggle for central hegemony amongst the Chinese dynasties and kingdoms. These disturbances produced a large number of refugees who were exiled or forced to escape from their own countries. Immigrants to Japan included the privileged classes, such as experienced officials and excellent technicians. Many of them were hired in the Japanese Court, and some were included in the official rank system which had been introduced by the immigrants themselves. It is possible that many other legal institutions were also introduced, although partially rather than systematically, and this was probably the first transplantation of foreign law to Japan.[24]

[3. 2]

During these periods, Japanese law was unwritten and immature, and thus was far from comprising any official legal system. Nonetheless, Japanese society could not have functioned without some sort of law, however unofficial. The law regulating people's social lives can be found in contemporary general descriptions in Chinese historical books. The most noted of these is *The Record on the Men of Wa*, which was found in the Wei History, describing the Japanese state called Yamatai (or Yamato) ruled by the Queen Himiko (or Pimiko) in the second and third centuries. According to this account, Japanese indigenous law was based on the clan system, with each clan forming a collective unit of Japanese society. A clan comprised extended families and was controlled by its chief, who protected the rights of the members and enforced their duties with occasional punishments for crimes. The law of the court organised the clan chiefs into an effective power structure, in order to control the whole of society through the clan system. The form of these laws is not clearly known, but they may be characterised as indigenous and unofficial, as official power can rarely be identified.

In this period, a more powerful polity and a more developed legal system than the unofficial clan law of the struggling clan chiefs was required effectively to govern the society as a whole. Yamatai must have been the first central government which succeeded in securing the required power through the leadership of Queen Himiko, who was reputed to be a shaman. This leads to the assertion that Yamatai had its own primitive system of law, perhaps court law, which enabled it to maintain government over competing clan laws. As a result, the whole legal system formed a primitive legal pluralism of court law and clan laws. It can also be asserted that this whole legal system was ideologically founded on the indigenous postulate which adhered to the shamanistic religio-political belief in polytheistic gods called *kami* [25] and which was later developed into Shintoism.

Two qualifications can be added to these assertions. First, some Korean law must have been transplanted, albeit unsystematically; this can be seen by the rank system in the court law and local customs among settled immigrants. Second, official law was not clearly distinguished from unofficial law; this was due to its lack of written formalities, although court law was gradually emerging into a formal state law as far as central government was concerned. For these reasons, it cannot be denied that a primitive legal pluralism had developed based on court law and clan laws, partially with transplanted Korean law and overwhelmingly with indigenous law. These traits of legal pluralism, however primitive, were the prototype of the Japanese legal system which developed in later periods into more organised legal pluralism.

Transplantation and acculturation of Chinese law

[3. 3]

Soon after, the Japanese legal system advanced beyond the primitive legal pluralism for the following reasons. Internally, the central government needed to strengthen its political foundation, for reasons of self-preservation, by successfully accommodating two growing powers, the local clan chiefs and the Court nobles. Clans were made up mostly of native Japanese descendants, although some of them included descendants of immigrant Korean families who had intermarried with native Japanese. Nobles working in the Court formed an elite group of descendants of former Tennos (emperors) or clan chiefs. A few powerful clans, such as the Soga clan, began to scheme to control, or even usurp, the throne. The situation demanded a drastic reform similar to that observed in other nations just prior to national integration.

Chapter 2. Legal Pluralism in Japanese History and Society **23**

Reform was also required for external factors such as national pride and safety, being brought about through Japan's relations with Korea. As mentioned above, Japan had received Korean manpower which was skilled in various advanced arts and techniques, and Japan had, in turn, taken up activities affecting Korea. The most conspicuous of these was the peaceful trade with Korea by Japanese activists from western islands, such as Tsushima and Kyushu, which resulted in a so-called Japanese colony settling in a southern Korean locality for a number of years. These positive relations fostered a friendly relationship between both peoples. However, ironically, due to Japanese territorial advancements into Korea, a hostile relationship also existed, the first signs of which were occasional piracies around Korean coastal areas and the more distant Chinese coasts.[26]

Soon after this, in the eighth century, the government compiled a first official history. The myth of the unbroken line of the reigning Tenno family was created, into which the people were authoritatively indoctrinated, and of which critical examination was not allowed until the end of World War II.[27] These efforts were part of a policy to transplant an advanced legal system from China, rather than from the hitherto familiar Korean countries. After several decades of both open and secret struggles among powerful nobles and clan chiefs, Prince Shotoku was appointed to a regency in 593 until his death in 622. Every successful reformative movement during this time was ascribed in official Japanese history to Prince Shotoku, including elevation of courtlaw to unique Court Law.

His alleged achievements include the institution in 603 of the Twelve Grades of Officials, a revision of the long-established ranking system modeled on the Chinese system. In 604, he promulgated the Seventeen Article Constitution, a declaration of the responsibility and duty of the officials working for the absolute authority of Tenno.[28] The Constitution further declared the obligation to respect the highest value of *wa* (harmony) and the three 'treasures' of Buddhism, that is, Buddha, Dharma and Sangha. It was also the responsibility of the officials to faithfully obey the order of Tenno, by fulfilling the duties derived from their ranks and statuses. These rights and duties designated in the Constitution might have been, in reality, no more than a proclamation of the fundamental principles of the national polity, an amalgamation of indigenous philosophy and transplanted

Chinese ethics and Buddhist ideas. Their ideological impact was enormous, because these principles appeared repeatedly in the history as an alternative legal postulate outside of the law, as will be discussed later [3. 9; 3. 4,10 & 6. 4].

[3. 4]

Then the Japanese government made major changes in terms of its international relations, by replacing that which had been dominated by the relationship with the Korean countries, to that of closer ties with China.[29] The turning point was marked by the first Japanese official envoy to the Sui Dynasty in 607, dispatched by Prince Shotoku. This was followed by envoys of the Tennos to the succeeding T'ang Dynasty in 630 and thereafter. One of the most significant results of the exchanges with China was the transplantation of Chinese law, which became the only model of the reformative Japanese law. The Chinese Code, completed by the T'ang Dynasty, had been framed in four different structures: *ritsu* (penal law), *ryo* (administrative law), *kyaku* (imperial edicts temporarily to supplement the preceding two), and *shiki* (by-laws for operation). This system was called *ritsuryo*. Along the lines of the Chinese model, the Japanese *ritsuryo* was completed in 701 but followed by later supplements and revisions, and thus the whole politico-legal institution maintained the name of the *Ritsuryo* System. The main characteristics of this institution were as follows.

The population was classified into a hierarchical system. There were nobles or officials, and commoners who were subdivided into the ordinary and the humble. Rice fields, the basic productive land of the country, were divided into the official (further divided into the Tenno and government lands) and the private (divided into allotments for farmers or allotments associated with the holding of different offices). People were obliged to pay taxes in the form of products from their allotted rice fields, and to engage in public labour and military service. The central government was constituted by the eight ministries of *Dajokan* (office of the Prime Minister) and the independent *Jingikan* (Ministry of Serving the Gods). Local administration was organised in a hierarchical order of provinces, counties and villages. These local governments communicated with the central government by the *ekiden* (post horses). The main criminal punishments were whipping, stick-beating, imprisonment, exile and death; punishments were ordered by governmental authorities in the absence of a specialised judicial institution.

The overall effect was a well-organised system of official law composed of meticulous legal rules, at least in regard to public law. Like the Chinese T'ang Code, the Japanese *Ritsuryo* System did not deal with private law.

[3. 5]
Nonetheless, the *Ritsuryo* System was never a complete copy of the Chinese model. Among the many revisions made by the Japanese, particular mention must be made of four features of the system. First, people's private rights and individual duties were left out of official law unless they directly related to the official regulation of public law. This had the effect of eventually promoting the unofficial development of indigenous law in people's social lives, both in the family and at the local level. Second, the people were officially incorporated into national status hierarchy by their graded ranks, and unofficially, into a local one by the social statuses of familial and local ties. Third, the traditional position of *Jingikan*, which had administered provincial and local Shinto shrines, was retained under the *Ritsuryo* System, although the shrine system was finally completed later in 927.[30] Fourth, the position of Tenno was ordained with supremacy to create and authorise a valid legal system; it was thus the source of law, not inside but outside of the law. The importance of these elements of the *Ritsuryo* System is indicated by the fact that some of them have survived and can be found in a different guise in the present legal system.

Although the new *Ritsuryo* System brought about remarkable changes, its reform had begun in earlier years. As early as 645, a prince and his comrade from the noble class named Kamatari of Fujiwara Family, succeeded through a *coup d'état* in expelling the then most powerful clan, Soga, who had been representative of the traditional power structure. The victors then issued an imperial rescript on reformation of policies and measures, which was generally called the Taika Reformation. The *Ritsuryo* System was the result of the rescript on establishing the official state law under the supreme authority of Tenno.[31] The form of the *Ritsuryo* was a transplant of Chinese law, but its substance concerned indigenous matters. The Seventeen Article Constitution was to declare the spirit of ongoing reformation, and the purpose of the reformation was officially to base the authority of the central government upon Tenno, while private law was to be left untouched. In reality, however, unofficial law was working as a form of private law, regulating the lives of people in families and societies. Ironically, the official law demanded in fact the latent function of the unofficial law due to its limited character, and this resulted in a pluralistic existence of official law and unofficial law.

[3. 6]

Two of the oldest literary classics, written by the order of a Tenno, had been regarded until the end of World War II as the standard sources of Japanese history. These were prepared and completed during the reformation period, for the purpose of the reformers' self-legitimisation. *Kojiki*, completed in 712, was a formal but personal record of the mythical legend designed to authorise the unbroken line of the sacred Tenno family. *Nihongi* (or *Nihon Shoki*), completed in 720, was an official compilation designed to justify Japanese history under the reign of Tenno. These records have been found to include many dubious legends, such as the expedition of Empress Jingu to Korea. Also, according to the records, most Tennos are reputed to have had a lifespan of over 100 years. Such mythical creations tended to disregard the then working Korean law, presumably in order to flaunt Japan's hegemony over Korea. This resulted in no historical records left to prove the transplantation of Korean law into Japan preceding the later transplantation of Chinese law. The Japanese inclination to ignore the sovereignty of Korea and make light of Koreans is further evidenced by the invasion of Toyotomi Hideyoshi in 1592 and 1597, and by the modern colonisation of Korea from 1910 to 1945. This course of events has reinforced the Korean tendency to hate the Japanese, leading to the contemporary ambivalence toward Japan.

Development of indigenous law

[3. 7]

Thus the transformation of Japanese official law during nearly 1200 years began with the importation of ancient Chinese law and later consisted of the importation of modern Western law. The process is known through the achievements

Chapter 2. Legal Pluralism in Japanese History and Society 27

of legal historians, both Japanese and foreign, and it will suffice to describe it briefly below, focusing on the destiny of the *Ritsuryo* System between these periods. The following is a brief list of important historical events which may suggest some remarkable phases in the destiny.

866   A descendant of Fujiwara Kamatari assumed the post of *Sessho* (Regent). Following this, members of the Fujiwara Family continued taking the post of *Kanpaku* (chief adviser to Tenno).

around 1088 Emperor Shirakawa successfully contested, after his abdication, the supremacy of the Fujiwara. He established the rule of retired emperors (*insei*) on behalf of the reigning emperor.

1167 Kiyomori of Taira Family, leader among warriors and a descendant from an ex-Tenno, became *Dajo-daijin* (prime minister), the first from among the warriors.

1192 Yoritomo of Minamoto Family, leading warrior descended from another ex-Tenno, was appointed by Tenno, after defeating the Taira family, to *Seii-taishogun* (or simply *Shogun*, Commander-in-Chief of an Expeditionary Force against the Barbarians, in fact a universal agent for Tenno).*

1585 Hideyosni of Toyotomi Family was appointed to the post of *Kanpaku* in place of *Bakufu*, after suppressing a long civil war.

1603 Ieyasu of Tokugawa Family was appointed to *Shogun* and ruled the country from Edo (Tokyo). The Tokugawa Shogunate lasted until 1868.

* He opened the first *Bakufu* (office of the Shogunate Government) in Kamakura. His *Bakufu* was substantially succeeded after 1219 by Hojo Family in Odawara, and after 1338 by Ashikaga Family in Kyoto.

The above events suggest that there had been a dual power structure of legal authority throughout this whole period. At the beginning, Tenno maintained real power being assisted by the ruling nobles. But later, the real power was entrusted to *Bakufu* to make the authority of Tenno nominal. The structure necessitated an interlinking functionality between the two different powers, for such a dual structure is likely to cause conflicting outcomes. As a result, this dual structure and its outcome have produced some important legal postulates which, as argued later [3.11 & 5.3], continue to this day.

[3. 8]

The *Ritsuryo* reformation of official law was required to meet the central government's perceived development needs. There was remarkable economic development at this time occurring all over the country. Changes in the social structure accompanied various innovations in unofficial law which regulated familial and village lives of people. Primitive local governments headed by local rulers emerged with their own law. To meet ongoing development, the *Ritsuryo* official law gradually began to be altered soon after its institution, first by partial revisions of some constituent regulations, and then by the creation of new offices outside of the *Ritsuryo* System. The latter was so regularly practised as to be formally called by the specific pronoun, *Ryoge-no-kan*. The most influential of the offices created was *Kebiishi* (Police and Judicial Chief) set up in the early eighth century with the aim of controlling the police and judiciary in Kyoto: it was a position somewhat similar to the Anglo-American magistrate. This office soon developed into the central authority of both the police and the judiciary for the whole country, for *Kebiishi* were also set up in important provincial towns, modelled after the Kyoto *Kebiishi*. Having been promoted and enforced by the Court officials, these new positions which were occupied by the *kuge* (nobles) advanced the system so far as to form a new category of law: the *Kuge* Law. The edicts or ordinances which formed *Kuge* Law were compiled in 927 in a systematic code called *Engi-shiki* (Code of Engi, after the name of the era) to become the first formal system of indigenous official law.

The trend similarly developed in local areas, before and after the tenth century. Emerging local rulers enclosed some areas called *shoen* (manors) to ensure their control over certain lands and people. Their regulations developed into another category of law, namely *Shoen* Law, similar to the European manor law. Large Shinto shrines and Buddhist temples which received large grants of land from central nobles or local rulers produced still another category of law, *Shaji* (shrines and temples) Law, which had an independent jurisdiction. As both

Shoen and *Shaji* Laws were concerned with land title and ownership, called *honjo*, those two forms of law were categorised as *Honjo* Law. *Honjo* Law was absorbed before long into another new form of law, which emerged among the ruling *buke* (*samurai*, warrior). *Buke* Law grew to be the valid legal system for all Japan from the opening of the first *Bakufu* in 1192, and came to replace existing *Kuge* Law.

Buke Law may be grouped roughly into two categories, according to modern classification: public law, which regulated the lords' relations to *Bakufu*, other lords and people under their rule, similarly to European feudal covenants among landlords, and private law, which regulated the duties of serving warriors in order to maintain their prestige or status, in a similar fashion to the European knighthood. Public law was further hierarchised into the central and the local. The central one, called *Bakufu* Law, was issued and administered by *Bakufu* with jurisdiction over the whole country.[32] The local *Buke* Law was issued by each lord to maintain his rule over his estate and people. This vertical structure later led by the Tokugawa *Bakufu* to a completion of the systems of land, tax, industries and other matters, after the preceding Toyotomi's countrywide standardization.

[3. 9]

The Tokugawa *Bakufu* incorporated the precedents set by *Buke* Law into a coordinated *Bakufu* Law as the legal basis of their regime which lasted over two and a half centuries. In the early seventeenth century, the founder of the Tokugawa *Bakufu* issued three brief but fundamental laws: Law for the Lords,[33] Law for the Imperial Court, and Law of Temples. These laws were to secure the rule of *Bakufu* over the other powers and expand the coverage of central public law to local private law. In 1742, the *Kujikata-osadamegaki* (Code of Public Power) was promulgated to compile the basic regulations for administration of public power in criminal and civil affairs into 100 articles.[34] These central *Bakufu* laws were faithfully followed by the feudal lords in the administration of their granted fiefs, which were called *Han* (feudal domain). Those laws of the local lords (*Han* Law) represented a local form of public *Buke* Law. The Tokugawa *Buke* Law thus formed an indigenous legal pluralism, consisting of *Bakufu* Law and *Han* Law in a hierarchy.

Law emerging after the *Ritsuryo* System was not limited to the above-mentioned official *Buke* Law, but expanded into various forms of unofficial law. For example, people who were engaged in agriculture or fishing in their village communities had 'communal law', constituted by their agreements regarding common use of water for rice fields, waters and seas, and other resources such as fuel and grass. The communal law was also called villagers' law or village law, for it contained rules concerning worship at local shrines and joint works for communal needs. At the same time, familial and marital ties among people produced other categories of law.[35] People living in such big cities as Kyoto, Osaka, Tokyo and capital towns of the lords' fiefs, similarly produced their own communal law, with the calling of townsmen law, for their various local and commercial activities. The communal law was used to regulate markets, guilds and transactions, as well as neighbourhood community and familial/marital ties.

The above forms of unofficial law differed and often overlapped with one another, in their sources of authority, extent of jurisdiction and formality. Still, during the Tokugawa *Bakufu*, these forms of unofficial law shared some common features. One of the most important was that each form of law was constructed on the principle of status hierarchy. Each community member had duties corresponding to his status. The duties owed by the people to their feudal lords were obvious. Each community was hierarchically structured: for instance, the villages would be headed by large landowners of highest status to control landed farmers of middle status and tenant farmers of lowest status. Another important feature was that the hierarchically constructed communities or relationships were all guided by the principle of community solidarity, a contemporary variation of the ancient *wa* (harmony).

Traits of the legal pluralism

[3.10]

In summary, in the period after the introduction of the *Ritsuryo* System, but before the existence of modern Japan, the Japanese legal system, a well-organised system of plural laws, was first derived from Chinese sources but then

Chapter 2. Legal Pluralism in Japanese History and Society 31

later wholly indigenised. Thus, the whole working system of Japanese law after the establishment of the *Ritsuryo* System should be characterised not only as indigenised Chinese law, but rather as a 'developed' indigenous law which was based on transplanted Chinese law but almost completely modified by Japanese culture. It formed a distinct legal pluralism of a complex nature. This pluralism could be broadly classified into official law and unofficial law, both of which included further sub-classes. A first form of official law was Imperial Court Law, directly dependent on the authority of Tenno, which initially had been effective prior to *Ritsuryo* law and then developed into *Kuge* Law. Its authority gradually eroded, and its jurisdiction was finally limited to Court matters alone under the real power of *Bakufu*.

A second form of official law was the dominant *Buke* Law (replacing *Kuge* Law in the *Ritsuryo* System) which represented the valid official law during the whole period under the nominal authority of Tenno. It was again divided into the central *Bakufu* Law and local *Han* Law, accompanied by the religious law of big Buddhist temples and Shinto shrines which enjoyed respect and immunity from secular powers, somewhat similarly to the churches in Europe. Unofficial law was also incorporated into a pluralistic legal system. Its forms were varied by differences in the socio-legal entities it regulated, such as village communities, familial or marital ties, city and town communities, and professional organisations. Most of these laws were not always written or applied through distinct legal rules, but tended to be administered on legal postulates at the discretion of the authorities. Some unofficial laws were written in legal rules, but these tended to be revered by responsible authorities as the sacred symbols of their members rather than being promulgated in public. Despite such a lack of structure and formality, unofficial laws were valid, and affected the daily lives of the people who fell within their jurisdiction.

Such varied forms of law, both official and unofficial, could not emerge and work consistently within the whole structure without primary principles or underlying structural or functional mechanism. Each socio-legal entity was characterised by two main structural features: community solidarity and a status hierarchy, as mentioned above. The principle of solidarity is often compared to

Genossenschaft⁽³⁶⁾ among German people, or a *Gemeinschaft*⁽³⁷⁾ against *Gesellschaft*,⁽³⁸⁾ for its feature of common responsibility and interest among members. It was originally fostered in village communities and then extended to other social groups, especially face-to-face groups. Later, it was applied to larger societies, finally leading to the policy of national isolation by Tokugawa *Bakufu*. The status hierarchy originated from the ancient clan system, which was composed of a leader and his families, and it then reformulated into a patriarchal family system among warriors with the infusion of Confucian ethics and the Zen Buddhist idea of life and death.

[3.11]

Also remarkable is that some mechanisms connected official law with unofficial law. Official law was furnished with concrete measures to control various forms of unofficial law.⁽³⁹⁾ First, *Bakufu* issued various regulations, directly or indirectly through local lords, requiring people to be obedient to the duties of their given status.⁽⁴⁰⁾ Second, *Bakufu* nominated leaders of the highest status in rural communities to be the official village heads to enforce their regulations. Third, the *Bakufu*'s Court of Justice adopted various forms of unofficial law to pass judgment upon disputes in cases of familial, civil, commercial and agricultural matters.⁽⁴¹⁾ Fourth, the above-mentioned community solidarity and status hierarchy worked as the leading postulates in both official and unofficial law.

Additional to these matters is the remarkable dual structure of the nominal authority of Tenno and the real power of *Bakufu*. This dual structure often created difficulties for persons involved with both, which had to be avoided by choosing one of them tactfully. A symbolic example of the problem took place when Tokugawa *Bakufu* wanted to reopen the exchange of official envoys with Korea after its suspension following Toyotomi's Korean invasion. The Korean king first required an exchange with the corresponding supreme Tenno, while *Bakufu* wanted to undertake the exchange as the real ruler in place of Tenno. A solution was devised by the lord of Tsushima, who had been closely associated with Korea. The word *Ohkimi* (meaning Tenno in the Japanese pronunciation but 'great lord' in Chinese character) was used to refer to the title of *Shogun*: the Korean king attributed the former meaning to the word and *Bakufu* did the latter. Similar solutions to conflicts have often been employed in Japan to accommodate apparent incompatibilities, thus producing the phrase 'tactful use of either formal excuse or true intention' (*tatemae* or *honne*). This approach has prevailed as a useful legal postulate outside of the law, both in the official and unofficial domains.[42]

4. The modern legal system

[4. 1]

The modernisation of Japanese law by transplanting law from Western countries began after the Meiji Restroration in 1868, in which Tenno was restored to real power. The first major legislation was the Criminal Code of 1880, followed by the Constitution of the Empire of Japan in 1889,[43] the Commercial Code, Criminal Procedure Act and Civil Procedure Act in 1890, and the Civil Code in 1896 and 1898. These were called the *roppo* (six codes) and the term began to be used to mean the whole of Japan's statute law. The *roppo* thus also included administrative law of both central and local governments and international law in the treaties and agreements of the new government under Tenno (in addition to the former agreements with the United States and other countries, which had been entered into by Tokugawa *Bakufu*).[44]

Preparation for modernisation

[4. 2]

The majority of references to Japan's transplantation of modern Western law ordinarily start by describing the historical facts after, or soon before, the Meiji Restroration in 1868. However, an accurate grasp of the meaning of such a huge national undertaking is gained, first, through comparing this transplantation with that of neighbouring countries in similar circumstances and, second, through studying the preparatory development, both manifest and latent, of the Japanese people and society preceding the formal transplantation.

Among the North-East Asian countries, China was the first to have encountered Western civilisation. A Jesuit, Matteo Ricci, one amongst visiting Catholic priests in the late sixteenth century onwards, brought Christianity and Western sciences such as astronomy and mathematics into China. Chinese rulers reacted to the visitors with the national principle of *Chung-hwa* (China-centrism), armed by Confucian cosmology and ethics, allowing no room for heterogeneous religion and the sciences.

China's oppression of Western ideas culminated with the formal prohibition of Christianity in 1723, and her resistance to the Western invasion resulted in battles in the nineteenth century, most notably, the Opium War with Great Britain in 1840-42. China kept closing her door to Western civilisations until the Kuomintang succeeded in the revolution of 1911.

Koreans achieved their culturall, political and military development under Chiniese influences so that they called themselves the inheritors of China-centrism. They learned Western Catholicism and sciences through China. As with China, the opening of Korea to Western civilisations did not occur until the late nineteenth century, after the armed intervention of Western powers (in which Japan also joined to annex Korea in 1910).

Japanese attitudes were different. It is not incorrect to regard Japan as similar to both China and Korea because of Tokugawa *Bakufu*'s general policy of national isolation excluding foreign people and culture wholly. On the contrary, the policy was not so rigidly applied as in the other two countries. Even under the Tokugawa policy, the Japanese had begun to learn of some of the advanced technology of Western civilisations which emerged in the middle of the sixteenth century, the most notable of which was the gun, introduced in 1543 by Portuguese cast ashore on a small southern island. Powerful lords then struggling for national hegemony vied not only for the purchase of guns, but also to master novel techniques of manufacture by applying their traditional technique of producing Japanese swords. Further, Catholicism and accompanying Western knowledge introduced by another Jesuit priest, Francisco Xavier, in 1549, were initially welcomed by powerful lords, although the beliefs were later expelled by Toyotomi Hideyoshi in 1587. This initial welcome exerted a considerable influence, as exemplified by missions to Rome dispatched by local lords two times in 1582-90 and 1613-20 respectively, and by the mortal combat of Catholic lords around Na-

Chapter 2. Legal Pluralism in Japanese History and Society 35

gasaki with Tokugawa *Bakufu* when the latter formally prohibited Catholicism in 1634.

In addition, the Dutch were allowed to engage in trade with Japan during the period of national isolation, on the condition that their goods and activities should not relate to religion and that trade transactions should be restricted to a small place called Deshima in Nagasaki. This was a small and limited exception, but it produced a great deal. The Dutch introduced not only goods and language, but also sciences such as mathematics, astronomy, electricity, the calender system, surgery, and information about other countries in the world. The learning of languages and sciences was rapidly spread, initially by those who learned directly from the Dutch in Nagasaki, and later by Japanese intellectuals in the country, who were limited in number but inspired by a thirst for knowledge of unknown worlds. This evidences that not only low-grade warriors but also commoners had begun to gain the social freedom to participate in learning, and that the society was developed enough to demand advanced scientific and other information from the Westen world. Even *Bakufu* opened in 1811 an office responsible for the study of Western books, despite the existence of the isolation policy.[45]

[4. 3]

The remarkable development in Japanese society was symbolised by the Genroku era, a time of unprecedented growth in economic and cultural activities among common people.[46] For instance, rice fields were reclaimed with the support of local lords, *Bakufu* and emerging local leaders; river control and irrigation systems were also improved; agriculture and handicraft developed, with localities establishing various specialties in arts and crafts, many of which are produced today. The national economy developed beyond the bounds of local areas to accelerate the growth of such economic concepts as private ownership, loan and mortgage, credit and exchange, and partnership and guild. This eventually made some merchants and landowners sufficiently wealthy to lend money to local lords and even to *Bakufu*. As a result, various types of popular culture were created, representing the Genroku cultures, among others, in the three large cities of Tokyo (then Edo), Kyoto (then Kyo) and Osaka (then Naniwa). These included novels and *ukiyoe*,[47] polite accomplishments, public undertakings such as the *ka*-

buki play and *sumo* wrestling, and many other arts, most of which are today included in Japanese traditional culture.

The development of Japanese society was a result of the transformation through economic development of the vertical structure which had formed the basis of Japanese society for many centuries. Some scholars have claimed that the Genroku era marked the beginning of Japanese modernisation or capitalisation. However, it is argued below that this modernisation was not, in the true sense, based on a Western model.[48]

Modernisation practiced

[4. 4]

It might take many more centuries finally to ascertain whether the Japanese transplantation of modern law has succeeded. However, judging from world history hitherto, the transplantation certainly appears to be one of the most successful for several reasons.

First, the new Meiji leaders unanimously shared a goal of establishing a centralised nation under the Tenno regime, comparable with Western power structures. Domestically, the main policies were to promote capitalist industry and establish military forces. Several years after the Meiji Restoration, revolutionary reforms were implemented, such as the abolition of feudal class discrimination, feudal estates being replaced by private ownership and taxation, the enforcing of nationwide family registration, the appointment of new local officials in place of feudal village heads, the creation of compulsory elementary education, the adoption of a conscription system, and the reform of the calender system from the traditional lunar system to the Gregorian solar system. The most urgent, but difficult, policy for the government was to revise existing unequal treaties with Western powers, not only for the benefit of Japan itself, but also for the recognition of Japan as a fellow member of the international community.[49] A reforming legal system was required effectively to realise those policies, and there was no choice for Japan but to transplant modern Western systems.

Second, the leaders were wise to choose particular countries as their models

Chapter 2. Legal Pluralism in Japanese History and Society *37*

for Western law. The first modern political ideas which stimulated Japanese intellectuals in the early Meiji years were British and French liberalism and democracy, as can be seen by the translation of books by J. S. Mill and J. J. Rousseau. Under the circumstances, it was necessary to uproot feudalistic powers. In order to affirm the centralised authority of Tenno, however, a strong central government model was adopted from Prussia, about 10 years after the Meiji Restoration. The Constitution was drafted to reinforce the authority of Tenno, and other legislation was developed so as to reconcile the Tenno system with the requirements of national goals and a capitalistic economy.

Third, to accommodate the apparent incompatibility of incorporating traditional culture and new national goals into the legal system to be transplanted from Western law, considerable endeavours were undertaken. For instance, an effort was made to compare the different constitutional systems of the main Western countries. The American Constitution was rejected, perhaps on the basis that its political structure was democratic, the Great Britain's system was also rejected because it was based on unwritten law, and the French system was rejected because of France's unstable dynasties. In private law, the Japanese preferred the German and French models, and thus four pieces of legislation among the six main codes were directly drafted by advisers from these two countries: that is, the Criminal Code and the Civil Code were drafted by a Frenchman, G. Boissonade, and the Constitution and the Commercial Code were drafted by a German, K. F. H. Roesler. The other two main codes, the Criminal Procedure Act and the Civil Procedure Act, were also based on German and French models.

In addition, a special commission visited leading scholars in Germany, Austria, Great Britain and the United States to ask questions about the drafting of the Constitution and other legislations. Also, the government attempted a national survey of indigenous law which affected people's daily social lives, in order to assess whether to incorporate it into the new civil code. The survey's immediate effect on the Civil Code was limited to the insertion of a few articles: one article stating the conditions to allow limited use of customary law, two articles to permit common rights, and several individual references to customary law. It is doubtful whether the governmental surveys for new legislation, both international and national, were as effective as hoped. Nonetheless, the processes at least prove both sensitivity to foreign influence and an inclination for domestic tradition.

Fourth, the government took particular measures to provide the personnel required for the new legal system. A large number of specialists in law were needed, such as administrators, judges, prosecutors and attorneys to enforce the new legal system, and professors to conduct research and educate those personnel. The main institution for this last purpose was the Tokyo Imperial University, the present University of Tokyo, which was formally established by the government in 1877. The government had adopted in 1872, together with compulsory elementary education, the French mode of the centralised school district system. The University was initially given the power to administer the whole school system, although this power was soon transferred to the government.

The University had the mission of providing the knowledge, science and personnel required for the new Japan, in the same way as the Berlin University was established in 1810 for the development of Prussia and the University of London was established in 1828 for the benefit of Great Britain. The University's faculty of law monopolised the training of higher administrators, lawyers and professors until a second national university was established in Kyoto in 1897. Later, new faculties of law at private universities began turning out graduates for lower official positions. The preponderance of University of Tokyo graduates amongst higher officials is today still apparent.

Finally, efforts were made by the government to obtain capable drafters of new legislation. Among the measures taken soon after the Restoration was the invitation extended to a few foreign specialists from those Western countries which had been taken as models. Boissonade and Roesler were two representatives, both of whom had profound influence upon not only the drafting of bills, but also the education of bureaucrats. Another step taken was to send young Japanese students to London, Paris and Berlin to learn Western law. When the government decided to establish Tokyo Imperial University, select individuals were sent to Western countries, and then appointed on their return to professors

Chapter 2. Legal Pluralism in Japanese History and Society 39

of the University in order to spread knowledge of Western science, including jurisprudence. Professors of law were thus disseminators of the new jurisprudence for the new Japan, and many of them were asked by the government to be drafters of, or advisers on, new legislation. Every law student was required to learn not just Japanese law, but to study one of either the German, English or French legal systems. This study of foreign legal systems continues today with comparative law courses.

Modernisation featured

[4. 5]

The development of the Japanese nation functioned to complete the modernisation of its official state law, which is usually called Meiji Legal System, covering the modernisation period until the end of World War II; a typical transplantation of a modern civil system, with some indigenous factors incorporated. The Constitution[50] gave the legal system its basic structure, composed of several modern legal essentials: that is, national sovereignty, fundamental human rights, separation of powers, a representative government and state-controlled finances. At a glance, the system appeared equivalent to the modern model, for the reason that such institutions as absolute ownership in private freedom, freedom of contract and business, and the principle of *nulls poena sine lege*[51] were declared by the Constitution, and that these institution were given effect by the Civil Code, Commercial Code and Criminal Code, as well as by the civil and criminal procedure legislations.

The modernisation allowed Japan to achieve important goals. On the international front, it enabled Japan to revise the unequal treaties in 1911, which the Tokugawa *Bakufu* had concluded with Western powers earlier. Domestically, it enabled a capitalist economy to advance national productivity for peacetime industry and military forces for an emergency. These advances allowed Japan to conclude a military alliance with the much more advanced Great Britain (1902–23) and to conduct wars with bigger countries, that is, with China in 1894–95 and with Russia in 1904–05. After World War I, Japanese leaders were proud that the nation's growth was comparable to the five most advanced nations, being Great

Britain, France, the United States, Germany and Italy.

[4. 6]

Tradition was not disregarded in this process, as essential elements of the Constitution incorporated many traditional indigenous principles. Tenno held sovereignty with 'divine authority', while people were designated as 'subjects' with no liberal democratic power and whose fundamental human rights could be restricted by parliamentary statute. Tenno was vested with imperial prerogatives, particularly as follows:

1. The Tenno Family was to be given royal status and legal autonomy, thus establishing a new Court Law.
2. Tenno established an official rank system among the subjects, more elaborately organised than the preceding systems:
   a. a new nobility (with five ranks) was chosen from descendants of the feudal land lords and from those appointed after distinguished service to the new country;
   b. a new court rank was established, by which every public servant was ranked in one of the hierarchical orders; and
   c. a hierarchically ordered decoration system was to be conferred on subjects for their services to the country.
3. Tenno established a new shrine system to rank all the Shinto shrines in the country hierarchically under Ise Jingu, the supreme shrine of the Tenno Family. Worship at Ise Jingu was obligatory during World War II for every subject.
4. Tenno issued the urgent imperial ordinances. Although the use of the ordinances was conditional on the approval of parliament, no objections were ever raised.
5. Tenno assumed supreme command of the military forces and could make military law, apart from government law. This situation gave rise to potential conflict between two divided legal authorities under Tenno.
6. Tenno appointed a governor-general to Taiwan, which was ceded from China in 1894, and conferred Taiwan with its own jurisdiction separate from the central government, according to the British and French models. This

Chapter 2. Legal Pluralism in Japanese History and Society *41*

formality was also applied to South Sakhalin, which was ceded from Russia in 1904, and to Korea, which was annexed in 1910, thus generating new overseas land law as a whole.

[4. 7]

The Meiji Legal System was thus characterised as the law of Tenno authority. At this point, it may be useful to explain the concept of shrine law. According to earlier studies by myself, the shrine law developed in two domains, official and unofficial. The official shrine law originated from the ancient rank system of shrines in the Code of Engi in 927, applying to nearly 300 big shrines all over the country. After frequent revisions, it was reorganised by the Meiji Legal System. The main body of the law constituted a new rank system of all the shrines, however small they may be, which then numbered nearly 190,000, and elaborate formality of annual rituals and ceremonies to be performed by the shrine. In the rank system, all the shrines were classified (under the supreme Ise Jingu) into three major categories. First, there were national shrines comprised of sub-categories of big, medium, small and special shrines, all of which were supported by national funds and voluntary donation. Then there were local shrines with prefectural, county and village subdivisions, supported by corresponding local governments and people. Lastly, and rather curiously, there were 'non-ranked shrines' which had no officially approved rank but were supported by worshippers in small localities, and which comprised half the total number of the shrines. This rank system was an ideological attribute of national and local government hierarchy. The standard sources of shrine law were ordinances issued by the Minister of Interior Affairs and, where relevant, Court Law.[52] Unofficial shrine law developed in two directions: on the one hand, a bigger shrine or its denomination was endowed with a corporate nature, enabling the shrine to work like a social organisation similar to a Christian church or its denomination; on the other hand, a smaller local shrine in a village community was alive supported by village law. The unofficial shrine law survives today, with some modifications.[53]

[4. 8]

There was another important indigenous factor essential to the Meiji Legal System: that is, the protection of the patriarchal family by the Civil Code. The

Civil Code, which was first drafted by Boissonade, was criticised bitterly when it was first promulgated in 1890. Traditionalists objected to its two parts concerning family and succession (although there was no objection to the other three parts concerning general provisions, real rights and obligatory rights). The reason for the objection was that the new system would destroy the traditional 'good morals and manners' which had been practiced among Japanese.

Eventually, the Code was rewritten by three Japanese jurists to accommodate the above violent debate (one which could be compared to the debate between Savigny and Thibeau in 1814 on the suggested form of the German Civil Code). The rewritten Civil Code was finally enforced in 1898. The family chief was empowered to control his extended family, as registered in the national census, wherever its members might be living. The chief's main legal functions were to mediate officially between the government and members drafted for national defence, to give approval to marriage of underage members, and to detect any members who were suspected criminals. His unofficial function was to maintain the social status of his extended family in its local community. Thus, one can see the incorporation of unofficial law, that is, communal law and status hierarchy, into the official Code.

[4. 9]

For these reasons, the Meiji Legal System was an amalgamation of transplanted principles, represented by personal rights and parliamentary government, and indigenous rights, represented by the authoritative Tenno and the patriarchal family chief. Without any accommodating mechanisms, the different, or rather competing, principles might have been unable to coexist in a whole system. There were three official mechanisms for accommodation of competing interests. One was to make the Tenno's prerogatives nominal. Thus, four of the highest officials were responsible for each of the Tenno's separate prerogatives: that is, the Minister of the Imperial Household for Court Law, the governors-general for overseas land law, the Army and Navy Chiefs of the General Staff for military law, and the prime minister for governmental law, formally including shrine law. This structure was a reformulation of the earlier relationship between Tenno's nominal authority and *Bakufu*'s real power, one which was likely to cause conflict in the system, especially between the prime minister and the military chiefs.[54]

There were some legal measures with the intention to restrict personal rights. An electoral system of restricted suffrage was introduced by the Meiji Constitution, under which the right to vote was limited to a small number of people who were large landowners or who had great income. This continued until universal suffrage came into being in 1922 for men and in 1945 for women. The landowner system was legitimised by new legal measures regarding private ownership and free contract in the Civil Code, for it enabled landowners to accumulate more agricultural lands to replace feudalistic practices. There was a reformulation of the feudal status hierarchy into a new hierarchy in local areas comprising three ranks: a few privileged landowners (the higher class), common farmers (the middle class) and a large number of farm tenants (the lower class).

[4.10]
The Meiji Legal System allowed the reformulated status hierarchy to function for purposes of administrative efficiency. For example, feudal village communities, which had worked as the smallest socio-legal entities under their communal law, were incorporated into the new official local government system as subdivisions of the new official unit called village, town or city. Then, top leaders in the status hierarchy in each of these local communities were officially incorporated into the governmental structure through two ways. The first of these was by their appointment as official chiefs of the above subdivisions, their election as assembly members or headmen of their local governments, and their eventual decoration for official services. The second of these was, though limitedly, granting of the membership to the House of Peers to the largest landowners and distinguished persons of learning and experience.

It may be wondered how those mechanisms of official state law could function so as to accommodate the competing principles. The answer could lie in the traditional legal postulates of *wa* and others working outside of the law, as mentioned earlier. For example, there was the Imperial Rescript on Education, issued by Meiji Tenno in 1890 to enunciate the fundamental goal of school education.[55] According to the Rescript, the ultimate purpose of national education was to cultivate loyal subjects of the Tenno, subjects who were so deeply indoctrinated that they would sacrifice their lives for their country. This goal was to be attained by developing the intellectual faculties of the Japanese people through modern learning and the arts, and basing this development on the traditional *wa* principle and Confucian ethics which emphasised loyalty to Tenno and fidelity to parents, as well as inculcating a high respect for the Constitution and tha law. Everyone at school was required to repeat whole sentences of the Imperial Rescript from memory.[56] Those postulates were never manifestly defined as legal ones in any part of the official legal system, but in reality they played a fundamental role outside the law to orient the real effects of the legal system in the whole working structure.

5. The contemporary legal system

[5. 1]

The Meiji Constitution was wholly replaced by the new Constitution of Japan[57] in 1947 (under the reign of the late Showa Tenno) and Japan was occupied by the allied forces until 1952 after its defeat in World War II in 1945. The revision of the whole legal system, the Showa Legal System, followed immediately in accordance with the new constitutional principles. This Constitution is characterised by three basic traits: first, it was a transplantation of the American common law model,[58] second, it overturned the former divine authority of Tenno to found the legal system on democracy in accordance with modern civil liberties, and, third, its ninth article renounced war and the military, thus causing it to be named a 'peace constitution'.

A revolutionary change from earlier official legal system had thus taken place. Sovereignty vested in the people, while Tenno was deprived of its divine sovereignty simply to be 'the symbol of the State and of the unity of the people' with no political power, except in some ceremonial acts. Any restriction on fundamental human rights, even by parliamentary statute, was prohibited. All of the prerogatives of Tenno disappeared:

1. The administration of the Tenno Family was moved into governmental law;

Chapter 2. Legal Pluralism in Japanese History and Society   45

therefore, the former Court Law lost its independent authority.
2. Every form of discrimination was prohibited; therefore, the official rank system was abolished.
3. The official shrine system was also abolished; therefore, shrine law lost official support.
4. Urgent imperial ordinances would not be made, and parliament was declared to be the sole law-making organ.
5. The Tenno lost the supreme command of the military forces, and military law was to disappear.
6. Three overseas lands were returned to their former countries: Taiwan to China, South Sakhalin to Russia, and Korea regained its independence; therefore, overseas land law lost its reason for existence.

The previous system that established the powers of the patriarchal family chief to control family members was abolished. A new system based on personal dignity within the nuclear family was established, and the individualisation of common land was encouraged. The former mechanisms which allowed for possible conflicts between dual competing sources of authority were totally abolished.[59] Restricted suffrage of women and the privileged landowner system were also abolished. The impact of the new system seems to have been surprisingly powerful, and has affected all sections of society. People were liberated from earlier legal and social bonds of loyalty to the Tenno nation, faithfulness to the affiliated communities, and status hierarchy. The move to democracy was accomplished without serious conflict or civil war (unlike many other non-Western countries) and a miraculous prosperity has existed since the 1960s.[60]

Does a revolutionary change as apparent as the above mean complete modernisation of the legal system so that it is the same as those of the Western countries upon which it was modeled? The answer should be 'no', judging by discussions having taken place between Western and Japanese scholars. For example, it has been debated that people tend to maintain a reluctance to accept legal measures such as formal contracts, claiming of rights and actions before the courts,[61] that judicial review has seldom taken place because of the balance of functions between the courts and administrative agencies[62], and that conservative political forces have intended to preserve the pre-war family system.[63] However, I hesitate wholly to support these partial assessments. Japanese circumstances should be judged within the whole working structure in place. Observations must not be limited to official law and its legal rules; unofficial law and its legal postulates must also be considered.

[5. 2]

Regarding the structure of the official law as a whole, the new system has made state law the only one to unify the whole system, as ideologically demanded by modern law. The preceding system of official law was, in fact, a mix of more or less heterogeneous systems: court law, military law and overseas land law, along with the main governmental law which formally contained the official shrine law. The new system of official law consists of state law alone, with no other coexisting or competing systems of law. This simple structure may be unique in comparison with other countries. For example, in Christian countries, various systems of church law have their own jurisdictions independently of state law, whether or not offcially approved by Constitutions. In Muslim countries, Islamic law prevails along with state law, functioning as an underlying but in fact leading legal postulate for it. In the Theravada Buddhist countries, Theravada Buddhist law operates in society, whether or not authorised by the Constitutions.[64]

Among the real structure of the Japanese state law, there are various indigenous laws coxistiong whether officially or unofficially. Two examples may suffice as evidence of the essential importance of such laws living in the Japanese legal system. One is the constitutional position of Tenno. Tenno was deprived of its political powers, but it continues to be an indispensable constitutional organ which is supported by national funds conferred because of its symbolic function. This function unofficially operates postulatively much more widely than was anticipated by the relevant official legal rules.[65] The other is found in the family system. The previous official system of the patriarchal extended family was abolished, causing an enormous social impact which has been called the 'disorganisation of family'. However, there are some legal measures which may be used by those who want to maintain some elements of the traditional family;[66] these measures might appear to be of negligible significance within the official system, but, in reality, they offer the opportunity to maintain a traditional family under the present system. It should be noted that the previous law on the family was, even under the Meiji system, not always practised among people in society as rigidly as prescribed. The importance of the law had been maintained rather by its ideological function as a legal postulate. In summary, the offical abolition of both the Tenno authority and the family system did not mean their total disappearance in society but rather retain a covert reversion to their former influence as unoffical law.

[5. 3]

It can be seen from the preceding information that what gives the law real significance in its social function is not official legal rules alone, but the unofficial practices and postulates which are part of enforcing the rules. There are many examples of practices of this kind:

1. Tenno continues to receive, officially and unofficially, the utmost reverence, as is indicated by the term 'chrysanthemum curtain', the chrysanthemum being part of the official crest of the Tenno family.
2. The expenditures for the funeral of Showa Tenno and the enthronement of the present Heisei Tenno in 1989-90, were disbursed from the national treasury. This was despite legal opinion that the disbursement was unconstitutional under the principle of the separation of state and religion, because it meant official support of the Shintoist rituals which formed the basis of the two official ceremonies.
3. A noted judgment of the Supreme Court in 1977 concerned a case brought regarding the disbursement from a local government's treasury for a Shintoist ground breaking ceremony for a gymnasium. The Court ruled that the disbursement was constitutional because the ceremony was a 'traditional custom', not a 'religious ceremony'.[67]
4. The most obvious is the 'Self-Defence Force', which exists despite the ninth article of the Constitution, to prohibit use and maintenance of military forces. Since its creation in 1950 as a 'Special Police Force', the self Defense Force has grown substantially, so as to be called a military force by other countries.

5. The Japanese judicial system and people's attitudes towards it also reveal indigenous peculiarities. It is well known that arbitration, mediation or conciliation are official means of conflict management, as alternatives to judicial judgment.[68] Allegedly, there is a Japanese preference for private conciliation, mediation or arbitration, ordinarily presided over by an influential third person such as a chief or senior family member of the conflicting parties.[69]
6. Administrative systems do not work without certain practices entrenched in the bureaucracy. Notable amongst these is the functioning of the informal law. *Naiki* (internal regulations) are issued by agencies in the form of written bylaws, to announce uniform practices for the related legal rules. *Gyosei kanrei* (administrative precedents) is the practice, written or unwritten, by which agencies manage special cases when there is a vacuum in legal rules. *Gyosei shido* (administrative guidance) is an informal instrument of agencies, with which to inform private organisations of guidelines regarding legally acceptable acts.[70]

Points one to four exemplify, first, that traditional Tenno adoration and *kami* conception still operate as legal postulates for the related legal rules, second, that the universal constitutional principle of the separation of state and religion is interpreted flexibly enough to allow traditional practices and, third, that legal concepts are not clearly defined but are applied using the principle of 'true intention or formal excuse'. In other words, state law accommodates indigenous practices based on unofficial legal postulates. Furthermore, it is clear from points five and six that judicial litigation is not the only means of conflict management, that there are other indigenous means, official and unofficial, and that the national government is vested with influential administrative power through informal, unofficial law.[71] These approaches are nothing but a continuation of the traditional systems and practices.

The clearly recognisable traits of the whole system of current Japanese law are as follows. First, the revision of the Constitution aftar World War II was of great significance in the transformation of the legal system from one mainly influenced by German law to one greatly influenced by American law. Second, because the previous system and practices developed along the German model still

Chapter 2. Legal Pluralism in Japanese History and Society 49

underlie the present system, the latter is coloured by a mixture of German and American models. Third, and of most significance in such a transplanted system, is that indingenous law is extensively adopted within the formal structure of the official legal system. The various legal postulates operate to allow incorporation of indigenous factors into the whole working structure of law, through formal and informal means.

6. The whole working structure of Japanese law

Unofficial law at work

[6. 1]

Various forms of official indigenous law, adopted by the Meiji Legal System as mentioned above, were apparently abolished, and new legal principles and systems for democratisation of Japanese politics and society substituted. As noted, the impact of this abolition has been enormous. Such radical changes in official law and society might lead observers to presume a similar change was effected in unofficial indigenous law, too. As also suggested above, this was not the case.

The basic Japanese social organisation and accordingly the Japanese socio-legal entity before World War II, was generally represented by the local community in a rural *buraku* (hamlet), *mura* (village) or a cluster of seveal *buraku*. Each local community developed its own communal law, a system of rights and duties of the member families for the maintenance of their communal lives. Its purpose was mainly to regulate the use of common lands or waters for productive activities, and to manage cooperative work for the community's daily life and worship at the community's shrine. The community was, of course, organised hierarchically, but aspired to a common duty in communal solidarity. This type of socio-legal entity was incorporated as a sub-system of the official local government structure under the Meiji Legal System.

[6. 2]

Transformaion of the community, which had begun in urban areas before World War II, also affected rural areas, and it accelerated under the Showa Legal System for community members to begin to seek work outside their rural communities. Capitalist economic advances had the effect of liberating people from the bond of their local communities and the status hierarchy. As a result, common lands and waters, upon which they had relied for their productive activities in their communities, tended to become the subject of individual control or ownership. The movement towards this was finalised by statute in 1966.[72] In addition, common works for community became difficult to maintain due to the decrease in number of rural youths. The solidarity of the local community thus appeared disintegrated, and eventually became recognised as the 'disorganisation of the village community'.

[6. 3]

However, commumuty solidarity has not totally disappeared; rather, it has been preserved in other forms. The most conspicuous example of this has been the survival of the unofficial shrine law, or shrine community. The shrine community has evolved, leading to complaints by traditionalists about the said decay of the shrines. For example, previously, every family in a community was formally obliged to be a member of its shrine community. This no longer applies today, and thus a shrine community is transformed into a voluntary association in a local community. Also, people who took part in the rituals and festivals of a shrine were chosen from among the young men of the regular member families of the community, but today they are also chosen even from women and non-memder volunteers, due to the lack of qualfied members. Still, the shrine communtiy is maintained by an enduring indigenous law and forms a socio-legal entity for worship of its own guardian god. The shrine and its *matsuri* (rituals and festivals) regulated by a shrine law, are maintained as an important social symbol of the local communtiy.

Changes being made to the shrine community and shrine law did not only occur after World War II. The so-called typical form of the shrine and *matsuri* before the war,[73] which traditionalists take for the model, was not the original, but an outcome of the preceding transformation resulting from the official reorganisation of the shrine system by the Meiji government.[74] Therefore, the transformation today is only part of the evolution of shrine law since Meiji. In addition, many other forms of shrine law have been maintaned since preceding feudal periods, their traditional structures and function enduring despite the general transformation which has recently occurred.

In summary, the complex forms of cotemporary shrine communities can be classified into three ideal types in Weber's sense. First, there is the *miyaza* (a shrine fraternity) which maintains the original form of a closed, small shrine communuty. It is formed by a small hereditary group of privileged families trusted by its communuty to support the shrine and hold its rituals (the unique cultural heritage of which is often noted today). This type is conserved largely in some rural areas in the western part of the main island called Honshu. The second prevalent local type is the *ukijo* (community residents worshipping at a local shrine) group, which is a transformation of the original *miyaza* form expanded to the whole of a local community.[75] The third type is the *sukeisha* (voluntary worshippers at a shrine) group, which is based around a larger shrine and draws its voluntary members from different localities. The worshippers of this type support even a remote shrine and participate in its festivals, not only because of their belief in the enshrined god, but also to gain the god's divine favour in such matters as personal and familial happiness or success in examinations, marriage and business. There are many shrines such as these which are renowned for their special features: for example, Ise Jingu in Mie Prefecture enshrines Amaterasu, the founding god of Japan, and is also recognised for its traditional style of building, and Atsuta Jingu in Nagoya enshrines Yamato Takeru, younger brother of Amaterasu. Many others are famous for their spectacular *matsuri*, which attact a large number of spectators, including foreign sightseers.[76]

From the perspective of official law, the above might not seem to be relevant. However, from the perspective of unofficial law, the shrine law and its legal postulates, through a variety of socio-legal entities, supplement the function of official state law. The concept of the socio-legal entity with its own unofficial indigenous law is not limited to the shrine community, but appears within other social organisations. One example is temple law of Buddhist temple communities and various Buddhist sects, the former of which are established around each temple by affiliates of the temple. As is clear from the existence of shrine law and temple law, religious organisations cannot function without their own law. Many religions besides Shinto and Buddhism are also prevalent in Japan and are armed by their own law: for example, Tenri, Kurozumi and many others, not to mention Christianity. In summary, indigenous religious law has an unofficial role in comparison with the official workings of transplanted law which is based on the Judeo-Christian tradition.

[6. 4]

Another Japanese unofficial law which should not be disregarded is the *iemoto* law, which founded the *iemoto* system. *Iemoto* originally meant the main line of an extended family, but now refers to the headmaster of a school of traditional arts and accomplishments. These kinds are exemplified by the tea ceremony, flower arranging, *no* plays, traditional music and traditional military arts.[77] The ordinary members of a school choose their schools voluntarily, but are obliged upon entrance to be faithful to the school's discipline. The headmaster is as a rule a descendant or adopted heir of the former head, is vestd with supreme authority, and is assisted by sub-masters in training and administration. *Iemoto* law is the system of norms and rules to be found in this type of organisation, based on community solidarity and status hierarchy. The *iemoto* system has been maintained as Japan's unique socio-cultural feature, being called 'the heart of Japan'.[78]

Fictitiously, the structure of the *iemoto* system is extended in its essence to various social organisations. It is often found in modern business companies, in the relationship between main and branch shops, in special combinations of companies such as the *zaibatsu* (large industrial and financal conglomerates) and *keiretsu* (a network of interrelated companies).[79] The structure is also applied to underground organisations, such as the *boryokudan* (gangster organisations) and other secret or criminal societies.[80]

From these examples, it can be argued that unofficial indigenous law has been incorporated into many other social organisations, as ideological legal postulates and/or strict legal rules. Assuming this is correct, more assertions about unofficial indigenous law arise. For example, there is an indigenous inclination to

Chapter 2. Legal Pluralism in Japanese History and Society 53

nakama (comradeship). *Nakama* does not mean simple fellowship or group membership, but rather refers to a group of people connected for a specific purpose in a closed community. Its original purpose may have been to maintain shared belief in a shrine or to provide training in an accomplishment. It may sometimes arise out of parochial insularity and lead to discrimination against persons strange to a community, such as *gaijin* (foreigners), handicapped persons, or even the opposite sex and minors. There are some parallels between past and present discrimination; in the past, people outside a group were discriminated even on official legal rules, while today, outsiders may be discriminated on the hidden operation of the unofficial legal postulate.[81] Society's inclination towads *mibun* (status) and *ikka* (a family), both of which are variations of the above-mentioned status hierarchy and family system repectively, illustrates how discrimination can arise latently from unofficial legal postulates. These unofficial laws require further examination because of their overt or covert influences upon official law.

7. Conclusion

[7. 1]

In reviewing the history of Japanese law, no one would deny that the country experienced two reformational changes through the transplantation of Chinese law in ancient times and Western law in modern times. Despite these facts, the Japanese pepole have maintained their indigenous laws, and Japan is characterised by the apparently peaceful transplantation of Western law, as opposed to other Asian countries, many of which have suffered constitutional crises. Looking at the difference between the official law as it previously existed and that of present system which was transplanted, the change may be described as revolutionary or radical. However, taking into account the effect of unofficial and indigenous law, the process of change is rather a consistent development of an indigenous legal culture.

Prior to the seventh century, Japanese law featured a primitive legal pluralism of ancient state law and clan law, and another pluralism of indigenous law and sporadically transplanted Korean law. The following systemisation was extensive, in that the result was the first codification of state law modeled upon the Chinese

Codes. On the other hand, the leading postulates of the codification were, as expressed by Prince Shotoku, a combination of the *kami* conception and Tenno adoration under the *wa* principle, produced an amalgamation of indigenous postulates with the Confucian ethics and Buddhist ideals. Furthermore, the Chinese-modeled official state law, which was limited to administration of public power, left the wide domain of private relations to indigenous, unoffigical law to be developed in the course of the application of official law. The *Ritsuryo* System was therefore a genuine form of legal pluralism which included both Chineae law and indigenous law in official and unofficial law.

Eventually, the *Ritsuryo* System soon began to be wholly acculturated by the development of indigenous law in two domains: official law, formed initially by *Kuge* Law and later by *Buke* Law, and unofficial laws in various forms of community life among people. The Japanese legal system in feudal ages had for nearly ten centuries maintained an indigenous legal pluralism, as represented by the last Tokugawa system constituted by official *Bakufu* Law and *Han* Law together with unofficial communal law, familial law, *shaji* law, *iemoto* law and many other types of law.

After the Meiji Restoration, the indigenised system appeared wholly to have been replaced by the modern legal system which had primarily been modeled on the German system and secondarily modeled on the French system. This modernised system was again reformed after World War ll, based on the model of the Anglo-American system. However, it is argued that indigenous law was not totally cast out; rather, the transplanted official law has more or less been indigenised, while indigenous law is prevailing as unofficial law.

In reviewing the historical development of the Japanese legal system with the mind of Geerz,[82] one overriding principle has been identified, which allowed the previously discussed legal postulates to work effectively under different circumstances throughout Japanese history. This fundamental overriding principle is here termed the 'identity postulate of a legal culture'. In the Japanese context, the identity postulate can be seen by the flexibility of the Japanese people, something which can be characterised by the term, an 'amoeba-like situationism'.[83]

Chapter 2. Legal Pluralism in Japanese History and Society   55

This identity postulate has allowed the Japanese to be able to select one outcome of their legal system among two or more competing possibilities.

The 'amoeba-like situationism' is evidenced by three more particular characteristics. First, there is the accommodation of seemingly different or opposing principles in the Japanese legal system, for instance, *tatemae* or *honne*, formal versus informal means of dispute resolution,[84] a bureaucratic leadership exercised through an informal process,[85] and law which paradoxically appears to be without power.[86] Second, there is some fundamental principle ever working with Japanese law.[87] Third, there are some conditions which allowed for accommodation and indigenous development: for example, 'social relativism' or 'social preoccupation and inter-relational relativism'.[88] and 'flexibility' to 'symbolically create and manipulate a dualistic universe'.[89] I am convinced thus that the hypothetical propositlon, 'amoeba-like situationism' is without doubt verified.

Glossary

amae	indulgent dependence, initially referring to the relationship between an infant and mother, but extended also to the relationship between the protected and protector
bakufu	Shogunate government or office
buke law	law made by samurai (warriors) as represented by the Code of Joei in 1232 and the Code of Public Power in 1742
buraku	hamlet
boryokudan	gangster organisation
Dajo-daijin	prime minister under the ancient *Ritsuryo* System, or in the early Meiji government before the modern cabinet system
Dajokan	office of the *Dajo-daijin* under the *Ritsuryo* System, or in the early Meiji government
dozoku	a group of related families based around a main family and its branches
ekiden	post horses
gyosei kanrei	administrative precedents
gyosei shido	administrative guidance
han law	laws of the local lords under the Tokugawa *Bakufu*

honjo law	laws of the landowners in early medieval ages, such as *shoen* law and *shaji* law, concerned with matters of land title
honne	real motive, true intention
iemoto	headmaster of a school of traditional arts and accomplishments
ikka	initially referred to a solidary family, but later extended to mean a solidary social organisation of various kinds
insei	rule of retired emperors
Jingikan	minister or ministry of serving the gods and *jinja* administration under the *Ritsuryo* System and in early Meiji government
jinja	enshrinement of Shinto gods, worshipped by *ujiko* or *sukeisha*
kami	gods in Shintosim, not only enshrined in *jinja* but also deified as governing human affairs and natural occurrences
Kanpaku	chief adviser to Tenno
Kebiishi	police and judicial chief, created outside the transplanted *Ritsuryo* System
keiretsu	companies linked by continuous business relations, network of interrelated companies
kuge law	law made by nobles working for the Tenno's rule, as represented by the Code of Engi in 927
kyaku	imperial edicts in the *Ritsuryo* System
matsuri	annual rituals and festivals held at Shinto shrines
mibun	status
miyaza	a closed shrine fraternity
mura	village
naiki	internal regulations
nakama	members of a closed group
oyabun-kobun	fictitious parent-child relationship
ritsuryo	literally *ritsu* (penal law) and *ryo* (administrative law); the term extends to the whole legal system in ancient Japan
roppo	literally 'six codes', referring to the main codes in the Meiji Legal System but extending to the whole legal system based on Western law
Ryoge-no-kan	indigenous offices created outside the transplanted *Ritsuryo* System
Seii-taishogun	or *Shogun*: Commanders-in-Chief of an Expeditionary Force against the

Chapter 2. Legal Pluralism in Japanese History and Society 57

	Barbarians, in fact, universal agent for Tenno
Sessho	regency or regent
shaji law	laws of Shinto shrines and Buddhist temples
shiki	bye-laws in the Ritsryo System
shinrui	lineal and collateral relatives
shoen law	manor law
sukeisha	voluntary worshippers at a shrine from different locolities
tatemae	stated reasons for opinion, formal excuse
Tenno	Emperor of Japan
ujiko	a community resident worshipping at a local shrine
wa	harmony
wako	Japanese pirates
yakuza	traditionally booth-keepers, but the term now often refers to organised gangsters
zaibatsu	large industrial/financial conglomerate

Notes

(1) During nearly 200 years of national isolation under the Tokugawa *Bakafu* before the Meiji Restoration in 1868, exchange and trade with foreign countries was formally prohibited. However, *Bakafu* continued regular official exchanges with Korea, and smuggling was organised by a number of powerful merchants and lords in Kyushu to southern countries across the East China Sea. Such exceptions to the enforced isolation eventually contributed to Japan's pre-modern economic development.

(2) The general background of Japanese law is easy to ascertain from other sources. I have referred to legal sources and academic works only where necessary. Western curiosity regarding Japanese law has produced so many works as to make it impossible to deal with them satisfactorily here. The following references may be noted: Coleman and Haley 1975; Steenstrup 1991:160-191; Scheer 1993; Britt and Strouse 1995, for bibliographical purposes; Hall 1979; Ishii 1980; Steenstrup 1991: 1-159, for legal history; von Mehren 1963; Igarashi 1990; Coing et al, 1990; Menkhaus 1994; Centre Français de Droit Comparé 1989; Oda 1992; Port 1996, for the contemporary official legal system; Noda 1976; Port 1996; Tanaka 1976, for a general overview.

(3) These are minor additions and revisions to my basic scheme as described in

former publications. See Chiba 1989; chap. 12, reprinted in Sack and Aleck 1992.
(4) See Gilissen 1972 and Merry 1988.
(5) It is beyond the scope of this chapter to consider other forms of social norm and its sociological units.
(6) The socio-legal entity of state law is the national country which is legally and politically represented by the sovereign state.
(7) These have so far been left undiscussed by legal pluralists.
(8) The term was formerly used by myself, Chiba 1989: 207.
(9) See Renteln and Dundes 1994: sec. 8.
(10) See Introduction in Grahl-Madsen and Tomen 1984.
(11) The term is used among international lawyers to mean interpersonal law working among human beings which is not connected with national sovereignty, Grahl-Madsen and Tomen 1984, Vol. VII.
(12) Attemprs were made in Morse and Woodman 1988; von Benda-Beckmann et al. 1988.
(13) *See* for example, Ehrmann 1976; Berman 1983; Snyder 1985. Note that another objective is indigenous law working without reference to state law.
(14) See, for example, Podgorecki 1974: 224-226; Friedman 1975: chaps. 8 and 9; Macaulay 1989; Blankenburg & Bruinsma 1994.
(15) Blankenburg & Bruinsma 1994: 13-14.
(16) See Chiba 1989: 203.
(17) Benedict 1934: 42-43, 225-227.
(18) Some suggestions can be found in the preceding section ([2.1]) regarding legal pluralism. For example, the concept of 'a socio-legal entity' may be useful, as it corresponds to the anthropological concept of 'a significant sociological unit'. Please note the concept of the 'whole working structure of legal pluralism' as being the legal culture of a socio-legal entity.
(19) Some preeminent scholars are particularly relevant to this definition of law: Hoebel 1954: chap. 4 on 'fundamental legal concepts', in which he discusses four different sets of right-duty relationships, that is, those based on a supreme legal idea, whether philosophical 'justice' or anthropological 'native justice'; Weber in Rheinstein 1967: 5-10 on the elemental mechanism of legal authority.
(20) See, for example, Burman & Harrell-Bond 1979.
(21) This is because strict law is elaborated by meticulous formalities and systems of legal rules, while legal ideas, such as justice, equity and natural law, are defined according to their roles in the system.
(22) This explanation of historical development is based on data from other references, as well as my recent studies of Japan's history focusing on the cultural region of Chinese characters. See also, generally, Coleman and Haley 1975; Noda 1976: chap. 2; Ishii 1980; Steenstrup 1991; Oda 1992: chap. 2; Yasuda 1995. For the Tokugawa period, see Henderson 1965; Wigmore 1967-86; Hall 1979.

Chapter 2. Legal Pluralism in Japanese History and Society 59

(23) This may be shown by reference to some epochal events in Japanese relations with three Korean sub-state during this period: with Silla in 205 AD, Paekche in 247 AD and Kogryo, bordering upon North China, in 297 AD.

(24) However, Japanese legal and general historians have not overtly affirmed or denied this facts supposedly for two reasons: first, because there are no written records left and, second, because Japanese official history tended to devaluate, or even deny, any Korean influence. See further below[3.3 & 3.6].

(25) See translation in the glossary at the end of this chapter.

(26) A Chinese record of early fifth century named these *wako* (Japanese pirates) and the term was also used in Korea. These pirates caused much more damage to Korea than to China.

(27) For example, the tale that, in 200 AD, following divine revelation, Empress Jingu sent an expedition to Korea to subjugate Silla is not proven by historical evidence.

(28) See Lu 1974. Vol. I: 21-23 for the text.

(29) The reason for this shift is clear. Korean civilisation, which had once amazed the Japanese, was now found to be no more than transplantations from, or imitations of, Chinese civilisation. Thus, Japanese leaders must have wanted to learn the models directly from China.

(30) All Shinto shrines were formally given hierarchical positions. The highest shrine, called Ise Jingu, has long retained this position to enshrine the Gods of the Tenno family.

(31) In continuation of earlier religious beliefs, the ideology of the Tenno was based on the religio-politico belief of *kami*: see [3.2]

(32) Under the Hojo Shogunate, *Bakufu* law was codified in 1232 into 51 articles. It was called *Joei-shikimoku* (or *Goseibai-Shikimoku* or Code of Joei). See Lu 1974, Vol. I: 102-109 and Hall 1979: 19-42 for the text.

(33) Called *Buke Shohatto*, see Lu 1973, Vol. I: 201-204 for the text.

(34) See Hall 1979: 145-266 for the text.

(35) For example, *dozoku* (a group of the related families composed of the main family and its branches) as in Lebra 1992: 16-17, *shinrui* (lineal and collateral relatives), and *oyabun-kobun* (fictitious parent-child relationship) as in Nakane 1970: 40-46.

(36) A term referring to the prototype of the community in medieval German agricultural village, derived from Otto Friedrich von Gierke.

(37) Society of communal relationship, one of the antonym derived from Ferdinand Tönnies..

(38) Society of mechanical relationship, the other of the above antonym.

(39) Note the nature of modern pluralism, in which unofficial law is usually left to the private domain.

(40) Examples were edicts for hard work, keeping to a simple life, respect for gods and Buddha, observing village law and the 'five family groups', the last of which placed collective responsibility for public order on the neighbouring five families (see Lu 1973, Vol. I: 205-213 and Hall 1979: 132-143 for examples).
(41) Examples are collected in the volumes of Wigmore 1967-86.
(42) See Haley 1991: 186-190 and Goodman & Refsing 1992: 1-25 for details.
(43) See Tanaka 1976: 16-24 for the text.
(44) The modern system of Japanese law, together with the process of the transplantation and its socio-cultural background, has been studied by many Western and Japanese scholars. Prominent are von Mehren 1963; Takayanagi 1963; Tanaka 1976; Oda 1992 in English; Murakami 1974; Igarashi 1990; Coing et al. 1988; Scholler 1993; Menkhaus 1994 in German; Scheer 1993 in both German and English; Centre Français de Droit Comparé 1989; Maison du Japon 1991; Matsukawa 1991 in French.
(45) This office finally became the present University of Tokyo, after repeated reorganisations.
(46) A chronological period of 1688-1704.
(47) The genre of pictures on colour prints of everyday life in the floating world.
(48) Related to the above-described preparatory processes is the development of another cultural postulate: a generous allowance of the 'exception to general principle' according to differing circumstances. This allowance can be observed, first, in *Bakufu* allowing Dutch foreign trade and in the Japanese learning of foreign sciences under the isolation policy. Second, an important exception, was Korea being the only country with which *Bakufu* continued official exchanges by large delegations after its reopening. Third, the regular contact and trade with Korea were not directly handled by *Bakufu*, but entrusted to the lord of Tsushima, the island nearest to Korea. The best use of exceptions was to be made without marring general principles; that is, there was a general flexibility to select either principle or exception in given situations, a form of situationism. This cultural postulate is not new, but rather a developed variation of the abovementioned tactful use of either *tatemae* or *honne* [see 3.11].
(49) See Chang 1984 for details.
(50) See Tanaka 1976: 16-24 for the text.
(51) This maxim translates as 'no punishment except with the law'.
(52) The Court Law included Tenno's acts of worship at Ise Jingu and some limited particular shrines.
(53) Out of the changes was the decrease of the total number of shrines to around 100,000, as the result of a half-successful national policy in later Meiji years to amalgamate the smallest of local shrines. See Fridell 1973 for details. See also [6.3].
(54) This conflict was partially responsible for Japan's entry into World War II.

Chapter 2. Legal Pluralism in Japanese History and Society 61

(55) See Lu 1974, Vol. II: 70-71 for the text.
(56) The English translation of the Imperial Rescript on Education consists of over 200 words. The effects of this indoctrination were evidenced by the suicide parties during the various wars: for example, bomb-carrying soldiers in 1932 and bomb-laden Kamikaze planes in 1943.
(57) See Tanaka 1976: 3-15 and Port 1996: 268-278 for the text.
(58) The earlier Constitution was based on a German model.
(59) See [4.9].
(60) Those radical changes developed more under the new Constitution than was expected, producing such symbolic phrases as 'rooting the new Constitution in society', in contrast with the 'disorganisation of the traditional family and village community'.
(61) See generally Kawashima 1963 and Port 1996: 607-628.
(62) Hashimoto 1963: 242 and Port 1996: 248-262.
(63) Watanabe 1963: 378.
(64) Refer to Ishii 1993. In most countries, autonomous laws are often authorised by Constitutions as with Tibet, as well as scheduled tribes in the Indian mountains, and a variety of ethnic and religious minorities on the Asian continent.
(65) In addition, the revision of law has, in fact, not been a turning away from the traditional nature of Tenno, but rather a return to the principles founded on Japan's long history. The measures taken in the Meiji Constitution regarding Tenno were seen as going too far. Tenno authority, as such, is today still in existence in a different mode.
(66) For example, some provisions which allow the only one successor to inherit genealogical records and ancestral graves of a family, instead of having those records and graves divided up equally among beneficiaries of an estate, are often used to realise traditional primogeniture. There is also provision for maintenance of the family name to symbolise a traditional family, by free choice of the parties at marriage, although there is an option to allow a married couple to retain a different family name.
(67) See Port 1996: 206-211 for the judgment.
(68) See Henderson 1965, Vol. II and Port 1966: 458-476.
(69) See discussion on the 'reluctant litigant' in Haley 1978: 81-119.
(70) See Oda 1992: 61-63 and Port 1996: 645-689.
(71) See Upham 1987 and Haley 1991 for details.
(72) Common Lands and Forests Modernisation Law 1966.
(73) See [4.7].
(74) See Fridell 1973 for details.
(75) Before the present 'disorganisation of village communities', the local community included the whole local population, but since Japanese modernisation, a local community means a voluntary group of local residents who consider the commu-

nity to be their home, generally limited to farmers and shop-owners.

(76) See Sonoda 1975 for exmples.
(77) Variations upon, and adoptions of, the *iemoto* system are broadly prevalent in, for example, *kabuki* play, *sumo* wrestling, *waka* (31 syllable poem), *haiku* (17 syllable poem), and others.
(78) Hsu 1975.
(79) See Hamada 1992: 139-140, 163; and glossary at the end of this chapter.
(80) See Haley 1991: 183-186.
(81) See De Vos & Wagatsuma 1966 and Port 1996: 562-593.
(82) He explained the need to identify a particular 'legal sensibiliry' of a socio-legal entity, which is invoked by the entity's 'inward conceptual rhythm' and furnished with its 'symbols and system of symbols'. See Geertz 1983: 69, 182, 214.
(83) See Chiba 1989: 156 for details.
(84) See Kawashima 1963.
(85) Upham 1987: 21, 207-208.
(86) Haley 1991: 197, 199.
(87) For instance, the finding of *jori* (nature of things or reasonableness) in variations through history. See Röhl 1994.
(88) Lebra 1976: 27.
(89) Ohnuki-Tierney 1984: 70-74.

Chapter 3. Legal Pluralism in Sri Lankan Society
Toward a General Theory of Non-Western Law

1 Introduction

1 From non-Western law to legal pluralism

What is non-Western law ? This question has been regarded as if meaningless since the latter half of the nineteenth century. In reality, non-Western law has outwardly appeared to have been overwhelmed by transplanted Western law which was involuntarily imposed or voluntarily received. Non-Western law has been deprived, as a result, of the nature of 'law.' An exceptional minority of scholars who perceived its nature as 'a law' did not go so far beyond calling it, at first, 'ancient law' and then 'primitive law'.[1] Western law has been believed to be the authentic type of law with universal applicability. Accordingly, Western jurisprudence which has been charged with the mission to foster as well as justify Western law was also believed to be the universal, orthodox science of law not only by Western scholars but, in fact, by marginal non-Western scholars. (For details, see Chiba 1989: chap. 3)

During the following century, however, the believed-in universality of Western law and jurisprudence had to be crucially swayed two times by the revelation that their universality has, in reality, been accompanied by the cultural and social particularities embedded in Western history, in brief, 'relativizing of Western law and jurisprudence,' as I would call it. The first shock came from the legitimization of socialist law and jurisprudence in the new U.S.S.R after World War I and in the other socialist countries which successively gained independence after World War II. The main reason for the shock was the occurrence of the socialist legal system and principles to have intended to reject the capitalist ones. The second shock came from the disclosure of legal pluralism existent in non-Western countries which gained independence from colonial status after World War II.

Truly, during a short period soon after gaining independence, 'unification' of indigenous law by state law transplanted from Western countries, along with economic development, was the most important target of the new nations. The target has been never abandoned, but the new state legal system was soon found inseparably permeated by and, therefore, coexisting with indigenous law so conspicuously that the concept of legal pluralism was needed (cf. Gilissen 1972; Hooker 1975; Jørgensen 1982; Sack & Minchin 1986; Griffiths 1986; Merry 1988; Chiba 1989).

By way of contrast, 'primitive law' had increasingly attracted attention among anthropologists during the period before and after World War II because of the significance of its function in primitive societies of Oceanic islanders, African tribes and American Indians (cf. Malinowski 1926; Hoebel 1954). Their empirical method was truly different from the normative one of the orthodox jurisprudence, but the perspectives of both disciplines were not so different in that they had the tendency to isolate law from the rest of the total culture in society. Their features were invitations for criticisms from two sides. Criticism from one side characterized non-Western law as traditional against modern Western law and insisted upon its modernization for the development of non-Western countries; but such an idea was recriticized before long as justifying Western ethnocentrism or imperialism in law (for a review of the discussion, see Chiba 1989: chap. 2). Criticism from the other side, starting from the concept of 'tribal law' which redefined primitive law as inseparably interconnected with the total phase of tribal life (cf. Gluckman 1965a), reached the idea of 'legal pluralism' which observes non-Western law as comprising both transplanted state law and indigenous law, but which puts emphasis on the latter in opposition to the ethnocentric Western view (cf. Marasinghe & Conklin 1984; Allott & Woodman 1985; Renteln 1990).

2 The concept of non-Western law

Then, has the study of legal pluralism succeeded in representing the contemporary non-Western law correctly and clearly as it exists under its circumstances ? The question might be answered 'yes,' when we look at the considerable amount of reliable data on the topic. Still, it may be duly answered 'no,' when we find the shortage of information and lack of theory of the existing non-Western law in those data.[2] The following reasons may be given for such a negative answer.

Firstly, the concept of non-Western law accepted so far is not a substantial one which is constructed inductively from empirical data in variety, but rather an expedient one which is used to provisionally conceptualize all kinds of law other than Western law which the orthodox jurisprudence has taken for granted to be the only law. The concept of non-Western law in this inexact meaning is nothing more than a rudimentary, at best heuristic, one which is destined to be revised as researches present more and more meaningful data.

For this reason, secondly, its definition may vary according to the difference in research plans. For instance, to mention a common concept, some may define non-Western law as the state law of non-Western countries, individually or collectively. However, this is meaningless for our purpose, because our study is meaningful only when it treats the existing non-Western law as a whole which is pluralistically constructed of not only state law but other kinds of official law such as religious law or tribal law, and furthermore, unofficial law in various forms, whether supporting or conflicting with official law.

Thirdly, some other specialists being aware of such facts define non-Western law as indigenous law of non-Western people, individually or collectively.[3] This definition is somewhat meaningful, because it focuses upon the existing non-Western law which has been unreasonably underrated in the study of law. Recent anthropological achievements have made a valuable contribution to revise the aforesaid heuristic definition. Still, contrary to our purpose, they tend to lack, by and large, the perspective of the interrelation and interaction between indigenous law and state law.

Thus comes the fourth definition: non-Western law as the 'working whole structure of law in non-Western countries,' individually or collectively. In this, the structure is fundamentally constructed by official law on the one hand, which, besides keynoting state law formally transplanted from Western law, includes religious law, tribal law, local law, family law, minority law, and the like, insofar as adopted in or authorized by state law, and by unofficial law on the other, which, originating as a rule in various indigenous sources, works with different functions such as supplementing, opposing, or undermining official law especially state law. Its variation in each country and theoretical formulation as a whole should be pursued by the study of legal pluralism.

3 Research project under consideration

In the late 1970's while Western specialists started to pursue the above fourth concept of non-Western law, I had an opportunity to be inspired for joining the pursuance of non-Western law at an international conference in 1975 I assisted to organize,[4] and then organized two research teams to explore non-Western law in pluralism, among others, Asian law, on which meaningful research had been lagging behind compared with African tribal law and American Indian law, and which I had felt obliged to try to attempt as an Asian scholar. The basic aspiration for the projects was kindled by the following perception:

> Non-Western people have each cherished their indigenous law as integral part of their cultural heritage. During their long histories their law has on occasions encountered foreign law, whether voluntarily or not, and these encounters have led sometimes to peaceful assimilation and other times to destructive struggle between indigenous and foreign laws. The indigenous law may sometimes have failed to maintain itself, while at others it may have succeeded either by rejecting the foreign law or by adapting itself to conserve its cultural identity. Contemporary non-Western law is thus seen as one in a current state in an ongoing process of self-developing indigenous law whether successfully or not. Truly, the reception of Western law by non-Western countries in modern times is the most influential encounter of non-Western law with foreign law. However, it is still only one of many encounters in the long history of each non-Western law. (Chiba 1986: v)

The first project, in collaboration with specialists from each of six countries of Asian culture, aimed to present comparative features of the interaction between indigenous law and transplanted law in the countries characterized by traditional cultures originated in Asia: Sunni-Islamic Egypt, Shii-Islamic Iran, Hindu India,

Chapter 3. Legal Pluralism in Sri Lankan Society 67

Buddhist Thailand, multi-religious Sri Lanka, and Shintoist Japan, as well as to formulate the first theoretical scheme to apply to legal pluralism in general. Its final report was published in a book form (Chiba 1986).

For the second project, in collaboration with ten Japanese specialists from law, anthropology and South-Asian studies, chose Sri Lanka in 1979 as their objective of the intensive survey. The reason for the choice was mainly that Sri Lanka has a most complicated history of transplantation of foreign law, and that it is not so large a country which would be greatly beyond the capacity of our team. After a preparatory survey by four members in 1980, the team performed the main survey in the summer of 1982.[5] Data obtained from individual survey by some members before and after the main survey having been added, this project was finally completed in 1988 in a book written in Japanese.[6] The following sections of this Chapter are a summary of the book.

2 Whole structure of Sri Lankan law working officially or unofficially

1 Structure of the book and working hypotheses

The project had two purposes. The immidiate purpose aimed to accurately observe the working structure of Sri Lankan law as a whole and correctly analyze its elemental factors into a theoretical system. The final purpose aimed to formulate a general theoretical scheme enough to accurately observe and correctly analyze the existing complexities of Asian law, with still further expectation of its applicability to human law, including Western law.

At the outset, the immediate purpose required us to critically examine our methodological standpoint to ensure that it was free from the Western bias which had been disclosed in recent related discussions. We adopted three specified approaches in consideration of the enlightening discussions. First, our main target of research should be indigenous law working in contemporary society rather than transplanted state law, because the former has, in general, not been treated in jurisprudence compared with the attention given much more to the latter. Of course, while it should be observed and conceptualized distinguishably from the transplanted law, it should not be isolated from the working structure as a whole together with the keynoting state law and other socio-cultural factors.

Second, the indigenous law should be identified in both domains, if existing in the working whole structure, that is, in official law as adopted in the transplanted legal system and in unofficial law as functioning in socio-cultural settings. This may be a new approach among the fellow researches on legal pluralism. The four Chapters 3 to 6 in Part I of the book are thus devoted to exploring indigenous law in the official system, and another four Chapters 7 to 10 in Part II to that in the unofficial settings.

Finally, such a working whole structure should be meaningfully understood only when observed as a result of the historical endeavors, struggles and achievements, including some bewilderments and failures of the Sri Lankan people as the responsible socio-legal entity, not as a smooth nor agreeable result from the imposition of Western law. Chapters 1 and 2, in addition to scattered descriptions in other chapters, thus examine the cultural heritage of Sri Lankan Law.[7]

As was the case with the above immediate purpose, the final purpose required us to formulate two working hypotheses, because we could not find any reliable tool concepts and theoretical scheme available for our undertaking. Their nature should, firstly, enable us to accurately observe and correctly analyze legal pluralism, especially unofficial indigenous law, and secondly, be operational for and revisable by succeeding reseaches. They were as follows, although they were soon reformulated in the final stage of our research as described in the last paragraphs of this article.

One of the hypotheses was the 'three-level structure of law' which was to include in a whole system the other kinds of law which the orthodox jurisprudence had refused to regard as law in spite of their significant effects on the working whole structure of law. 'Official law' was law authorized by the legitimate authority of a country, including state law and some of customary law such as religious law, tribal law and the like as far as authorized by the legitimate state law. 'Unofficial law' was such a law not officially authorized by the legitimate authority, but sanctioned in practice by the general consensus of a certain circle of people, caus-

Chapter 3. Legal Pluralism in Sri Lankan Society   69

ing a distinct influence upon the effectiveness of official law, positively or negatively. 'Legal postulate' was a value principle or system which specifically connected with and worked to justify particular official or unofficial law.

The other hypothesis, 'interaction between received law and indigenous law,' was to take serious consideration of the fateful encounter that non-Western law had to face. 'Indigenous law,' in a broad sense, was law originating in the native culture of a people and, in a narrow sense, law existing in the culture of a people prior to the reception of Western law in modern times. 'Received law' was broadly that which was received by a country from one or more foreign countries, and narrowly Western law received by non-Western countries in modern times. 'Interaction' includes both acceptance and rejection or modification of foreign law by receiving countries.[8]

The society chosen for our study in which the above working hypotheses are to be validated is an old island country well-known by the name of Ceylon in the region of Indian culture. The image of the gem island in the Indian Ocean or the native country of Ceylon tea may sound beautiful, but, in fact, the island was colonized by the West. The majority Theravada Buddhists and minority Hindus had founded dynasties respectively with scattered Muslims and Christians. The people finally gained independence in 1948 and adopted the native name of Sri Lanka for their state in 1972. Their future was hopeful, but in recent years especially since 1983, their national unity has been jeopardized by the so-called ethnic conflict. Such a history of the Sri Lankan people has developed in close connection with its large neighbor India in every phase of culture, society, economy and politics.[9]

2   Development of the pluralism seen from changing official law

Sri Lanka has been a typical multi-ethnic society. The aboriginal Veddhas had earlier been outrivaled by foreign ethnic groups who transmigrated from the Indian continent. One of them were the Dravidians represented by the Tamils who brought in Hinduism, the caste system, and Hindu law. But, the Arians represented by the Sinhalese succeeeded in establishing the first kingdom between the fifth and third centuries B.C. with the political idea of the 'region of the Buddhist King' founded on their Theravada Buddhism. The kingdom continued, with changes in dynasties, until it finally was subverted by the British power in 1818. In the course of their history, they developed their own legal system, a Buddhist law which is called Kandyan law after the name of the last dynasty, the still remaining indigenous law of the Buddhist Sinhalese. On the other hand, the Tamils established an independent Jaffna Kingdom after new immigrants occupied the northern area between the thirteenth and fourteenth centuries. It was subverted by Portugal in 1619, but their own indigenous Hindu law of the Jaffna Tamils with some variations with the caste structure is known at present as Tamil law called *Tesavalamai* after the name of the most popular one. Both of these indigenous laws were deprived of their official status after the Western invasion, but were never totally outlawed. Their essentials were frequently incorporated into the new official systems transplanted from Western law. In fact, the colonial governments attempted to record them for selective adoption; and in this attempt, after the first (Portuguese) and the second (Dutch) failed, the third (British) succeeded. Both Kandyan and *Tesavalamai* laws are truly of different origin and history, but they clearly belong commonly to the basic Indian culture legally represented by the ancient Indian Code of Manu which was also transplanted to other Theravada Buddhist countries like Thailand and Burma.[10]

Thus, the legal pluralism developed out of indigenous laws to a typical one of indigenous laws and transplanted laws. After the Portuguese law left no significant influence, Dutch law, different at that time from the contemporary one, was so influential that its legacy was carried into the present law of libel, unjust enrichment and *fideicommissum*, now called Roman-Dutch law. Of this, some high ranking legal agents today often speak proudly of their contributions to the preservation of such an old law.[11] But, subsequently, British common law exerted deeper and wider influences such that Sri Lanka today is a representative common law country. Still contemporary Sri Lankan law adopts various other laws of different origins, such as some Roman-Dutch law as well as indigenous laws, not only Buddhist law among the Sinhalese and Hindu law among the Tamlis, but also religious law among Muslims and Christians. This must show the unyielding socio-cultural tradition of the Ceylonese, which was actively working under the British policy of indirect rule.[12]

With the national independence after World War II, such a tradition worked out manifestly as clearly seen in the transformation of the judicial system into one with more national features. For instance, traditional village courts which had been functioning among people were made official as the lowest Rural Court. The unique Conciliation Board instituted in 1958 was devised to realize popular justice by layman. The importance of conciliation for the judicial procedure seemed increased in some procedures for various conflicts even after the suspension of the Conciliation Board in 1978. In the Constitution of 1972, the movement for nationalization was symbolically declared together with an article to specifically protect Buddhism,[13] and also secured by instituting their own Supreme Court instead of the preceding British Privy Council. Subsequently, the Constitution of 1978 adopted a de Gaulle style presidential government from a French system.[14]

The above Conciliation Board was, in fact, created and abolished in twenty years. Its life was complicated. First, the reason for its institution was furnished by three conflicting camps demanding the revival of indigenous popular practice, transplantation of the Indian *Panchayat*, and taransplantation of the popular court in socialist countries (cf. Tiruchelvam 1986). The interest in socialism is worth noticing, for it was later developed into an overt constitutional policy with various social welfare measures in education, medicine and livelihood assistance. Then, its nature of deprofessionalization of the judicial process brought about opposing effects among people: it freed people from the foreign-made strict pressure of the judicial system, on the one hand, but it invited some confusion on national justice and negative criticism from lawyers, on the other. For the reason of these negative effects, it was abolished by the power of the de Gaulle style President.[15]

Legal pluralism at present is much more conspicuous when various indigenous laws are found incorporated into the official state legal system. First, family law is legislated in accordance with its differentiation in the religious practices of marriage, divorce, matrimony and inheritance. Second, religious laws are also enjoying their autonomy. Buddhist law among Sinhalese is particularly protected by a constitutional article and accompanied by some legislations for *Sangha*, temples and their property, while Hindu law among the Tamils and Islamic law among the Muslims are protected by particular legislations and established judicial precedents under the constitutional freedom of religion. Third, some local laws are adopted, too, because the above Buddhists and Hindus are largely living in localities and some special local practices are made official as in conciliation procedures.[16]

Such a pluralism is nothing but a result of the wisdom of the people to maintain their cultural identity, though with some failures. This is clearly seen by reviewing the judical system working in actuality among people. The old Kandyan dynasty had authorized the indigenous village court called *gamsabhave*. The court was officialized under the later British rule after having been outlawed in earlier years. There was another quasi-judicial practice before and after independence, in which the official village headman kept the official record of unofficial hearings of conflicts between villagers. This practice and record seem to have been replaced by the new local administrators such as the Cultivation Officer who is entitled to manage agricaltural conflicts.[17] Both official system and the unofficial are found here to have been inseparably connected in function.

3 Unofficial law composing the pluralism

In order to observe such influential unofficial law functioning in people's daily life, intensive surveys were conducted in several villages. One of them done of a village called Beralapanatara, which is divided into two sub-villages, revealed a norm structure of a Sinhalese society. Among various norms contributing to the social integration of the village, both conventional and current norms are found conspicuously working independently or dependently. Of the conventional norms, there are two sets of basic importance. One is those of the villagers to maintain Buddhist temples and their activities: for instance, villagers are obliged to make offerings to the temples, participate in the *poya* observances at the temples in all days of the full moon, and invite monks to their domestic events such as marriages, funerals, house-building, prayers for recovery from diseases, etc. In return for these obligations, they are privileged to cultivate paddies of the temples or borrow money from the temples when needed, and participate in educational and cultural events at the temples. The other set of conventional norms is those related to a Himdu caste system; for instance, prohibition to select spouses and associate with people from different castes, though working latently. The current norms, originating in the official authority of the state, are working in different ways according to the different state functionaries in the village. Noticeable among them are regulations of the aforementioned Cultivation Officer for agricultural activities and the Development Officer for the cooperative development of the village. Those and others are compoundedly contributing to the social integration of the village.[18]

Among those social norms, the most fundamental are those supposed to be originating in Buddhist law, except among the seven hundred Tamils working in isolated tea estates. There is historical evidence that the traditional Buddhist worship has long been offered not only to the Lord Buddha but to syncretized Hindu gods, local deities/demons and spirits, and that these practices are prevalent beyond differences in castes and localities. Most important among the norms of Buddhist origin may be the duty of the layman to offer meals and goods to the monks at the temple, unlike to the visiting mendicants in Thailand, in the hope of 'merit-making for happiness in the next world.' In contrast to such an unofficial law among people, the practices of *Sangha* and temples had been made official by the Kandyan dynasty and are protected by the present official law as seen by the aforementioned constitutional article and the prevailing national worship to the Temple of the Tooth in Kandy. Judging from the historical facts above, Buddhism has been generous enough to give the multi-religious people a national integration. However, considering the recent bloody and exhausting conflict between the Sinhalese and the Tamils since 1983, the Buddhist idea seems to be utilized, according to reliable observers, as a political ideology to forcibly realize an integration.[19]

Farmers composing the majority of the entire population have also unofficially developed some system of agricultural regulations for themselves, among which the most characteristic is one to self-control the water system for paddy farming especially in the Dry Zone, North-Eastern plains. In unidentified early times, farmers had created many tanks to reserve water and developed regulations to utilize them. With more water being required for post-war rural development, an ambitious project is in operation to introduce some water of the Mahaweli, the longest river on the island, to those areas mentioned above. Still, tank irrigation obliges farmers to observe their practiced rights and duties to control utilization and administration of the water. The rights and duties are unofficial but perhaps more vital to the farmers concerned as an agricultural law than official law.[20]

Finally, the social status of women composing another half of the population is discussed in respect to its traditionality toward modernization in the recent trend. Women laborers were chosen as the sample from two factories, traditional tea making and modern porcelain production to validate the well-known rule that a positive will to work and ordered discipline by the laborer tend to decline under bad working conditions and alienated humanity in a rationalized system. The results obtained from both factories rather invalidated the rule, for the laborers are used to working hard in spite of unfavorable conditions. The reason is analyzed differently for each of the factories. The tea factory laborers are induced to work by the manifest or latent pressure of the family and caste structure, obedient attitudes toward authorities, and their own plans to earn money for their dowry. Among the porcelain factory laborers, however, the pressure of the caste is replaced by their desire to earn money for their families. The analysis gives evidence that contracts under official law together with the traditional duties under unofficial law gave a positive motivation to those women laborers to work.[21]

3 Conclusion

As stated above, the field survey of Sri Lankan law has disclosed its working structure as a whole. It is found forming a most complicated legal pluralism composed of both official law and unofficial law or else both indigenous law and transplanted law, under the guidance of some legal postulates such as the Buddhist, the socialist, and an unidentified one which has enabled such plural forms of law to work as Ceylonese/Sri Lankan law distinct from the other peoples. Its invalu-

Chapter 3. Legal Pluralism in Sri Lankan Society 75

able contribution to our purpose is, we believe, that it has validated the basic idea of the two working hypotheses as well as invalidated some minor factors to be further reformulated. An attempt at the reformulation is finally described below.[22] (For further detail, see Chiba 1989: chap. 12.)

The initial two working hypotheses have been reorganized into a new theory called 'three dichotomies of law.' Its main structural variables are arranged into three different dichotomies, and integrated into a system by the basic postulative value called the 'identity postulate of a legal culture,' which was first obtained from my other researches and then found in the data from this survey though not precisely. The new theory is formulated originally to apply to Asian situations, but extendedly to the other non-Western and forthermore to the Western as well.

The first dichotomy comprises, in relation to the different modes of the authority of legal sanction, *official law* vs. *unofficial law*, terms which are defined respectively as the "legal system and its components authorized by the legitimate authority of a country," and the "legal system and its components not officially authorized by any legitimate authority, but authorized in practice by the general consensus of a certain circle of people, whether within or beyond the bounds of a country, when they cause distinct influences upon the effectivity of official law, supplementing, opposing, modifying or even undermining any of the official laws, especially state law." While state law, "the official law of a political body called state," is truly typical of official laws, it is not, as too often taken for granted, the only one. In addition to their state law, many capitalistic and some socialistic countries in the world are also officially regulated by religious law, local law, family law, ethnic law and others often collectively called customary law.

The second dichotomy is the contrast of positive rules, or legal rules, with postulative values, or legal postulates. *Legal rules* are "the formalized verbal expression of particular legal regulations to designate specified patterns of behavior," and *legal postulates* are "the particular values and ideas and their systems specifically connected with a particular law to ideationally found, justify and orient, or else supplement, criticize and revise the existing legal rules." Both the legal rules and legal postulates of a particular body of law coexist and cofunction, as a rule, interactingly. Among the various modes of the interaction between the two, particularly to be noticed is the independent function of legal postulates when the supported legal rules have become outdated or disappeared; while they may be easily deserted from lack of a sound basis fortified by legal rules, or, in the contrary, invoke the potential of reactivating outdated legal rules or even creating new legal rules to embody themselves.

The third dichotomy is especially serious to contemporary non-Western countries, though applicable to Western countries as well. It relates to the different origins of law in human society. The contrast here is *indigenous law*, broadly defined as "law originating in the native culture of a people" and narrowly as "the law existing in the indigenous culture of a non-Western people prior to their transplantation of modern Western law," in contract to *transplanted law*, broadly defined as "law transplanted by people from one or more foreign cultures" and narrowly as "the state law of a non-Western country transplanted from modern Western countries." It is noted that, as mentioned above, the contrast of indigenous law vs. transplanted law is a relative one to be exhibited differently with the degree of assimilation of foreign law, and that transplanted law may be typified by two types: that which is voluntarily received and that which is involuntarily imposed.

In sum, the law of an individual country may be accurately observed and analyzed in its working structure by the above analytical tool scheme of the three dichotomies of law. In other words, it may be elucidated as comprising different types of official law and unofficial law, each of which is constituted of legal rules and legal postulates as well as of indigenous law and transplanted law, received or imposed. The combination of the three dichotomies in reality vary from country to country. Such variations will exhibit diverse legal examples of the proportion of two polar variables in each dichotomy and transformation of those combinations and proportions with time, including the case when transformation may result in the total replacement of a state's legal system.

Still, except in rare cases, people who have cherished their indigenous culture may preserve their legal culture through transformation of the combination and proportion of the three dichotomies. In so far as a legal culture is preserved, a "basic legal postulate for the people's cultural identity in law," which I would call the *identity postulate of a legal culture*, must be presupposed as functioning. It guides a people in choosing how to reformulate the whole structure of their law, among others, the combination of indigenous law and transplanted law, in order to maintain their cultural identity in law under changing circumstances.

In conclusion, the three dichotomies of law, comprised of official law vs. unofficial law, legal rules vs. legal postulates, and indigenous law vs. transplanted law, combined into a legal culture under the guidance of the identity postulate of the legal culture, is a useful analytical tool scheme for accurate observation and analysis of the working whole structure of law of a people, individually or comparatively. It awaits empirical verification and further theoretical elaboration.

Notes

(1) Still other terms were used such as customary law, native law, local law, unwritten law, preliterate law, etc.

(2) See, for instance, Arnaud 1988, which includes two items, 'pluralisme juridique' and 'pluralisme juridique (théorie anthropologique),' but never mentions empirical traits nor theoretical schemes of non-Western law. This lacking was corrected in Arnaud 1993.

(3) Instead of indigenous law, other rubrics such as customary law, folk law, unofficial law, primitive law, etc. may be used, each with a different meaning as found when precisely examined but with a common nature being conceptually outlawed from state law.

(4) Annual meeting of the ISA Research Commitee on Sociology of Law, Hakone, Japan, September, 1975. It adopted a topic on Asian and African law for the first time at the occasion of its first meeting in non-Western countries. For details, see Chiba 1976.

(5) The expenses for the survey and publication of the results were granted mainly by Japanese Ministry of Education, Science and Culture.

(6) *Suriranka no Tagen-teki Ho-taisei: Seioho no Ishoku to Koyuho no Taio* (Legal Pluralism in Sri Lanka: Transplantation of Western Law and Counteraction of Indigenous Law), edited by Masaji Chiba, Tokyo: Seibundo, 1988. I am grateful to the Sri Lankan people who kindly helped us carry on our survey, including the

late Neelan Tiruchelvam and other specialists in law who gave us invaluable instruction (cf. Tambiah 1950, 1968, 1972; Cooray 1971; Nadaraja 1972).
(7) The above description is summarized from Section 1 of 'Introduction' on 'Purpose and Significance' by Chiba.
(8) The above, from Section 2 of 'Introduction' on 'Working Hypotheses'.
(9) A brief summary of 'Outlines of Sri Lanka' in three sections: on cultural history by Yoshio Sugimoto, social characteristics by Yoshiko Taniguchi, and ethnic problems with relation to India by Teruji Suzuki.
(10) From Chapter 1 on comparative features of traditional law by Ryuji Okudaira.
(11) They share the proud role with South Africa.
(12) From Chapter 2 on transplantation of Western law by Takao Yamada.
(13) It reads: The Republic of Sri Lanka shall give to Buddhism the foremost place and accordingly it shall be the duty of the State to protect and foster the Buddha *Sasana*, while assuring to all religion the rights granted by Articles 10 and 14 (I) (e) (freedom of religion——Chiba).
(14) From Chapter 3 on the judicial system after independence by Nobuyuki Yasuda.
(15) From Chapter 4 on the socialization of the judicial system attempted by the Conciliation Board by Teruji Suzuki.
(16) From Chapter 5 on family law especially the Islamic by Michio Yuasa.
(17) From Chapter 6 on the indigenous judicial system by Jini'chi Okuyama.
(18) From Chapter 7 on the social integration of a village by Motoyoshi Omori.
(19) From Chapter 8 on traditional Buddhist practices by Yoshio Sugimoto.
(20) From Chapter 9 on the traditional practices of tank irrigation by Hisashi Nakamura.
(21) From Chapter 10 on tradition and modernization among women by Yoshiko Taniguchi.
(22) From Section 2 of 'Conclusion' by Chiba. (Section 1 summarizes each Chapter.)

Chapter 4. Islamic Law transplanted in Asian Countries*

1. As it is unusual for an editor to review a book he edited, this piece might miss just criticism a third party could offer. The reason why I dare to attempt it is that I wish to present the contents of this unique collection by Japanese contributors[1] to interested foreign scholars in the hope of furthering the studies of Islamic law, non-Western law, and legal pluralism in the world.

Islamic law has been written about a great deal and is well known among Western legal scientists by the countless works on it. However, the related works are mostly produced by theoretical or ideological interests with little attention of its working reality by a wide variety of peoples and countries. Truly, some exceptional works have been presented, but, generally speaking, their number is too small and the scope is too limited to convey a variety of accurate information.

The working reality of Islamic law in the contemporary world are grouped tentatively for a heuristic purpose into three areas according to the cultural characteristics of its geogrphically different prevalance. The first area is made up of Near and Middle Eastern countries from which Islamic law, after having been founded in earlier times, has disseminated itself among surrounding heterodoxy peoples. For this reason, I call it the "home of Islamic law." The second area covers African countries in the West. The third area includes Asian countries in the East other than the home countries. Both the second and third areas developed Islamic law in their characteristic legal pluralism combined with their own traditional cultures.

Such a grouping might be criticized by some specialists in Islamic law. I would not rebut them, on the one hand, for I admit their supposed grounds, the "Umma Community" as a whole. However, I have to rebut them, on the other, when we observe the working reality, as is clearly shown by the fact of so many Islamic peoples and countries coexisting in the world with their own cultural identities.

The division between African and Asian Islamic law might also be doubted. There are, however, reasonable grounds to make a distinction between the two continents based on their socio-cultual and historical circumstances: 1) traditional cultures as world of kinship-based societies versus world of multi-cultural societies, 2) colonization in modern times of all countries except Ethiopia versus many independent countries having survived colonization, and 3) revival of Islamic law after World War II with more attempts for modernizing Islamic law in Asia[2] than in Africa. It is therefore a reasonable scientific requirement to try to identify the different ways in which Islmic law has been transplanted in each area, as is suggested by the slogan "Islam toward East" which Muslims proudly cry of the East.

Islamic Law transplanted in Asian Countries examines the state of transplanted Islamic law in eleven Asian countries.[3] There are three reasons why other Asian countries are excluded. First, countries in Near and Middle East, the home of Islamic law, are out of my definition of transplanted Islamic law. Second, countries such as Japan and Korea present no reliable information about Islamic law because the percentages of Muslims[4] in the populations are too small. Finally, those countries around Indo-China, includig Brunei, also lack enough informaion to be compared with the eleven countries discussed in the book. Afghanistan and Turkey, which may be counted among Near- and Middle-Eastern countries, are included to contrast their situation with the home and transplating countries.[5]

2. China is a country from where news of Muslims or Islamic law is rarely heard. In fact, however, as many as 190 million Muslims are dispersed throughout the total population of the country. In each of the 127 local areas where Muslims occupy a majority population, ranging from the biggest Autonomous Districts such as Sinkiang Urgur and Nigsia Hui, to many provinces, prefectures, cities, and even the smallest villages, the central government authorized its self-government. This is the outcome of a long history of a considerable number of Chinese people having indigenized transplanted Islam. This can be seen in their contemporary home-born denominations, peculiar forms of schools and mosques, various daily practices against traditional Confucianism, Taoism and Mahayanist

Chapter 4. Islamic Law transplanted in Asian Countries *81*

Buddhism, as well as the postwar oppression of the socialist government especially during the Cultural Revolution from 1966 to 1977.

The current Chinese regime admits freedom of religion in the Constitution but places particular administrative restrictions originating in its socialist policy on Muslims, For instance, the Chinese central govenment prohibits the Shari'ah Court, religious education and marriage, and organizational activities including liaisons overseas except for those specifically permited. Muslims are allowed by local legislations, on the other hand, to observe their precepts of specific food and drink with adequate ones provided by their local governments, religious festival days, burial instead of regular cremation, and other daily practices including the five virtuous deeds. The people's behavior thus waivers between Islamic and Chinese laws. As a result, there are found both routinized conflicts and accommodation, including Muslim practices with no visits to mosques, only irregular or totally unserve of five daily worships, festival days and Ramadan.[6]

News of tough struggles of Muslims is often heard from the Philippines, where not more than five percent of the whole population are Muslims. The Muslims in the Philippines are mainly living on Mindanao and neighboring islands. The purpose of their struggle against the Christian majority government had been to enjoy autonomy. In other words, they wanted to legally elevate the status of unofficial customary Islamic Iaw to official law. After independence in 1946. gradual advancements helped finally reach the goal by having the government enact the Code of Muslim Personal Laws of the Phlippines in 1977, and establish the Autonomous Region in Muslim Mindanao and Shari'ah Court in 1990. While some activists still complain of the unsatisfactory results of these new policies, most Muslims today enjoy being able to choose their legal identities between governmental and Islamic laws.[7]

Indonesia, with the biggest Muslim population in the world, is noted as one of the representative Islamic countries in Asia but in fact there has formed a typical multi-racial and religious society constituted of indigenous peoples and immigrants from surrounding seas. After independence in 1945, the legal target of the Muslim majority was to elevate customary Islamic law to offical law. The advancement of the movement faced a difficult course, for conflicting requirements of various peoples of different religions and racial origins had to be taken into consideration. Their target may be said to have been realized, though with some limitations, when one sees it to be a success that a new marriage law was enacted in 1974 to admit Islamic marriage and that a Religious Court was authorized in 1989. In contrast, an official project in codifying Islamic law remains unrealized, which started in 1985 but still is continuing today due to the conflicting pluralism of various laws, each based on different religious or secular or else indigenous or transplanted origins.[8]

Malaysia is another representative Islamic country in East Asia made up of multi-cultural societies, being unique in preserving the former Sultun System in her regime. It is symbolized by two constitutional principles: 1) the status of Islam as the national religon and 2) the authority of the King as the supreme Islamic ruler, for the King, elected from among the Sultuns of constituting nine Islamic states, also rules the other five states which are governed by secular Governors. The Islamic principle has thus permeated into every phase of such official systems of the law as the political, court, administrative, educational, as well as personal and marriage. It should not be overlooked, however, that Muslims, being little more than half of the total population, are facing difficult problems in achieving further accommodation with other powerful minorities such as the Chinese Malaysians.[9]

Few scholars would have information of Muslims in Thailand, for many scholars tend to believe that the people of this country are all occupied by Theravada Buddhists. However, four percent of the population are Muslims, living in the areas of the capital Bangkok, the old capital Chiengmai which has many Chinese immigrants, and four southern prefectures which border Malaysia with many Malays. This has been officially made possible by the policy of Buddhist Kings since the 17th century to protect Muslim merchants in the then capital Ayutthaya. After the officialization of Buddhist Sangha in 1902 together with religious freedom in their modern Constitutions, the policy was developed by the following Kings, finally to establishng the Mosque Committee in 1945.[10]

The Union of India, with 25 States and seven Territories, is noted for its Hinduism but in fact presents a most complex legal pluralism that had developed before her independence and after separation from Islamic Pakistan in 1947. Islmic law was gradually tansplanted in earlier times to the whole of India into three modes: Hinduized Islamic law widely practised among Hindu people, Anglo-Muhammadan law acculturated with the transplanted Common law by the official court decisions and legislations under the British rule after the 19th century, and the original Islamic law with rare acculturation with other laws. The Union of India today provides as many as nearly 100 million Muslims with official laws, mainly as personal law including marriage and *Waqf*, while the Islamic laws of commerse and crimes were replaced by transplanted modern law.[11]

Together with acculturation, however, various conflicts between Islamic law and other laws, whether official or unofficial, caused difficult accommodation. The recent Shah Bano case was most noted for two reasons: 1) it was a frontal clash between the official Indian Shari'ah Act to limit the responsibility of a Muslim, in conformity of the original Islamic law, to pay alimony to his divorced wife within the remarriage restriction period of three months, and the Criminal Procedure Act which orders such a man to continue payments with no temporal limitation. The clash was finally resolved by the decision of the Supreme Court in 1985 to favor the modern principle. And 2) the judicial decision advised the government to enact a new Muslim Women (Protection of Rights on Divorce) Act in 1986 with a clause enlarging some rights of divorced wives.[12]

Pakistan separated from Hindu India in 1947 to gain independence, and Bangladesh did from Pakistan in 1971. However, both countries received most of the official Islamic legislations of personal law from India. In addition, they of course enacted their own laws. Among some legislations which Pakistan enacted on Islamic principles, the Muslim Family Ordinance in 1961 is most remarkable. It is a small but epoch-making legislation in two ways. First, its purpose was to achieve modernization of an Islamic principle to protect devorced wives against what was viewd as unfair treatment for the reason of traditional Islamic polygamy. Second, the Ordinance was followed by Bangladesh, too. Isalmic law in both countrise is thus generally of a common nature but, when the particulars are compared, some differences are found. It is the contributor's assertion that such differences were mainly caused by the fact of a fundamentalist trend in Pakistan and more acculturation with Hinduism in Bangladesh.[13]

Sri Lanka, which was also separated from India in 1948 and is often said to be a Common law country together with India, Pakistan and Bangladesh, presents another similar but different acculturation of Islamic law. The working whole of its Islamic law can be seen in the official system of personal law. Under the Constitution which declares to uphold seemingly heterogeneous Buddhism and Socialism, Western-style personal law is made up with some influences of five different legislations: the Common law of marriage with some influences of survived Roman-Dutch law, customary law for people preserving Buddhist practices in Kandyan District, Hindu law among the minority Tamils mainly living in Jaffna District, Islamic law among the Muslims who amounts to five percent of the population, and a special law for foreigners. As to Islamic law, two characteristics are to be remarked on: that practiced discrimination against women is mitigated by the modern official law but not to the extent of the above-mentioned three countries, and that disputes among Muslims are treated by the Kadi of Shari'ah Court.[14]

People living in Afghanistan formed an Islamic nation in the early 18th century. This was long after having transplanted Islam and converting from indigenous Zoroastrianism, overcoming inside struggles among tribes and factions, as well as outside threats from the east by Great Britain and later Pakistan, and from the north by Russia and later the Soviet Union. Under such a complicated international circumstance, their modern nation has had to suffer from repeated fluctuations between monarcy, socialism and democracy. Their Constitutional laws accordingly repeated revisions. For instnace, the Fundamental Principles of Politics in 1931, Constitution of the Kingdom in 1964, Constitution of the Republic in 1973 after a *coup d'état*, Fundamental Policy of the Democratic Republic in 1978 after the socialist revolution, Fundamental Principles of the Democratic Republic in 1980 under the Soviet invasion, Constituion of the Republic in 1987 and continuing suspention of Constitution since the retreat of Soviet army in 1989. Still, the Islamic principle has survived such fluctuations in the variant constitutional principles, though with different importance attached to them. In contrast, Islamic law has remained with rare remarkable changes as seen by farmers observing customary Islamic law, both official and unofficial, in their daily life.[15]

Turkey presents a more striking sxample of Islamic law differing between the official and unofficial levels. Such a detachment originated during the reformation of the Islamic Ottoman Empire in the early 19th century to westernize their legal system based on the model of France. The Civil Code, delayed after some trial laws, was finally enacted in 1926, being copied from the Swiss Code, together with seven other modernized codes enacted by the Republican Turkish government which had been established in 1923. The new Civil Code aimed to replace traditional Islamic personal law almost totally. In contrast, people especially those living in agricultural areas, still have tended to observe Islamic law in their landholding and familial matters of marriage, divorce and inheritance.[16]

3. My abridged descriptions above of eleven Asian countries may contain some points to be criticized from two sides. One is from the contributors who may feel that my abridgement of their works is missing what they intended to write in each chapter. I hope, however, that they may understand my intention to present our general results in an abridged form before an international forum in order to add important data regarding hitherto neglected Islamic law in legal pluralism of Asian countries. The other group of scholars who are focussing on legal pluralism and comparative law may argue that what I have presented does not cover the whole bird's-eye view of Islamic law in Asian countries. I also hope that they may accept my both intention and inevitable limitations as written in the outset.

I am convinced that *Islamic Law transplanted in Asian Countries* has added some impoprtant information that was lacking in the related circle of study. First, the book discusses Islamic law in representative Asian countries in its variant modes of acculturation with other laws. Second, different modes of legal pluralism which Islamic law forms with other laws, whether officially or unofficially, are dealt with. Third, a suggestion to promote the comparative study of the transplantation of law and its outcome in non-Western countries is given.

Even if my conviction is supported by readers, the book is known to have left some neccessary works undone, on the other hand: To make an accurate view of the whole structure of legal pluralism in the world and transplantation of law which caused it. I would appeal to interested scholars to further advance such works.⁽¹⁷⁾

Notes

(∗) This chapter is originally a review essay of the book in Japanese, edited by myself and published by Seibundo, Tokyo, in 1997, with the title of *Ajia ni okeru Isuramu-ho no ishoku* (Islamic Law transplanted in Asian Countries).

(1) See note 3.

(2) People's efforts to modemize Islamic law is written in Chapter 2 of the original book: "Tradition and Modernization of Islamic law" by Michio Yuasa, specialist in family law and Islamic law.

(3) There are no Japanese specialists in Islamic law, except Yuasa and a few other theorists. I was successful however in finding some other scholars who do not specialize in Islamic law but had obtained important data on it in the pursuit of their particular specilizations. They met, to my happiness, my desire to cover the eleven significant countries.

(4) In Western jurisprudence, the word "recipient of law" is reasonably distinguished from another word "observer of law." However, as far as Islam and Islamic law are concerned, both words may be used alike in most cases. For this reason, I use here "recipient" and "observer" of Islamic law and "Muslim" synonimously.

(5) The above-mentioned is abridged from Chapter 1 "Problems in Transplanted Asian Islamic Law" by Masaji Chiba, specializing the anthropology of law.

(6) Chapter 3 "Islamic Law in China" by Ken Suzuki, specialist in Chinese family law.

(7) Chapter 4 "Law among Muslims in the Philippines" by Masami Mori, specialist in anthropology.

(8) Chapter 5 "Codification of Islamic Law in Indonesia" by Yasuko Kobayashi, specialist in international relations.

(9) Chapter 6 "Islam and Marriage Law in Multiracial Malaysia" by Yoshiyuki Hagiwara, specialzing in Malaysia, and Jiro Kojima, specialist in family law.

(10) Chapter 7 "Thai Muslims and King's Protection of Religion" by Yoneo Ishii, specialist in South-Asian History, translated from English by Junzo Iida, specialist in international law.

(11) Section 1 of Chapter 8 "India" by Michio Yuasa, note 2 above.

Chapter 4. Islamic Law transplanted in Asian Countries *87*

(12) Section 2 of Chapter 8 by Nobuyuki Yasuda, specialist in Asian Law.
(13) Chapter 9 "Pakistan and Bangladesh" by Michio Yuasa, note 2 above.
(14) Chapter 10 "Sri Lanka" by Atsuko Tanaka, specialist in family law, and Jin'ichi Okuyama, specialist in Sri Lankan society.
(15) Chapte 11 "Acculturation and Development of Islamic Law in Afghanistan" by Mitsue Kobayashi, specializing in agricultural law.
(16) Chapter 12 "Modernization of Turikish Civil Law and Islamic Law" by Yoko Hanawa, specialist in family law.
(17) Chapter 13 "Problems Left on Asian Islamic Law" by Masaji Chiba, note 5 above.

Part II

NON-WESTERN LAW

Chapter 5. Droit non-occidental*

L'expression 《Droit non-occidental》 peut désigner: (1) le droit des pays non-occidentaux, (2) le droit étatique des pays non-occidentaux, (3) le droit non-officiel des sociétés non-occidentales dans les pays capitalistes et socialistes, (4) la coexistence du droit étatique avec le droit non-officiel dans les pays non-occidentaux, (5) ou bien, encore, la culture juridique des pays non-occidentaux.

Définitions

Contrairement à l'usage qui est en fréquemment fait, la notion de droit non-occidental n'est ni simple ni scientifiquement établie. On en compte de nombreuses acceptions. Ainsi, la première définition, 《droit des pays non-occidentaux》, sert à distinguer le droit des pays non-occidentaux du droit occidental. Cependant cette distinction ne possède pas vraiment un caractère scientifique: elle ne fait que mettre en relief une différence sans viser son contenu, en particulier la signification des termes 《non-occidental》 (*non-Western*) et 《droit》 (*law*). De ce point de vue, la seconde définition, 《droit étatique des pays non-occidentaux》, est plus élaborée; elle applique la conception du droit des pays occidentaux à la situation occidentale, qu'ils s'agisse des pays socialistes ou des pays capitalistes.

Mais on peut regrouper autrement ces diverses définitions. Dans un premier groupe, on trouverait les conceptions qui ne tiennent pas compte du droit non-officiel et accordent peu d'attention au droit étatique d'origine autochtone (*indigenous*)[1]. Dans un second groupe, on pourrait classer celles qui rendent comptent des influences socio-culturelles sur le droit étatique[2] et qui insistent sur l'existence de droits hétérogènes aboutissant à la formation d'un pluralisme juridique incluant le droit étatique[3].

Dans un troisième groupe, on trouve des définitions critiques par rapport à celles du groupe précédent, qui insistent sur les influences autochtones sur les législations coloniales et néocoloniales[4], attirent l'attention sur le caractère étatique[5], dénoncent le caractère ethnocentrique des définitions employées[6], ou se prononcent pour une réforme du droit applicable aux pays du tiers-monde[7] ou au bénéfice des minorités[8].

Différentes de celles mentionnées initialement, les définitions à caractère anthropologique se relient plutôt à ce troisième groupe; elles se concentrent en fait surtout sur le droit indigène des tribus ou des minorités et s'appuient sur des enquêtes poussées, soit basées sur le terrain[9], soit d'ordre plutôt bibliographique[10]. Mais elles tendent à souffrir d'un manque de précision en ce qui concerne la définition de ce qui est nommé 《droit non-occidental》.

Récemment, les spécialistes du pluralisme juridique ont observé avec beaucoup d'attention la coexistence du droit étatique avec le droit non-officiel, particulièrement avec le droit autochtone. Leurs travaux justifient une quatrième définition, 《la coexistence du droit étatique avec le droit non-officiel dans les pays non-occidentaux》[11]. On trouve quelques différences dans leurs approches: les droits indigènes persistent, mais le droit étatique tend à les submerger[12]; il existe un indissociable processus d'interaction entre le droit étatique et le droit non-officiel[13]; on note un essai de classification générale des différents processus d'interaction[14]. Parmi eux, on peut trouver quelques partisans du second groupe de définitions, dans la mesure où ils acceptent l'idee du pluralisme juridique.

Avec la cinquième définition, 《la culture juridique des pays non-occidentaux》, le droit non-occidental non-officiel est caractérisé par les particularités culturelles de chaque groupe ou de chaque société, et le droit étatique coexistant est décrit comme interagissant plus ou moins avec les facteurs culturels spécifiques. Ce type d'approche est réservé à ceux qui ont une bonne connaissance des particularités culturelles du droit non-occidental.

La signification de l'étude du droit non-occidetal

Depuis que les sociétés occidentales ont élaboré un système juridique moderne fondé sur l'autorité légitime d'un État centralisé, tous les autres systèmes juridiques qui ont prévalu dans d'autres sociétés ont été l'objet d'un processus de disqualification. Le droit a été limité à la sphère étatique, sauf lorsqu'on prend la précaution de lui ajouter expressément des qualificatifs spécifiques. Une science du droit a été développée pour faire bénéficier cette conception du droit d'une théorie juridique qui la protège et l'authentifie — la légitime — en recourant à l' autorité étatique, comme le montrent les doctrines de John Austin et Hans Kelsen.

Ainsi, on observe des efforts de qualification de certaines normes sociales agissant en interaction avec le droit étatique, lorsque celles-ci comportent des aspects juridiques. Ainsi en est il des termes suivants: droit médiéval, droit féodal ou droit vivant, droit traditionnel, droit local, droit d'origine religieuse, droit de la parenté (*kinship law*); ou droit primitif, droit autochtone, droit tribal, droit populaire (*folk law*), etc.

Ces droits marginaux ont, en fait, été déterminants pour les peuples qu'ils concernaient avant la formation du droit étatique moderne; mais, dans les pays occidentaux, ils ont été incorporés dans le droit étatique et ont fini, en conséquence, dans les pays non-occidentaux, par être dévalorisés par rapport au seul ⟨véritable⟩ droit.

La situation a changé dans le courant de ce siècle. Quelques anthropologues ont démontré que la nature du droit primitif était indépendante du droit étatique, sans toutefois aller jusqu'à mentionner son caractère non-occidental. Après la seconde guerre mondiale, des juristes de plus en plus nombreux ont commencé à concentrer leur attention sur les aspects complexes du droit des sociétés non-occidentales, dans des perspectives sociologiques ou anthropologiques. Si l'on s'en tient aux résultats auxquels sont parvenus aujourd'hui les spécialistes à la recherche d'une définition plus élaborée, on doit particulièrement signaler l'activité de deux institutions: (1) l'IUAES (*International Union of Anthropological and Ethnological Sciences*), dont dépend la commission du *folk law* et du pluralisme juridique qui étudie ce dernier dans l'ensemble (CFLLP) du monde (et pas seulement dans le monde non-occidental); (2) l'*International Third World Legal Studies Association*, qui milite pour le développement des populations rurales du tiers-monde, et pour la création d'un nouveau type de droit.

Les études sur le droit non-occidental doivent parvenir à une définition telle que les différences entre les unes et les autres soient éliminées. En revenir à une définition ⟨authentique⟩ du concept de droit suppose que l'on mette sur pied une méthodologie également authentique.

Les traits fondamentaux du droit non-occidental

Parmi les nombreux traits du droit non-occidental qui ont retenu l'attention des auteurs, trois facteurs méritent d'être retenus en raison du contraste qu'ils forment avec le droit occidental moderne.

La diversité

À la diversité correspond le concept de pluralisme juridique. Le droit non-occidental est bien pluraliste, fondamentalement formé par le droit étatique et le droit non-officiel, ce dernier étant indubitablement le plus déterminant. Cependant, la réalité est plus complexe. Un système juridique étatique peut souvent autoriser officiellement l'autonomie d'autres systèmes de droit, tels que des droits religieux, local, tribal, etc., qu'on peut qualifier de «droit officiel» comportant du droit étatique. Mais, d'autre part, on trouve du droit non-officiel fonctionnant de façon indépendante dans des entités socio-juridiques allant des villages, de la famille, d'autres petits groupes, jusqu'aux nations et groupements de nations.

En même temps que le dualisme entre droit officiel et non-officiel, on trouve donc un autre dualisme : celui du droit étatique et du droit mondial. Le droit non-occidental est vraiment très diversifié.

On trouve encore d'autres formes de diversité. Si l'on s'en tient à ses origines, le schéma conventionnel de la distribution droit étatique/droit autochtone n'est peut-être pas complètement faux, mais il demeure trop simpliste. En réalité, un droit étatique transplanté incorpore très souvent du droit autochtone et peut être reçu ou rejeté au cours de longs processus historiques. En général, sa formulation ne vise pas à exprimer systématiquement des règles juridiques et tend plutôt, à l'exception de quelques droits religieux, à fonctionner à partir de postulats juridiques non-écrits. Ses effets sur le système social sont différents de ceux du droit moderne, dans lequel on doit raisonner logiquement à partir de règles juridiques écrites basées sur le principe de l'Etat de droit, le «Rule of Law».

Le type de lien qu'entretiennet droit et culture

Le second trait fonde la distinction entre droit occidental et non-occidental dans la différence culturelle. Sous cet aspect, l'approche anthropologique est parvenue à des résultats remarquables. Sans remonter aux études fondamentales de H.S. Maine, L.H. Morgan, A.H. Post, J. Kohler, R. Thurnwald et autres, les anthropologues occidentaux, après B.K. Malinowski, ont élaboré des perspectives générales sur les caractéristiques culturelles du droit non-occidental. Ainsi, le droit tribal africain a-t-il été exploré par les études du E.E. Evans-Pritchard, M. Gluckman, etc., tandis que le droit des Indiens d'Amérique l'était par E.A. Hoebel. Les autres régions du monde n'ont pas fait l'objet d'enquêtes aussi poussées, si bien qu'on manque d'éléments pour établir les caractéristiques générales des droits de ces contrées, quoiqu'on dispose de bonnes études ponctuelles sur des populations (notamment insulaires) d'Asie ou d'Océanie. On ne connaît presque rien des populations d'autres régions de l'Asie qui utilisent l'écriture chinoise: l'Asie du Nord et continentale, dominées par des régimes communistes, et l'Asie de l'est.

Sans enquêtes scientifiques fiables sur un certain nombre de populations, il sera probablement impossible, dans l'avenir, d'expliquer la dépendance du droit vis-à-vis de la culture. Cependant, si l'on considère les résultats obtenus par quelques auteurs, on peut identifier certaines zones régionales de cultures juridiques. Ce sont les cultures juridiques de l'Islam, de l'Inde, de l'Afrique et de la Chine telles que les ont étudiées les comparatistes. Les cultures juridiques bouddhistes et d'Océanie ont été étudiées par les anthropologues; la culture judaïque est apparemment isolée mais possède des relations essentielles avec le droit occidental moderne.

Les conséquences a posteriori du colonialisme

Le colonialisme est, à l'origine, engendré par l'autorité politique réelle et l'hégémonie économique des pays occidentaux sur les pays non-occidentaux. L'ère coloniale terminée, on s'aperçoit de la prévalence fictive de la culture moderne occidentale sur les populations non-occidentales, et on note, de plus, la croyance symbolique dans la culture occidentale. En bref, l'ethnocentrisme de l'Occident demeure.

La réception du droit par des pays non-occidentaux est dominée par un ethnocentrisme réel, fictif et symbolique. Il est prouvé que la soi-disant universalité du droit occidental moderne, inventée par les Occidentaux, sert en réalité à préserver le pluralisme juridique. Des études récentes placées sous le signe du pluralisme juridique ont montré la permanence du droit vivant non-occidental et autochtone, qui a survécu simultanément au droit reçu, que ce droit ait été imposé ou reçu volontairement. En fait, tous les peuples non-occidentaux ont veillé sur leur droit autochtone et combattu les droits étrangers pendant tout le temps durant lequel ils ont dû assurer le maintien de leur identité culturelle dans leur culture juridique.

Il a pu en résulter le rejet ou l'assimilation du droit étranger, ou, au contraire, leur insuccès dans cette aventure culturelle, de telle sorte qu'ils ont dû reformuler ou abandonner leur droit autochtone. Le pluralisme juridique contemporain chez les peuples non-occidentaux n'est pas autre chose que le résultat, ou plutôt l'expression, de ce processus conflictuel, qui est l'une des conséquences juridiques de la colonisation, postérieure à l'ère coloniale. On doit toujours porter attention à l'interaction entre droit occidental transplanté et droit non-occidental autochtone.

Méthodologie de l'étude du droit non-occidental

Les traits mentionnés ci-dessus montrent qu'il faut développer une méthode nouvelle pour observer avec précision et analyser le droit non-occidental tel qu'il existe et qu'il fonctionne[15].

Une approche sociologique peut servir de modèle. Appliquée à l'étude du droit non-occidental, elle est, en fait, parvenue à des résultats considérables. Mais, en même temps, la sociologie du droit a tendance à prendre le droit occidental comme son objectif essentiel. Cela est logique, car la sociologie a d'abord été créée pour comprendre la société moderne. Elle avait peu d'estime pour les sociétés prémodernes, et, pour elle, les sociétés non-occidentales devaient être classées en fonction de la distinction sociétés modernes/sociétés prémodernes.

Une approche anthropologique doit nécessairement compléter ou remplacer l'approche sociologique. Comme on peut s'en rendre compte à l'observation d'un grand nombre de bibliographies et de revues (*Journal of Legal Pluralism and Unofficial Law; Law aud Anthropology; Verfassung und Recht in Uebersee*; etc.), la connaissance contemporaine des droits non-occidentaux doit se faire à l'aide des résultats obtenus par cette approche. L'anthropologie juridique doit être de plus en plus développée car elle permet de mettre fin à de nombreuses interprétations fausses d'observations faites partout dans le monde. Mais l'anthropologie telle que la conçoivent généralement les spécialistes occidentaux ne semble pas complètement dégagée de l'ethnocentrisme occidental[16].

On a demandé à l'anthropologie d'être, avec la sociologie, objective et neutre dans ses observations et ses analyses. Cette exigence repose sur de bonnes raisons, mais, d'un autre côté, tend trop à cacher, sous le masque de l'objectivité scientifique, la prééminence des conceptions occidentales du droit et à légitimer des points de vue ethnocentriques. On doit, de façon urgente, formuler une méthode nouvelle pour corriger ou abolir cette tendance.

On peut tendre vers deux objectifs. L'un est la formulation d'un schéma analytique de concepts destinés à être appliqués au droit non-occidental. En bref, il faut rendre opérationnel pour des recherches empiriques le concept du 《folk law》, sur lequel il y a consensus. L'autre objectif est de pouvoir observer à la fois avec objectivité et un esprit ouvert le point de vue des populations non-occidentales dans leur lutte pour le maintien de leur identité culturelle sur le plan juridique. En bref, il faut transformer en concepts analytiques l'idée critique d' 《ethnocentrisme occidental》.

Une approche de ce type consiste à distinguer: (a) trois dichotomies du droit qui comprennent les différents types de 'droit officiel' et 'droit non-officiel', dont chacun est constitué de 'règles juridiques' et de 'postulats juridiques' aussi bien que de 'droit autochtone' et de 'droit reçu'; (b) le concept fondamental de 《postulat d'identité d'une culture juridique》[17].

Cette hypothèse doit être confirmée afin que le but projeté soit atteint, grâce à la coopération des auteurs intéressés, non-occidentaux.

Notes

(*) Les pages qui suivent constituent une version remaniée d'un texte paru au Arnaud 1993 et sont reproduites avec l'aimable autorisation de la Librairie Générale de Droit et de Jurisprudence (Paris). Traduction de Norbert Rouland.

(1) Cf. par. ex. David & Brietley 1985.

Chapter 5. Droit non-occidental

(2) Cf. par. ex. International Legal Center 1974.
(3) Cf. par. ex. Carbonnier 1978.
(4) Cf. Hooker 1975.
(5) Cf. Burman & Harrell-Bond 1979.
(6) Cf. Rouland 1988.
(7) Cf. Marasinghe & Conklin 1984.
(8) Cf. Tiruchelvam & Coomaraswami 1987,
(9) Cf. Malinowski 1926; Hoebel 1954; Gluckman 1965a, 1965b.
(10) Cf. Griffiths 1986; Merry 1988.
(11) Cf. Allott & Woodman 1985; Chiba 1986.
(12) Cf. Abel 1982.
(13) Cf. von Benda-Beckmann et al. 1988.
(14) Cf. Morse & Woodman 1988.
(15) Cf. par. ex. Marasinghe & Conklin 1984.
(16) Cf. Renteln 1988.
(17) Voir Chiba 1989: 177–180; pp. 16–20 de ce livre.

Chapter 6. A Horizon of Legal Anthropology*

1. The main part of this book is a collection of 26 articles written by 22 Japanese scholars to give a general view of contemporary topics in the anthropology of law.

In Introduction, Jin'ichi Okuyama first reviews the formation of the discipline by scholars such as Malinowski, Radcliffe-Brown, Hoebel, Gluckman, and others, and then Taro Kitakamae traces the develpment of main topics from primitive law and conflict management, through their socio-cultural contexts, to contemporary legal pluralism and legal culture.

Part I is to examine the possible contribution of the discipline to a further advancement of legal sciences in general. The viewpogints taken by six writers seem to diverge into two different orientations. On the one hand, Masayuki Koike is convinced of its essential contribution to the History of Legal Ideas in revealing unconscious group norms working in or as law; Tsuyosi Mori to the History of Japanese Law in disclosing magico-religious norms functioning in Japanese local societies; Teruji Suzuki to Comparative Law in examining plural legal cultures such as ones in Middle and Eastern Europe; and Takanori Kitamura to Legal Semiotics in exploring law as a cultural symbol.

On the other hand, Setuo Miyazawa asks legal anthropologists to extend their perspective to contemporary complex society for sociologists of law to make best use of their achievements on small-scale societies; and Shigeru Otsuka compares Legal Anthropology that focuses on the law of different culturs in non-Western society with Philosophy of Law that treats modern Western law.

Part II collects various examples of indigenous law or legal culture working without direct connection with state law.

First, *Daimonji-yaki*, popular yearly fire event in Kyoto, Japan, is described by Haruka Wazaki as regulated by an unofficial law similar to that of *matsuri*, festivals of the Shinto Shrine, although the event originated in a Buddhist practice. Another unofficial law is reported by Seiji Maeda of *rit* among the Lawa, moun-

100 Chapter 6. A Horizon of Legal Anthropology

tain people in Thailand, as functioning effectively by its postulated principles and concrete orderings. In contrast, *Dammathat*, legal idea transplanted from old India, was embodied, Ryuji Okudaira states, in the official legal system of the Burmese dynasties and still partially working among people under the present revolutionary regime of Myanmar.

Next, variations of Sri Lankan indigenous law are exemplified. A number of precedents of unofficial conflict management by an official village headman are reported by Jun'ichi Okuyama on the one hand, and, on the other, as Yoshio Sugimoto discloses, the legal idea combined with Buddhism *Damma* laid at the base of the royal authority of the premodern Kandyan Kingdom and is protected by a constiutional clause in force.

Followingly, three examples are described as working basically unchanged under seemingly changing circumstances. The elaborate procedure to manage conflicts by the popular judge is revealed by Masaru Miyamoto on the Hanunoo-Mangyan, Mindoro Island of the Philippines. The social order in Papua New Guinea is viewed by Hironari Narita as achieved by the rules of struggles among groups and the competent Bigmen of the groups. Another developed indigenous law is reported by Motoyoshi Omori of the Chiga, Uganda, with its systematic function.

Part III offers succinct illustrations of lagal pluralism, whether indigenous law is overwhelmed by or accommodated with state law.

The Ainu is found, according to th analysis of Toro Kitakamae, as having been deprived of their various indigenous titles by the modernized Japanese government. The Confucius human morals transplanted to Vietnam from old China is also found by Masanori Aikyo to be disappearing under the present socialist regime though with some survivals. It is made clear by Junzo Iida that the alleged modernization of Thai marriage law before 1935 adopted traditional polygamy in fact to mitigate a sudden change.

A severe struggle between state law and indigenous law is exemplified by Nobuyuki Yasuda in his description of a traditional Hindu practice called *Sati*, wife's death with her deceased husband, that took place in India in 1987 so influentially as to drive people to raise a shrine for the dead wife against official prohibition by state law. In contrast, three native laws are reported in regard to their

Chapter 6. A Horizon of Legal Anthropology *101*

official recognition in respective Constitutions, though still with some limitations: of the Indians in U.S.A. since later 19th century and of the Inuits in Canada since 1970s by Denmei Ueda, and of the Aborigines in Australia by Hideki Kaneshiro.

Last three chapters present examples of indigenous law which have survived unofficially or officially under the transplanted state law. The Mexican law to accomplish the agricultural revolution since 1910 as summarized by Narumi Hasegawa was in reality an encounter of three different systems: colonial plantation, pre-Columbian common, and modern individualism. Contemporary Islamic law is, Michio Yuasa views, partially officialized as of marriage and family by transplanted state law, and, simultaneously, prevailing unofficially among people as before. The legal culture of Middle and Eastern Europe is analyzed by Teruji Suzuki to be an amalgamation of Roman law or Islamic law, Canon law or Eastern Church law, socialist law or modern law, and folk laws of particular people.

Besides the above main part, Preface states the aim of this book in two: to produce the first text book in Japan for the anthropology of law and to commemorate my 70th birthday in 1989 for my alleged leadership in this new social science. With these aims, appendixes contain an essay by Andrzej Kojder, Warsaw University, to remark on my personality and international activity, and both a chronological table and a standard bibliography of legal anthropology arranged by Shu'ichi Sugita and Yoshindo Ohashi respectively.

2. It may be unusual for a scholar to review the book dedicated to himself. I am pleased to have this chance, however, to provide foreign specialists with a piece of information upon legal anthropology in Japan.

I feel some insufficiencies of the above contents compared with most advanced works abroad. I wish, firstly, that the contributors to Part II, mostly from anthropology, might have paid more attention to the interaction of indigenous law with state law, while the contributors to Part III, all from law, might have done to anthropological data; secondly, that the cases might have been collected from wider areas in the world; and thirdly, that any chapter might have attempted to make theoretical investigation of legal pluralism and legal culture.

Still, I evaluate the book as a significant one for the developing anthropology of law; for the insufficiencies mentioned above are not the defects particular of the Japanese contributors but also represent the general tendency of the achievements in the international circle. What is required at present to advance the anthropology of law is, I believe, to collect much more data on legal pluralism and legal culture as well as to refine the methodology and theory. I never doubt the significant role of this book from Japan to get nearer to fulfilling these requirements, and hope the contents of the book to be useful as a supplement to the recent French works by Rouland (1988 and 1990).

In Japan, my earlier book (1969) was the first introductory one to the anthropology of law, although its contents were occupied by a bird's-eye view of foreign achievements alone based mainly on African and American data. One of my recent books (1991) collected eleven articles written on various legal cultures in Japan and in the world. In contrast to these books of mine, this new one consists of a variety of cases of indigenous legal culture and legal pluralism gathered from wider areas together with the methodological and theoretical examination of this dicipline.

The description in each chapter is concise but reliable being based on each contributor's preceding intensive study. With these contents, this book deserves of the first text-book of legal anthropology in Japan.

I am pleased with the fact that such a book was produced by younger Japanese successors. Their academic circumstances are not always favorable. For instance, there is no regular chair of legal anthropology at the universities, most of them have to work for their major duties in other fields of law; foreign languages and travel expenses always form barriers against their international activity. Their aspiration may, I hope, push forward this science in spite of such difficult circumstances.

Notes

(*) This chapter was originally a review essay of the book in Japanese, entitled *Hojinruigaku no Chihei* (A Horizon of Legal Anthropology) edited by Michio Yuasa et al. and published by Seibundo, Tokyo, 1992.

Chapter 7. Une conclusion d'identité culturelles juridiques non-occidentales*

Ce livre (Capeller & Kitamura 1998) vise à présenter une vue d'ensemble de la culture juridique non-occidental, à savoir la culture juridique du monde non-occidental. Si l'on ne comprend pas correctement ce qu'est la culture juridique non-occidentale, les réalités et l'essentiel du droit non-occidentale échapperont à l'attention[1].

Ce livre peut sembler traiter d'un sujet nouveau ou plutôt insolite. Cela est vrai dans la mesure où nous avons présenté cinq cultures juridiques non-occidentales pour donner une vue d'ensemble de leur totalité. En même temps, nous devons garder à l'esprit qu'on traite d'un sujet relativement nouveau — la culture juridique — qui a ses exigences scientifiques propres.

Il y a, ainsi, deux modes d'approche: l'étude peut, en premier lieu, être concentrée sur son objectif premier, celui qu'on a à portée de main. Mais, en même temps, l'étude peut être rapportée à la carte générale des cultures — pour aussi hypothétique qu'on puisse considérer une telle carte — et au contexte d'ensemble. Alors apparaît un objectif secondaire, qui consiste à jeter un coup d'œil sur quelques autres cultures juridiques insignes non encore représentées, dans la mesure où il en existe dans le monde non-occidental, et de faire quelques suggestions utiles pour des recherches futures, à l'attention des chercheurs qui seraient intéressés à vérifier cette carte hypothétique.

Dans cette perspective, ce livre rassemble en substance trois groupes de textes distribués en deux grandes parties. Le plus important de ces groupes rend compte de cinq cultures juridiques non-occidentales; des sept auteurs de ces textes, tous sont natifs de la culture depuis laquelle ils s'expriment, ou suffisamment qualifiés pour en parler. L'autre partie traite de la culture juridique non-occidentale en général, d'un point de vue théorique, de la méthodologie et des objectifs, avec des commentaires et discussions, ainsi que quelques données personnelles[2].

Dans cette Conclusion, je voudrais d'abord mettre au clair la signification de

104 Chapter 7. Une conclusion d'identité culturelles juridiques non-occidentales

l'objectif de ce livre dans l'étude contemporaine du droit non-occidental, puis résumer et donner une estimation des résultats des contributions rassemblées, et, enfin, essayer d'indiquer quelques tâches à remplir, qui solliciteront des efforts de coopération de la part des chercheurs intéressés.

Dans cette perspective, et sur le vu du contenu, je suis convaincu du caractère unique de cette réalisation parmi celles, croissantes, qui se font sur le thème des droits ou de la culture juridique non-occidentaux, parce que les autres travaux semblent n'avoir pas réussi — malgré, parfois, des réalisations heuristiques remarquables — à fournir une vue générale précise de ce qui existe et fonctionne[3]. Il existe, heureusement, le précédent appréciable de l'*International Encyclopedia of Comparative Law*. Un de ses volumes donne un aperçu général des familles juridiques dans le monde, y compris les droits non-occidentaux, en plus de ceux de l'Occident et des pays socialistes[4]. Cette entreprise non seulement reflétait l'esprit d'une *Encyclopédie*, mais établissait également la doctrine de cette époque. Par rapport aux objectifs qu'elle s'était fixés et aux résultats qu'elle a atteints, les nôtres peuvent être décrits et évalués de manière distincte.

Réalisations et tâches laissées par l'*Encyclopédie*

On pourrait raisonnablement se demander, tout d'abord, quelle importance revêt l'objectif de cette Conclusion. On pourrait également se demander quelle est la signification des deux termes essentiels, 《non-occidental》 et 《culture juridique》, dans la perspective qu'on s'est proposée. En effet, le terme 《non-occidental》 a ordinairement été utilisé sans définition exacte, et 《culture juridique》 semble être utilisé sans définition claire, entre initiés. L'analyse de ces questions révélera des présupposés cachés derrière ces deux expressions, dérivées de l'opinion admise, et, en conséquence, l'importance de notre objectif, qui consiste à transgresser une frontière dans les sciences juridiques.

D'abord, l'usage de 《non-occidental》 est bien contrasté avec celui de son antonyme 《occidental》. 《Occidental》 semble être utilisé, souvent, aussi, sans définition spécifique, dans des citations individuelles. Cependant, on ne se trompe globalement pas sur le sens du mot, sans qu'il soit besoin de définition, parce que les utilisateurs connaissent bien ses significations, et l'utilisent aussi simplement

Chapter 7. Une conclusion d'identité culturelles juridiques non-occidentales *105*

que lorsqu'ils évoquent l'Europe, l'Amérique ou le monde, selon le contexte. Pour cette raison, seuls quelques auteurs sensibles ont donné du terme des définitions spécifiques, quand ils l'utilisaient dans des sens un peu différents[5]. En contraste, 《non-occidental》 tend à être utilisé ordinairement sans signification précise dominante, ni définition spécifique. Cet usage de 《non-occidental》 prouve que le terme n'est rien d'autre qu'un nom sur une boîte noire, utilisé pour signifier un autre monde, un monde n'appartenant pas au monde occidental. Autrement dit, les utilisateurs n'ont pas ressenti la nécessité de discerner la nature ni les variations existantes dans le monde non-occidental, en réalité bien plus diversifié que l'Occident.

Par ailleurs, trois prémisses ont servi de base à la signification prédominante de 《droit》, qui sont rarement contestées à cause de leur évidence en soi, qui fait qu'on y fait foi. Je veux parler du *monisme* des droits étatiques limitant droits et légitimité au système juridique d'un pays souverain, de l'*universalisme* du droit occidental fondé sur la prédominance et la supériorité apparentes du droit occidental dans le monde, et de la *systématisation formelle* si présente et si imposante dans le système des droits modernes d'origine occidentale. La signification de ces prémisses ne mérite pas, en elle-même, d'explication complémentaire, ici, mais je vais expliquer les raisons pour lesquelles je les ai mentionnées.

Jusqu'à l'indépendance des colonies occidentales du monde non-occidental après la Seconde Guerre Mondiale, le droit non-européen reconnu sous ce nom était limité au droit de l'État de quelques rares pays indépendants autres que les pays d'Amérique latine: l'Éthiopie, la Turquie, l'Iran, la Thaïlande, la Chine et le Japon — sauf quand on en parlait du point de vue historique, colonial ou ethnologique. Ces systèmes juridiques étaient cependant considérés comme peu dignes d'intérêt, parce que la structure fondamentale des droits étatiques avait été transplantée à partir des droits occidentaux.

Pour cette raison, l'*Encyclopédie* est un outil appréciable, parce qu'elle a soulevé certains doutes sur les prémisses qu'on vient d'evoquer, même si l'expression en demeure peu claire, par le fait que les droits qui y sont présentés sont considérés d'emblée comme non-occidentaux. On y évoque les 《Structures et Divisions》 des droits islamiques, hindous et africains dans un chapitre, et les 《Différentes conceptions des droits》 parmi les peuples islamiques, hindous, d'Extrême-

106 Chapter 7. Une conclusion d'identité culturelles juridiques non-occidentales

Orient et d'Afrique dans un autre[6]. Il est vrai que les éditeurs semblent d'abord avoir reconnu, outre l'existence d'un ⟨droit non-occidental⟩ et d'un ⟨droit non étatique⟩, quelques systèmes juridiques qui paraissent assez étranges tant la ⟨systématisation formelle⟩ des droits non-occidentaux, qui fut adoptée, était rendue problématique par l'hétérogénéité de ces derniers. De plus, ils ont, dans un chapitre sur les ⟨conceptions du droit⟩, ajouté en fait, un nouvel attribut au droit en adoptant un nouveau thème discuté par les sociologues du droit avant et après 1970 sous des appellations variées telles que ⟨conscience⟩, ⟨attitudes⟩, ⟨connaissance et opinion⟩, ou expressions similaires.

Mais leurs doutes sur les théories établies n'étaient pas assez puissants pour parvenir à faire chanceler leur conviction. Premièrement, les droits non-occidentaux qu'ils reconnaissaient étaient limités aux droits islamiques, hindous et africains, connus pour former des familles juridiques indépendantes qu'il s'agissait de différencier par rapport aux droits occidentaux et socialistes; et aucune tentative n'a été faite réellement de détecter des droits non-occidentaux, individuellement ou collectivement, en explorant les variations existantes autres que celles qui étaient adoptées par les éditeurs. Ceci prouve que ces derniers ont considéré les droits non-occidentaux comme quelque chose de bizarre du point de vue des droits occidentaux.

En deuxième lieu, les droits qui ne sont pas du droit étatique et qu'ils reconnurent néanmoins comme tels étaient constitués de seulement trois familles juridiques régionales et de quatre conceptions de droits (dans le volume consacré aux généralités), ainsi que (de manière dispersée dans d'autres volumes) du droit positif et des coutumes adoptés dans divers domaines juridiques particuliers. Cela prouve que les droits qui ne sont pas du droit étatique étaient pris en compte dans la mesure où ils présentaient un certain rapport évident avec les droits étatiques, mais sans intention d'en identifier les différentes variations.

Troisièmement, comme on peut l'imaginer, ils ne pouvaient trouver suffisante, aux fins de comparaison avec les droits occidentaux, aucune ⟨systématisation formelle⟩ des droits non-occidentaux.

Bref, l'*Encyclopédie* était encore enchaînée à ces prémisses. Son traitement du droit chinois est un bon exemple de cet assujettissement. À première vue, il était raisonnable de traiter de la conception chinoise du droit comme des conceptions islamique, hindoue et africaine. Il peut donc sembler étrange que le système juridique chinois n'ait pas fait l'objet du même traitement que les trois autres. L'étrangeté n'est qu'apparente. En effet, il était logique, pour les éditeurs, de procéder ainsi puisque le droit étatique chinois, à cette époque-là, n'était considéré, par manque d'information, que comme une branche du droit socialiste, qui était tenu pour proche du droit occidental, conformément à la théorie des familles juridiques dérivée de l'opinion alors admise.

Globalement, l'*Encyclopédie* devrait être appréciée pour ce qu'elle suggère de tâches à accomplir par nous autres, chercheurs tard-venus: et notamment de développer les doutes non exprimés par les éditeurs sur les prémisses qui, loin de refléter la vérité, forment au contraire l'une des cibles de la doctrine post-moderne actuelle. En fin de compte, les efforts des auteurs du présent ouvrage sont une réponse à de telles suggestions, une tentative de progresser dans l'étude de la culture juridique et du pluralisme juridique.

Réalisations récentes dans les domaines de la culture juridique et du pluralisme juridique

La culture juridique est devenue un sujet de débats parmi de nombreux chercheurs juristes un peu avant la parution de l'*Encyclopédie*, un débat stimulé par les discussions des chercheurs en sciences politiques sur le nouveau thème de la «culture politique», en particulier parmi les non-occidentaux. Depuis cette époque, le sujet s'est développé au point de devenir l'un des plus prisés des chercheurs de tous les domaines de la théorie juridique, du droit comparé, en passant par la philosophie, la sociologie et l'anthropologie du droit, ainsi que des domaines spécialisés tels que les contrats, la propriété, les crimes et peines, et autres.

Les tendances générales du débat peuvent *grosso modo* être réparties sur deux axes. L'un concerne la culture juridique dans les pays occidentaux, qu'elle fasse l'objet de recherches à titre individuel[7] ou comparatif[8]. L'autre concerne la culture juridique au-delà de ces pays, pour l'intérêt qu'on peut trouver dans la classification des familles juridiques (par ex. l'*Encyclopédie* citée) ou la comparaison des traditions juridiques[9], ou encore par un intérêt émergeant pour le droit dit non-occidental[10]. Les discussions sur le sujet semblent vraiment prospères, mais, en les observant, je remarque leur manque de méthodologie,

Chapter 7. Une conclusion d'identité culturelles juridiques non-occidentales

comme une tendance générale à laisser le concept de culture juridique dans une boîte noire indéfinie[11].

L'étude du pluralisme juridique s'est développée un peu plus tard, et a donné des résultats remarquables quant au droit non-occidental. Elle a d'abord été l'objet de l'attention portée par des chercheurs francophones au pluralisme juridique dans l'histoire européenne et dans quelques pays africains et socialistes[12]. Elle s'est alors concentrée, comme tendance générale, dans les pays non-occidentaux[13] avec une variété de résultats obtenus par les sociologues/anthropologues du droit, au nombre desquels ceux de la IUAES *Commission on Folk Law and Legal Pluralism*[14]. Les résultats sont appréciables et prometteurs pour de plus amples progrès dans cette étude.

Vu de mes yeux non-occidentaux[15], l'étude de la culture juridique et celle du pluralisme juridique continuent à être des questions importantes à explorer, qui l'ont été, à l'occasion, par quelques chercheurs, mais dont le caractère essentiel semble passer inaperçu. De ces questions, j'en prend trois à titre d'exemple, parmi les plus urgentes.

L'une d'entre elles consiste à développer l'étude du pluralisme juridique dans les pays occidentaux. En général, il est vrai que les tenants du pluralisme juridique, en Occident, ont eu tendance à s'intéresser beaucoup plus aux questions non-occidentales qu'à celles de leurs propres pays. Un tel intérêt peut être naturel dans la mesure où l'on admet la prédominance du droit occidental dans le monde; mais, scientifiquement, la négligence d'une perspective équilibrée ne manque pas de paraître étrange. Il est appréciable que les chercheurs étudiant la culture juridique aient démontré un intérêt pour la culture juridique occidentale, et ne se soient pas confinés dans l'originalité au ⟨non-occidental⟩. Mais les pays occidentaux qui ont, jusqu'ici, fait l'objet d'un traitement sont limités à un trop petit nombre, et le droit non-officiel a rarement été traité dans ce cadre. L'étude du pluralisme juridique a produit moins de résultats concernant l'Occident. Cela constitue un obstacle à une comparaison équilibrée entre les droits occidentaux et non-occidentaux, et, donc, à la bonne compréhension de chacun d'eux.

Il faut ensuite incorporer dans les études le droit qui traverse les frontières nationales délimitées par le droit étatique — on parlera de droit mondial — dans la structure du pluralisme juridique. Le pluralisme juridique a été saisi comme

Chapter 7. Une conclusion d'identité culturelles juridiques non-occidentales   *109*

formé fondamentalement dans une structure double: droit étatique et ce qu'on pourrait appeler les droits mineurs, dont la vigueur est actuellement soumise à la juridiction du droit étatique. Il n'y a aucun doute sur cette double structure. Le mot 《pluralisme》, dans son sens littéral, suppose que l'on compte avec d'autres formes de droit à côté de ces deux-là, d'une part, et une autre forme de droit qui, actuellement, traverse les frontière nationales, de l'autre.

On se réfère, bien entendu, au droit international, à la fois privé et public. Évidemment, cela inclut des accords formels entre gouvernements nationaux, ainsi que des coutumes informelles applicables valablement d'une manière plus large que les droits coutumiers sous juridiction étatique. De plus, il convient de noter, comme le soutiennent beaucoup de spécialistes, qu'une autre forme de droit joue non seulement entre les pays, mais plutôt entre les individus et entre les organisations privées, comme le droit humanitaire[16], le droit populaire[17], le droit sportif[18]. 《Le droit mondial》 peut ainsi raisonnablement se classer en droit régional, droit par-delà les frontières nationales, mais délimité dans une région, et en droit universel, droit valable parmi les hommes au-delà des frontières nationales; d'où la nécessité d'examiner l'interrelation entre les deux. Alors, personne ne pourra nier que le droit sous juridiction d'un pays, qu'il s'agisse du droit étatique ou de droits mineurs, ne peut pas échapper aux influences manifestes ou latentes de quelque forme de 《droit mondial》. Le pluralisme juridique fonctionne donc ainsi en structure triple, puisqu'on y ajoute le droit mondial sans l'incorporation duquel la discussion sur la culture juridique manquerait d'un attribut essentiel.

Enfin, il faut essayer d'avancer dans la perception générale du droit non-occidental, ce qui n'a pas encore été tenté jusqu'ici, peut-être par simple manque d'intérêt sinon par partialité occidentale. Il est vrai que les données nécessaires pour brosser efficacement une vue générale n'ont pas été fournies en nombre suffisant. En même temps, chacun doit savoir qu'un projet individuel pour découvrir un certain groupe de données factuelles peut difficilement atteindre son but sans hypothèses de travail adéquates pour le fonder. Autrement dit, l'opération scientifique exige à la fois la découverte et la circonscription d'un certain nombre de faits et la formulation d'hypothèses de travail, qui doivent être avancées de manière interactive. Pour cette raison, il est indispensable, pour le bon développement de l'étude du droit ou de la culture juridique non-européens, d'essayer de formuler des hypothèses de travail pour le projet dan son ensemble.

Nous avons choisi le sujet de la culture juridique régionale dans le monde non-occidental parmi les problèmes urgents signalés ci-dessus, laissant les autres aux chercheurs qui y seraient intéressés. Mais, comment poursuivre efficacement cette éutde ? Il pourrait être sage d'essayer d'abord de formuler, disons, une 《carte des problèmes》. On entend par là la liste systématique des problèmes concernés par un certain sujet, incluant l'ensemble des faits et problèmes connus et dont on soupçonne l'existence. Il ne peut s'agir d'une liste complète à l'étape initiale, mais simplement de contribuer au progrès scientifique de la recherche sur le sujet en ménageant pour les chercheurs, au point de départ, la formulation d'une hypothèse de travail.

Le présent livre se veut, en fait, la tentative d'une telle carte des problèmes concernant le droit ou la culture juridique non-occidentaux. C'est, bien entendu, une tentative en vue d'atteindre l'objectif final. Tout autre chercheur intéressé est invité à faire sa propre tentative. Plus il y a de tentatives en ce domaine, et plus de pas seront accomplis vers notre but commun. Cette Conclusion n'est rien d'autre qu'un tel essai, bien que nous soyons convaincus de son caractère exceptionnel parce qu'elle est le résultat de la première tentative collective de spécialistes natifs — ou 《pro-natifs》 — de la culture juridique non-occidentale. La clé de cette conviction peut être fournie par l'analyse des significations de nos deux termes fondamentaux: 《culture juridique》 et 《non-occidental》.

De la 《culture juridique》

Il convient, en premier lieu, d'examiner la signification de 《culture juridique》. La doctrine occidentale, fidèle à la méthodologie moderne, a construit son concept de droit de manière isolée des autres normes sociales. Face à ce concept ainsi admis, le droit non-occidental apparaît être lié de manière inséparable aux autres normes sociales telles que coutumes, morales, croyances religieuses et autres, contrairement au droit occidental. Confrontée à cette contrariété, la doctrine pourrait négliger une telle relation. On peut apprécier, pour cette raison, les efforts sérieux accomplis par l'*Encyclopédie* pour saisir la relation entre le droit non-occidental et les autres normes sociales; témoin, l'adoption d'un nouveau

Chapter 7. Une conclusion d'identité culturelles juridiques non-occidentales 111

chapitre sur la ⟨conception du droit⟩, qui s'ajoute au chapitre traditionnel des ⟨systèmes juridiques⟩[19]. Ces efforts étaient destinés à se terminer par un échec; aussi je sympathise avec les éditeurs, qui ont œuvré dans des conditions défavorables à ce moment-là, parce qu'ils ne disposaient pas de la ⟨carte des problèmes⟩ du droit non-occidental. Depuis lors, le nouveau thème de la culture juridique, décrit précédemment, l'emporte et, en conséquence, les chercheurs se sont efforcés d'utiliser le terme plus sérieusement pour montrer également la relation entre le droit non-occidental et le droit occidental. L'expression ⟨culture juridique⟩ peut, ainsi, être considérée comme un équivalent avancé de la ⟨relation du droit avec les autres normes sociales⟩ dont on a parlé. C'est ainsi qu'il convient de comprendre l'expression du titre de ce livre, utilisée pour insister sur une telle signification, plus large, du droit.

L'importance réelle du terme réside cependant dans le fait que, dans un autre sens, nous voulons prendre en compte des considérations spécifiques. En vérité, la ⟨culture juridique⟩ est un des mots favoris utilisés par les personnes intéressées par cette relation du droit avec les autres normes sociales. Franchement, j'ai cependant saisi quelques imperfections dans l'usage qui en est fait. D'abord, la conception de la culture repose sur le critère du concept ⟨établi⟩ de droit; une telle relation est alors considérée comme quelque chose non pas d'intérieur mais d'extérieur au droit, considéré à partir des usages comme la tradition juridique, la conscience juridique, les attitudes vis-à-vis du droit, et autres. Deuxièmement, on a rarement tenté d'accomplir un véritable effort en vue d'une formulation scientifique et de l'application de sa définition opérationnelle, sauf dans la formulation par Blankenburg de la culture juridique comme constituée de quatre variables[20], qui, à mon avis, peut être applicable aux pays occidentaux avec plus d'efficacité, mais non aux peuples non-occidentaux. Troisièmement, les différents essais de définition ont rarement fourni des clés pour observer et analyser la culture juridique non-occidentale telle qu'elle existe. Quatrièmement, l'utilité de ces résultats, tout remarquables qu'ils soient, reste ainsi cantonnée dans le cadre du problème de la valeur heuristique de l'usage du mot ⟨culture⟩, pour faire percevoir aux chercheurs certaines caractéristiques du droit jusqu'ici restées dans l'ombre. Enfin, les chercheurs juristes qui défendent cette perspective ont démontré très peu d'empressement pour une coopération avec les anthropologues; ainsi la voie menant à une recherche scientifique constructive sur la ⟨culture⟩ juridique est-elle bouchée, sans possibilité de coopération avec les spécialistes de la culture.

Mon essai de définition de la culture juridique visait à présenter une tentative de remédier à ces défauts. Je vais, à présent, en résumer les points essentiels[21]. Face à la culture juridique, le droit est défini comme ⟨un type de normes sociales qui qualifie spécifiquement des modèles de comportement social autorisés comme droit, et la responsabilité correspondante à ces modèles de comportement obligés comme devoirs, sur le fondement d'un ensemble de valeurs et d'idées particulières d'une part, et de l'autorité légitime d'une entité socio-juridique de l'autre⟩. Ce qu'il faut spécifiquement remarquer dans cette définition, c'est que ⟨l'entité socio-juridique⟩ n'est pas limitée à un état souverain, mais étendue aux organisations sociales maintenant tout système juridique tel que défini ci-dessus, qu'ils s'agisse de groupes ethniques, locaux ou religieux ou d'autres classes ou stratifications sociales; et en conséquence, que la relation entre le droit et le devoir ne se cantonne pas à l'intérieur du système juridique, mais opère dans tout système juridique, pour autant qu'il a pu être observé au moyen du concept d'outil opérationnel de Hoebel[22].

Ainsi, la culture juridique peut d'abord se définir comme une ⟨configuration culturelle dans le droit⟩. Il est à noter que cette définition essaie de saisir la caractéristique générale de la culture juridique d'une entité socio-juridique plutôt que quelques caractéristiques individuelles observées dans une mentalité ou un comportement personnel, tels que conscience du droit, attitudes vis-à-vis du droit, et similaires. Par ailleurs, le principal composant de la définition ⟨configuration culturelle⟩ est redevable au concept établi en anthropologie depuis Ruth Benedict[23], ce qui confirme le caractère indispensable d'une coopération avec les anthropologues, spécialistes de l'étude de la culture. Bref, je supplie les chercheurs juristes et anthropologues d'essayer de formuler d'autres concepts et hypothèses de droit et de culture juridique, convenant à la fois à la culture non-occidentale et à la culture occidentale.

Supposons que ma définition de la culture juridique soit utile dans un but scientifique; on pourra se demander comment elle peut être effectivement utilisée pour une recherche empirique, parce qu'elle ne semble pas pourvue d'une défini-

Chapter 7. Une conclusion d'identité culturelles juridiques non-occidentales *113*

tion suffisamment opérationnelle pour être employée par un chercheur qui souhaiterait la vérifier ou l'infirmer. Je pense être capable de présenter ici une idée de sa définition opérationnelle comme suit, en disant — en bref — que la culture juridique d'une entité socio-juridique est 《l'ensemble des caractéristiques comparables dans la structure opérationnelle globale du droit, qui est composée de trois sous-structures 'dichotomiques' distinctes, sous la houlette du postulat d'identité》. Les trois dichotomies sont les combinaisons du 《droit officiel》 avec le 《droit non-officiel》, du 《droit indigène》 avec le 《droit transplanté》, et des 《règles juridiques》 avec des 《postulats juridiques》. On y reviendra plus loin en détail.

Le 《postulat d'identité d'une culture juridique》 est 《le postulat juridique de base selon lequel les gens se reconnaissent une identité culturelle en droit》; il sert à intégrer toutes les combinaisons dichotomiques en une structure systématique comparable avec d'autres, et à faciliter à l'entité socio-juridique concernée le maintien de son identité juridique dans des conditions changeantes. Le postulat d'identité peut ainsi à la fois symboliser toute la structure opérationnelle d'un droit maintenue par une entité socio-juridique, et être comparé lui-même à beaucoup d'autres.

Le postulat d'identité de la culture juridique japonaise, comme j'ai pu le vérifier, est un 《type de comportement quasi-amibien》 de par la fonction qu'il assure de permettre aux 《gens de se comporter de manière flexible pour pouvoir s'adapter aux conditions changeantes dans la mesure où il leur est possible de conserver leur individualité/identité》. La formulation de postulats d'identité d'autres entités socio-juridiques peut être tentée par des chercheurs natifs ou 《pro-natifs》 de chaque entité socio-juridique[24].

Du monde 《non-occidental》

La catégorie 'non-occidentale', en ce qui concerne le droit, dans l'*Encyclopédie*, a été représentée par les mondes islamiques, hindous, d'Extrême-Orient et africains, conformément à la théorie des familles juridiques chère aux éditeurs de l'ouvrage. Cependant, ces quatre catégories peuvent être considérées comme autant de types de mondes non-occidentaux, chacun fondant son type particulier de droit ou culture juridique — et de manière non exhaustive. Pour nous, la signification spécifique que nous leur attribuons est celle non pas de familles juridiques, mais de cultures juridiques régionales du monde non-occidental. Chacune d'elles, en effet, forme une région particulière qui s'étend au-delà des différentes frontières nationales et sur des gens disposant d'un ensemble de caractéristiques culturelles différentes, droit inclus. La nouvelle expression 'culture juridique régionale' a été adoptée pour utiliser un concept neutre exempt de toute déformation occidentale, comme l'implique en pratique celle de 'famille juridique'.

Cette précision apportée, deux questions peuvent être, entre autres, considérées comme urgentes. L'une concerne la signification plus profonde et/ou l'implication de la nouvelle expression par laquelle on introduit une différence avec celle de 'famille juridique', et les caractéristiques réelles des cultures juridiques énumérées que nous avons spécifiquement notées. L'autre vise la carte complète des cultures juridiques non-occidentales, incluant celles qu'il convient d'ajouter aux quatre précitées. Un examen individuel de ces dernières permettra de répondre à ces questions.

Le monde africain. — Tout le monde admettra que le continent africain, tel qu'il se définit géographiquement, a conservé dans son histoire ses caractéristiques culturelles, y compris le droit. Ce fait peut donner une ample raison pour catégoriser la culture juridique régionale africaine comme sujet indépendant. Compte tenu des trois ⟨traits fondamentaux⟩ du droit non-occidental[25], j'ai montré que les bases culturelles du droit africain se trouvent d'abord dans le système de parenté indigène à travers les différentes tribus, ce qui indique un type particulier de ⟨diversité⟩ non-occidentale combinée ⟨avec la culture⟩. Puis, dans toutes les sociétés tribales et culturelles, le droit occidental a été transplanté dans les Temps Modernes de manière telle qu'il y a laissé ⟨les conséquences à posteriori du colonialisme⟩, aujourd'hui, et y compris en Éthiopie, qui s'est frayée un passage à travers les pressions occidentales. Le trait de base contemporain de la culture juridique africaine doit être un combiné de deux caractéristiques fondamentales: pluralisme juridique du droit occidental transplanté et des droits indigènes diversifiés rencontrés, bref, un choc frontal entre le droit non-occidental et le droit occidental. La culture juridique africaine a un sens en elle-même, bien que des chercheurs tendent à justifier ce trait par comparaison avec d'autres cultures juridiques régionales[26].

Le monde dit *hindou.* — Le droit hindou a véritablement été établi en un

Chapter 7. Une conclusion d'identité culturelles juridiques non-occidentales   *115*

système très stable, nettement distinct du système positif du droit officiel indien, le droit anglo-indien. Le terme 'hindou' peut paraître approprié pour un tel système de droit. Simultanément, le droit hindou fonctionne dans la société par influences mutuelles manifestes ou latentes entre le droit officiel et d'autres droits non-officiels incluant le droit des castes, le droit de parenté, le droit local et d'autres encore. Saisi du point de vue de ses destinataires, le droit hindou impose ses propres normes juridiques de comportement aux Hindous, pas aussi exclusives, mais aussi sélectives que d'autres, rendant irréaliste le fait de l'observer de manière isolée de toute interaction inévitable avec d'autres. Cet état de choses chez les Hindous est similaire à celui qu'on trouve chez d'autres habitants de l'Inde qui observent différents droits non-officiels, par exemple, les croyants de religions aussi différents que les musulmans, sikhs, jaïns, et autres différentes communautés séculières de castes dépassant le cadre religieux, de tribus retirées dans les zones montagneuses et autres. Le qualificatif 'Indien' est ici adopté au lieu du nom limité 'Hindou' pour désigner l'ensemble des habitants de l'Inde. La culture juridique indienne est ainsi caractérisée comme pluralisme juridique constitué de divers droits indigènes et de droits officiels transplantés, en principe similaires, mais en réalité defférents de ceux d'Afrique.

Le soi-disant *monde d'Extrême-Orient.*— Cette dénomination, quoiqu'elle soit celle sous laquelle ce monde a été reconnu, introduit en fait deux difficultés lorsqu'on cherche à décrire le caractère réel de l'ensemble. La première est la désignation 'Extrême-Orient'. On pourrait rappeler à l'observateur avisé qu'une association internationale abandonna en 1973 son nom historique de *International Congress of Orientalists* pour *International Congress of Human Sciences in Asia and North Africa.* La raison principale a été, comme cela apparaît clairement, la volonté de remplacer le mot 'Orient', qui implique une prévention occidentale, par les mots neutres de 'Asie et Afrique'. La culture juridique 'd'Extrême-Orient' devrait, de la même manière, être remplacée par une autre dénomination, neutre. Parmi les candidates, la plus utilisée semble être 'région culturelle confucéenne'. Il peut y avoir une bonne raison à cela, mais elle tend à une focalisation excessive sur le Confucianisme, comme si c'était la seule philosophie dominante, sans prêter l'attention voulue à d'autres philosophies et cultures. Une autre possibilité pourrait être de parler de 'région d'Asie de l'Est'. Cette

116 Chapter 7. Une conclusion d'identité culturelles juridiques non-occidentales

dernière solution pourrait sembler raisonnable par sa neutralité, mais en fait, elle est embarrassante car elle ne permet pas d'opérer une délimitation exacte, à cause d'un désaccord évident entre des liens géographiques, culturels et juridiques.

Le terme 'région culturelle à caractère chinois' est une expression neutre adaptée. Elle permet de délimiter exactement les limites de la région en question. Le caractère chinois a eu un rapport fondamental avec la culture juridique de cette région; d'une part, il a servi de véhicule de communication de base aux différents peuples concernés; d'autre part, il est assez remarquable que beaucoup de termes juridiques écrits en caratères chinois aient été transplantés aux autres peuples, tels quels, sans être traduits dans d'autres langues. Évidemment, une nationalisation à la fois du caractère chinois et des termes juridiques a été opérée chez tous les peuples chez lesquels ils ont été transplantés et qui avaient conservé leur propre identité culturelle. De plus, le développement du droit, y compris la transplantation du droit occidental à l'époque moderne, a été mené de manière différente par les différents pays. Pourtant, la caractéristique de base de la région en tant qu'unité culturelle n'a pas été mise en doute. Là, réside une possibilité prometteuse pour une nouvelle dénomination permettant à la fois de reconnaître précisément la communauté et la différence dans la culture juridique des peuples concernés.

Cette possibilité s'accompagne en fait de la difficulté de reconnaître une culture juridique commune à la région. La difficulté tire son origine des différentes manières selon lesquelles la transplantation du droit occidental s'est opérée dans les différents pays. Il est vrai que les différents systèmes de droits étatiques contemporains apparaissent si hétérogènes qu'ils font abandonner l'idée de les inclure dans une seule orbite. Par exemple, le contraste entre le droit capitaliste et le droit socialiste divise tous les pays en couples d'opposition, comme on le voit pour le Japon et la Chine, Taïwan et la Chine, la Corée du Sud et du Nord, d'une part; et l'état du droit de peuples vivant sur le vaste territoire chinois comme les Mongols, les Tibétains, les Shinkyo-Uyghurs, les tribus des montagnes, est rarement connu à cause du manque de rapports fiables[27], d'autre part. Pour ces raisons, il n'est pas possible, pour le moment, de prétendre avoir une vue d'ensemble de la culture juridique dans cette région, considérée comme un tout. J'en suis désolé mais obligé de me satisfaire de l'inscription de la culture juridique chinoise seule pour toute la région, souhaitant que cette insatisfaction soit un jour comblée par une coopération entre chercheurs.

Enfin, *le monde islamique.* — Ce monde pris comme une culture juridique régionale, est certainement symbolisé, par comparaison avec les trois précédentes, par trois traits majeurs. L'un est que ce monde s'est consacré à élaborer un système de droit et de jurisprudence islamique sans rival avec aucun autre droit non-occidental, et comparable même avec le droit canonique et le droit occidental. Ensuite, il y a le fait que la région est représentée par le Centre et le Proche-Orient, d'où le droit islamique tire son origine, bien qu'il ait été transplanté des années plus tard dans diverses vastes régions tout comme le droit socialiste, qu'on n'abordera pas ici[28]. En troisième lieu, ses frontières géographiques recouvrent non seulement les trois mondes précités en Afrique et en Asie, mais aussi les droits occidental et socialiste en Europe et en Asie. Ce fait nous donne un exemple important de transplantation, et le résultat en est le chevauchement de différents droits — en réalité, une lutte et/ou une acculturation du droit islamique avec une variété de droits indigènes et de droits étrangers transplantés par la suite, et entre autres, le droit occidental. La culture juridique régionale islamique se caractérise ainsi par un pluralisme distinct d'un grand nombre de systèmes juridiques diversifiés et par le principe intégrateur de *Umma* auquel les musulmans adhèrent avec ténacité.

Cultures juridiques non-occidentales existantes

Il se confirme, ainsi, que les quatre mondes précités doivent être comptés parmi les cultures juridiques non-occidentales les plus représentatives, comme c'est le cas dans l'*Encyclopédie,* mais avec une approche différente. Alors, une question se pose, raisonnablement: est-ce là tout ce que nous devrions énumérer du monde non-occidental ? Ma réponse est absolument: 《Non》. Ma réponse est négative, parce que nombre de cultures juridiques non-occidentales ont été laissées dans l'ombre de la perspective occidentale malgré leur existence réelle et leur importance vitale.

Le monde océanique constitue la première d'entre celles qu'il convient d'ajouter ici. Les théories reçues le négligent complètement, parce que les deux principaux pays qui le constituent, l'Australie et la Nouvelle-Zélande, sont considérés comme faisant partie de la famille juridique occidentale.

En réalité, le droit indigène — en vigueur parmi tous les peuples des îles autres que ces deux pays, ainsi que dans les minorités d'Australie et de Nouvelle-Zélande — a été considéré comme invalidé sous les droits coloniaux et néo-coloniaux. Et le droit étatique que les peuples insulaires instituèrent après leur indépendance au cours de plusieurs décades a été complètement négligé, peut-être parce que leur droit était une transplantation du droit occidental sans raison d'être en soi et sans influence significative sur l'étude internationale du droit.

En fait, ils ont maintenu leur propre droit indigène, dans leur perception et leur pratique, de manière permanente, parallèlement au droit transplanté. La perception et la pratique ont été si fermement enracinées dans leur structure et leur fonction sociales qu'elles sont officiellement incorporées dans leur Constitution[29] et qu'on a pu noter que certains comportements minaient la validité officielle du droit étatique[30]. Ce potentiel officiel de droit indigène est le pluralisme juridique le plus mélangé qui soit dans le monde contemporain. La non-existence du droit océanique n'a aucun fondement, aucune réalité; elle n'a été rien d'autre qu'une apparence dépeinte par la perspective occidentale.

Un autre *monde* est celui *du bouddhisme Theravada* (petit véhicule). Ce dernier s'étend géographiquement du Cambodge, Laos, Thaïlande et Myanmar, à la péninsule indochinoise et jusqu'à Sri Lanka. La culture juridique spécifique à ce monde n'a jamais été remarquée en théorie. Il n'est pas difficile de supputer la raison principale de la perspective occidental: l'état du droit, dans ce monde, apparaît, en effet, fondamentalement similaire à celui du monde océanique, bien qu'en plus compliqué. Autrement dit, le droit étatique des pays concernés est une transplantation du droit occidental avec une note spéciale d'une importance rare. Certaines autres raisons semblent renforcer cette vue: d'abord, cette région peut sembler ne présenter aucune caractéristique juridique distincte dans son ensemble; ensuite, un trait distinctif, s'il y en a, peut consister dans la distorsion ou le chevauchement de différentes cultures juridiques, telles qu'indigène, hindoue, islamique, chinoise et occidentale; enfin, même si le droit bouddhique *Theravada* prévaut parmi les habitants, ce n'est peut-être rien de plus qu'un droit non-officiel formant un sous-système du droit indien ou hindou, qui ne mériterait, en

Chapter 7. Une conclusion d'identité culturelles juridiques non-occidentales   *119*

conséquence, pas d'être remarqué.

Perçue par les habitants de ces pays, cependant, la situation semble tout à fait différente. Sur la base de ce chevauchement tourmenté de cultures juridiques variées qu'on a évoqué, se sont développées une structure sociale et des fonctions particulières accompagnées d'une réglementation juridique indigène, communes à toute la région et différenciables des régions voisines. Elles tirent leur origine du bouddhisme *Theravada*, assez négligé, et ont, à leur tour, soutenu la pratique de ce bouddhisme. Depuis longtemps, la pratique de respect profond des moines, des temples et des *sangha* (ordre de moines) est répandue dans les villes et admise par les gouvernements. Ce phénomène a potentiellement été si important qu'il a établi une idéologie officielle des pays bouddhistes dans le passé, qu'on retrouve aujourd'hui en Thaïlande et à Sri Lanka. C'est pourquoi la culture juridique régionale du bouddhisme *Theravade* doit être ainsi ajoutée à celle des autres mondes non-occidentaux si l'on veut comprendre sa signification en comparaison des autres cultures juridiques voisines.

D'autre part, cette culture juridique régionale ne peut pas échapper à une interaction assez compliquée avec les autres cultures qui la chevauchent, voilant sa spécificité par rapport à celle des pays insulaires de la Mer de Chine méridionale, représentés, entre autres, par l'Indonésie et les Philippines. Ce n'est pas sans raison qu'on saisit globalement ces deux régions au travers d'une autre, plus large, appelée aujourd'hui l'Asie du sud-est et symbolisée par l'ASEAN *(Association of South East Asian Nations)*. Toutefois, étant une structure politique internationale créée après la Seconde guerre mondiale, l'ASEAN a progressivement changé après la fin de la guerre froide. L'appellation 'Asie du sud-est' tend à dénoter des liens différents correspondant à différents usages, et ladite région ne présente aucune caractéristique distinctive de droit ou de culture juridique, contrairement aux régions d'Océanie et du bouddhisme *Theravada*. Ce n'est pas le moment de pratiquer l'amalgame, même si des chevauchements désordonnés avec les précédents ne manquent pas d'attirer l'attention.

Outre ce problème du chevauchement de cultures juridiques, il reste encore quelques régions à énumérer pour leur importance, comparable à celle des six 《mondes》 précités. Il y a, cependant, eu peu de réalisations dignes d'être signalées dans l'étude de ces cultures, et l'on ne voit aucun spécialiste à inviter à se joindre à nous. Tout en pensant que c'est regrettable, on est bien obligé de reconnaître qu'il n'était pas possible de les faire entrer dans ce livre. C'est par l'énumération de ces cultures juridiques régionales non-occidentales que j'en terminerai, en ajoutant quelques commentaires particuliers les concernant.

La *culture juridique latino-américaine* est probablement la plus importante d'entre elles. Malheureusement, en dépit d'un intérêt sporadique de la part de chercheurs occidentaux et de quelques travaux de chercheurs latino-américains[31], ses traits dominants semblent ne pas encore avoir été formulés dans les termes d'un concept satisfaisant pour les juristes. Cela pourrait sembler logique — au sens commun de la doctrine occidentale — dans la mesure où chacun d'entre eux semble avoir achebé très tôt une unification officielle avec les droits indigènes, et où l'on se base sur le fait que le droit étatique transplanté des pays indépendants — souvent, d'ailleurs, par des gouvernements autoritaires, voire dictatoriaux — peut, de manière appropriée, être classé parmi les familles juridiques occidentales, contrairement aux droits étatiques des pays africains qui paraissent, aujourd'hui, n'avoir pas réussi à unifier les droits indigènes. Historiquement, le fait est qu'il y existe une similitude fondamentale de culture juridique entre l'Amérique latine et l'Afrique: je veux dire l'existence d'un pluralisme juridique issu d'une variété de droits indigènes et du droit occidental imposé à l'origine.

En réalité, les droits indigènes d'Amérique latine ont survécu. Premièrement, quelques royaumes d'Amérique latine — les Incas, les Aztèques sont bien connus — ont connus des régimes politiques et des constitutions politiques avancés incluant des systèmes juridiques, contrairement à certains royaumes africains qui avaient développé un système juridique correspondant au droit occidental[32]. Deuxièmement, le droit indigène latino-américain survit, en fait, encore aujourd'hui, bien que les rapports en fassent bien moins état que du droit indigène africain. Il suffit de se reporter aux rapports anthropologiques sur les habitants du Mexique et du Brésil, et d'écouter la voix des indigènes demandant la renaissance de ⟨l'identité culturelle parmi la population indienne⟩ (Déclaration de San José)[33]. Enfin, à en juger par ces faits, la culture juridique latino-américaine nous donne une raison suffisante de croire à des luttes et/ou une acculturation permanentes entre le droit indigène non-officiel et le droit étatique transplanté, avec quelques similarités et quelques différences avec l'Afrique. Elle nous invite donc

Chapter 7. Une conclusion d'identité culturelles juridiques non-occidentales *121*

à l'explorer pour tirer au clair ses réalités et les comparer avec d'autres cultures juridiques régionales.

Il faut encore signaler deux autres cultures juridiques régionales, bien qu'on leur prête rarement attention. L'une est, en gros, la *culture juridique du Nord*, à savoir la culture juridique qui a été maintenue sur la base de droits indigènes dans le cercle polaire, incluant l'Europe septentrionale, la Sibérie et le nord de l'Amérique du Nord. Le droit officiel qui régit cette région semble avoir rarement été remarqué, sauf la protection juridique des peuples indigènes par les droits nordique ou scandinave et le droit de la Communauté Européenne[34]. Le droit non-officiel aussi est resté inconnu, sauf quelques mentions de ses influences sur le droit officiel faites par les chercheurs scandinaves, et de coutumes et traditions dans les sagas faites par des historiens juristes. La culture juridique de cette région, s'il y en une que l'on puisse appeler de ce nom, mérite d'être étudié e pour son rapport avec les droits officiels contemporains et d'être comparée avec d'autres.

L'autre *culture juridique* est celle *de la région d'Asie centrale*. Il est, en fait, très difficile de délimiter géographiquement cette région et plus encore d'identifier une caractéristique distinctive du droit ou de la culture juridique prévalant dans la région. De plus, le droit étatique de cette région a été séparément institué par chacun des pays environnants, qui ont intentionnellement fait abstraction de toute forme de droit qui ne soit pas du droit étatique, et nous ne disposons d'aucune information à ce sujet. Toutefois, il existe des preuves historiques que différents systèmes juridiques y ont été transplantés, de tous les côtés, depuis les temps anciens, et que diverses formes de droit non-officiel ont joué dans la diffusion du droit islamique et l'oppression juridique officielle tant du Tsar que de la Russie socialiste[35]. Cette région doit, pour cette raison, constituer l'un des exemples représentatifs de chevauchement de cultures juridiques dans l'histoire et de nos jours.

Six cultures juridiques et les autres ont ainsi en fin de compte été identifiées comme principales cultures juridiques non-occidentales représentatives et susceptibles d'être décrtites sur le fondement de données sérieuses.

Revue des rapports individuels

Chacun des rapports présentés sur diverses cultures juridiques du monde non-occidental peut être évalué en mettant en lumière chaque sujet individuellement et la vue générale collective. Un examen détaillé de chaque rapport révèle bien les objectifs qui ont été atteints à titre individuel sur chaque sujet.

À propos de la culture juridique africaine, les deux auteurs présentent une opinion similaire sur la diversité apparente et la communauté sous-jacente du droit indigène. Cela confirme la vision fondamentale d'un auteur de l'*Encyclopédie* [36], mais pour s'opposer à la vision du droit indigène en voie de disparition d'un autre auteur [37]. Les auteurs de notre livre suggèrent de plus des points importants en suspens: Roberts, qui aborde la 《nature de l'ordre juridique》, reconnaît que 《Toutefois des signes récents montrent que les normes et les pratiques 'traditionnelles' sont perçues comme ⋯ symboles de cohésion dans un monde contemporain peu certain》[38], alors que Kludze, qui traite spécifiquement de la 《propriété》, précise que 《des questions de terminologie ont créé une certaine confusion⋯》[39]. Ils suggèrent ainsi — je le ressens ainsi — quelques problèmes fondamentaux pour notre recherche. L'un d'entre eux pourrait être la réalité du pluralisme juridique actuel et son évaluation à différents niveaux par des groupes ethniques, locaux et religieux; un autre concernerait les conflits terminologiques sous-jacents au pluralisme juridique et les dispositifs méthodologiques aptes à les gérer.

L'un des deux rapports sur le droit islamique publiés dans l'*Encyclopédie* a étonné les éditeurs par son argument basé sur la 《conscience des croyants》[40] en opposition avec une esquisse froide fidèle, ce qu'on appelle observation objective[41]. Les deux auteurs qui s'expriment dans le présent ouvrage résument harmonieusement les caractéristiques comparatives du droit ou de la culture juridique islamique d'une manière précise: Khadduri met l'accent sur sa nature philosophique (non pas 《le droit fait par l'homme》 mais 《les révélations divines》[42]), alors que Botiveau élucide le système de ses règles individuelles avec des expressions comme 《l'universalité de la sharî'a est potentielle》 et 《coexistence ⋯ avec les ordres juridiques des États-nations contemporains》, mais en bloc comme 《vie spirituelle selon un ordre de valeurs 'cachées'》 et 《Le droit est ambivalent: il est

Chapter 7. Une conclusion d'identités culturelles juridiques non-occidentales *123*

tantôt droit de l'homme, tantôt droit de Dieu⟫[43]. L'un et l'autre laissent entendre aux chercheurs qui s'appuient sur la méthodologie occidentale la nécessité qu'il y a à comprendre avec précision la philosophie et les règles du droit islamique selon la manière dont les musulmans perçoivent leur droit. Cette suggestion nous exhorte de plus à faire une comparaison minutieuse des systèmes et relations, à la fois dans l'histoire et aujourd'hui, entre le droit islamique et le droit occidental, pour élucider la vraie nature des deux droits cachée sous le sens commun juridique.

En ce qui concerne la culture juridique indienne, je vais faire ici quelques brèves observations personnelles, le chapitre attendu n'ayant malheureusement pas pu être remis en temps utile par l'auteur pressenti, un spécialiste de ce pays. Je voudrais d'abord mettre en garde le lecteur, l'expression ⟪culture juridique indienne⟫ pouvant recevoir trois acceptions qu'il convient de bien distinguer. On peut entendre par là, tout d'abord, selon les précisions que j'ai fournies plus haut, le pluralisme juridique de l'ensemble du peuple indien vivant dans l'aire géographique couverte par l'Inde, comprenant le droit étatique au sens moderne, le droit hindou, le droit islamique, le droit des castes, ainsi que beaucoup de droits mineurs locaux, religieux et tribaux, qu'ils soient officiels ou non. En second lieu, de la doctrine dominante, il ressort une identification de la culture juridique indienne avec la culture juridique hindoue, à l'exception du droit islamique, du droit moderne et des autres droits. ⟪Culture juridique indienne⟫ pourrait, troisièmement, à titre hypothétique, embrasser toutes les cultures juridiques qui puisent leur origine dans l'ancien droit indien, mais se sont développées sous des formes diverses à l'extérieur de l'Inde géographique telles que la culture juridique bouddhiste *Theravada* aux abords du sud-est et la culture juridique lamaïste au nord.

Si l'on s'en tient à théorie du droit admise, il semble raisonnable d'isoler le droit hindou et la conception juridique qui y est attachée, du reste du système juridique, contrairement à ce qui est présenté dans l'*IECL*. En réalité, le droit hindou est caractérisé par une nature spécifiquement basée sur les postulats fondamentaux du *Dharma* éternel et la prééminence — variable à travers l'histoire — d'un pouvoir juridique, moral et éthique placé sous l'administration du village et de la cour de caste. Le système a survécu aux efforts d'unification de l'Inde moderne qui ont suivi les ⟪changements catastrophiques⟫ introduits par les

Européens[44] et l'indépendance sous une constitution moderne. Concrètement, cependant, l'uniformisation n'est jamais autant à l'œuvre, structurellement, qu'il n'y paraît à l'observation théorique. D'abord, le droit hindou de la famille unie traditionnelle prévaut chez 《de nombreux musulmans et quelques chrétiens》[45]. Par ailleurs, il existe une différenciation qui tient à des formes diverses qui tiennent à des pratiques locales variables. Ces dernières incluent celles des tribus reconnues constitutionnellement, le droit religieux comprenant le droit islamique et le droit étatique moderne par lequel le droit anglo-hindou a été développé différemment du droit hindou vivant[46]. En troisième lieu, dans la constitution indienne modernisée, les croyances en Sikh, Jaïna ou les religions bouddhistes sont inclues dans les peuples 《hindous》, le mot 《Hindou》 étant conçu d'une manière aussi large que l'est la religion hindoue, ce qui n'est jamais le cas des Musulmans et des Chrétiens. Culture juridique hindoue, en réalité, désigne alors non pas la base culturelle d'un simple droit religieux susceptible d'être ainsi spécifié, mais un système pluraliste de diverses cultures juridiques liées l'une à l'autre et reliées entre elles par le principe fondamental du *Dharma*. À vrai dire, l'idée de *Dharma*, loin d'être confinée au droit hindou, est également répandue dans quelques autres droits de pays bouddhistes voisins. D'un côté, elle a été transplantée à travers l'ancien Code indien de Manu, jusque dans des pays de bouddhisme *Theravada* : ainsi le *Thammasat* qui est aux sources du système juridique Thaï, aussi bien traditionnel que moderne; ou encore le *Dhammathat*, droit officiel burman d'avant la révolution post-guerre et droit non-officiel contemporain du peuple; ou le 《Bouddhisme *Sasana* 》(*Dharma* dans le Bouddhisme) du droit officiel du Sri Lanka à travers l'histoire et jusque dans la constitution moderne. D'autre part, l'idée juridique du Bouddhisme lamaïste représentée par le Tibet et Butan constitue une autre manière de l'idée de *Dharma* [47].

Il en découle que *Dharma* peut être considéré comme formant le postulat identitaire des divers systèmes juridiques qu'on vient de mentionner. Cela constitue la quatrième raison de la structure plurale de la culture juridique indienne, sous réserve d'inventaire. En somme, la culture juridique indienne, du fait qu'elle n'est pas incontestablement une, comme l'est l'hindoue, paraît présenter un abrégé du pluralisme juridique complexe aux dimensions du globe. Ses amples terres attendent notre exploration, nous suggérant d'en réexaminer le sens au titre des

Chapter 7. Une conclusion d'identité culturelles juridiques non-occidentales

cultures juridiques régionales comme on les a décrites dans ce livre. Le travail dépasse de beaucoup mes seules capacités.

La culture juridique régionale du bouddhisme *Theravada* décrite par Ishii[48] doit être saluée pour sa première apparition sous un titre indépendant, différent de celui de plusieurs études antérieures qui ne jetaient qu'un coup d'oeil sur ce sujet[49]. Le droit qui a fondé cette culture juridique a été incorporé dans l'ancien Code indien de Manu. Étant la source la plus ancienne et la plus revêtue d'autorité du droit hindou, il a été transplanté, mais avec quelques modifications, en particulier l'exception du système de castes, comme seul modèle de base du droit officiel par des dynasties qui se sont succédées dans cette région en dehors de l'Inde hindoue.

Son autorité officielle semble vraiment avoir décliné depuis la socialisation de plusieurs gouvernements après la Seconde guerre mondiale, en comparaison de sa prospérité de jadis. Cependant, il reste non seulement l'un des plus hauts principes constitutionnels de la Thaïlande bouddhiste et du socialisme original de Sri Lanka, mais également un droit non-officiel profondément enraciné parmi le peuple qui le reconnaît《jusqu'à ce jour, [comme] la norme pour la conduite quotidienne des bouddhistes》[50].

Ce fait nous amène à rechercher la fonction réelle du droit traditionnel en tant que droit non-officiel et/ou officiel contemporain, et peut suggérer de plus, j'en suis convaincu, d'étendre la recherche à la culture juridique du Butan, du Népal, et du Tibet, symbolisée par la religion d'État ou quasi d'État du bouddhisme de Lama-Mahayaniste, afin de saisir en comparaison la culture juridique bouddhiste en bloc.

Culture juridique non-occidentale la plus fréquemment citée avec les cultures juridiques Indienne et Islamique, la culture juridique chinoise, qui a des caractéristiques de base telles que tradition confucéenne et légalisme, non-discrimination entre droit et morale, accent mis sur le droit public et le droit criminel, et d'autres encore[51] est bien connue. Les deux auteurs abordant ce sujet aussi bien dans l'*Encyclopédie* que dans ce livre semblent partager la même opinion sur ces caractéristiques de base. Toutefois, Tay présente, ici, une vision plus réaliste, comparée à celle de l'autre auteur qui avait tendance à une généralisation caractérologique du caractère national chinois[52], d'abord en élargissant ladite région à ⟨communauté chinoise surtout du sud-est asiatique⟩, puis en désignant la fonction du droit comme ⟨l'incessante malhonnêteté et la corruption⟩ sous le région nationaliste, et enfin en distinguant la culture juridique des ⟨usages et traditions⟩ populaires de la ⟨culture politique⟩ du Parti Communiste[53]. Ses suggestions peuvent être développées, à mon avis, par une observation plus réaliste, et étendues à l'étude de la culture juridique de la Mongolie, du Tibet, du Sinkiang-Uyghr et des tribus des montagnes. Tous ces droits indigènes ont été inclus dans la rubrique ⟨droit chinois⟩, mais, en réalité, ont maintenu un système indépendant de leur propre droit non-officiel et/ou officiel.

La culture juridique océanique, présentée par Sack, fait une première apparition au forum de la science juridique, avec celle du bouddhisme *Theravada*. Elle révèle des caractéristiques inconnues jusqu'à présent du droit indigène et du pluralisme juridique dans cette région symbolisée par les ⟨influences colonialistes⟩[54]. Le droit indigène se caractérise par ⟨plus de diversité aussi bien que plus de ressemblance⟩, soit un mélange complexe de cultures originales parmi des habitants d'innombrables îles dans les trois sous-régions de la Micronésie, de la Polynésie et de la Mélanésie, et de cultures transplantées des régions asiatiques environnantes, tels que la culture malaise, mongolienne et caucasienne[55]. Sack suggère expressément sur cette base ⟨une déconstruction radicale du 'droit' — processus qui vient à peine de commencer pour l'Océanie comme, à vrai dire, pour les pays de droit occidental⟩[56]. Cela peut sembler radical dans une perspective occidentale, mais est vrai aux yeux des ⟨natifs⟩, et peut nous encourager à étudier davantage les faits et à les formuler dans une théorie du pluralisme juridique, ainsi qu'à imaginer un ensemble adapté de concepts et d'outils qui y seraient applicables.

Récapitulation générale de cette anthologie

Au-delà des contributions individuelles qu'on vient de signaler, les cinq rapports établis, pris comme anthologie, indiquent à la fois ce qui a été réalisé et ce qu'il reste à effectuer comme recherche sur la culture juridique non-occidentale. Il ne fait aucun doute que chacun apporte respectivement des faits dénotant des caractéristiques générales du droit ou de la culture juridique non-occidentale, ce que j'ai mentionné comme ⟨diversité, lien du droit et de la culture, (et)

Chapter 7. Une conclusion d'identité culturelles juridiques non-occidentales   *127*

conséquences à postériori du colonialisme⟩[57]. En même temps, cette Conclusion semble suggérer que l'on poursuive l'étude plus avant à la fois au plan méthodologique et en ce qui concerne les objectifs.

La suggestion méthodologique est double. Il s'agit d'abord d'élucider des problèmes de terminologie, devant les conflits qui existent, par exemple, entre les concepts juridiques des droits occidental et indigène en Afrique[58] et devant l'impossibilité de représentation des conceptions juridiques indigènes par des termes juridiques occidentaux, comme c'est le cas en Océanie[59]. Ces problèmes existent, en fait, partout dans le monde non-occidental, bien qu'ils ne soient pas expressément mentionnés dans les autres rapports de ce livre. On se trouve, donc, dans l'attente d'un système terminologique intelligent, adéquat, applicable aux situations non-occidentales[60].

Il s'agit, ensuite, comme cela est exprimé dans l'appel de Sack à la création d'une perspective non-occidentale parallèle à la perspective occidentale, de cesser ⟨de considérer les formes de droit non occidental d'un point de vue occidental⟩ et ⟨de voir les formes de droit occidental d'une perspective non occidentale⟩, avec la perspective ⟨d'ajouter un troisième critère⟩[61]. Cela, c'est ainsi, du moins, que je le comprends, afin d'encourager les non-occidentaux à ouvrir les yeux sur une perspective scientifique, à la développer eux-mêmes et à demander qu'on la respecte, pour maintenir une norme équilibrée.

Je soutiens ces suggestions, ayant moi-même proposé trois systèmes méthodologiques relevant d'un point de vue similaire à celui de Sack. L'un d'eux propose une nouvelle approche scientifique du droit, destinée à interpréter le ⟨droit dans la subjectivité⟩, de l'intérieur du comportement des gens, sous la réglementation de systèmes juridiques pluralistes, face à l'approche communément reçue, qui observe le ⟨droit dans l'objectivité⟩, de l'extérieur des gens, comme sanctionné par l'autorité légitime[62]. La nouvelle approche a été proposée comme adéquate au droit non-occidental dans le but d'établir une perspective équilibrée avec la perspective traditionnelle.

L'autre dispositif méthodologique que je propose consiste dans un nouveau jeu de concepts-outils efficacement applicables et adéquats aux conditions non-occidentales, bien que je sois convaincu de son applicabilité à l'Occident également[63]. Cet ensemble se compose d'un concept de base d'*entité socio-juridique* et de six formes de droit réparties en *trois dichotomies* sous le *postulat d'identité*. Cela a été mentionné dans une section précédente, mais peut requérir quelques explications complémentaires. S'agissant des trois dichotomies, la première est formulée par rapport à la qualité de l'autorité légale face à l'existence de deux formes de droit qui s'opposent: le 'droit officiel' — qui comprend non seulement le droit étatique, mais aussi d'autres systèmis juridiques en tant qu'ils sont officiellement sanctionnés par le premier — et le 'droit non-officiel', qui prévaut parmi les populations des entités socio-juridiques, sans être officiellement sanctionné ni partiellement adopté par le droit officiel.

La seconde dichotomie est liée à la provenance du droit, qui tire son origine, pour ce qui est du 'droit indigène', de la culture indigène, ou du 'droit transplanté', de cultures étrangères, les deux se développant en interaction et dans un processus d'acculturation. Troisièmement, chacune des quatre formes de droit précitées est encore classée, selon son expression formelle, en 'règles juridiques', en expression verbales formalisées, ou en 'postulats juridiques', du point de vue du fondement des valeurs et des idéaux. Ce qui maintient un sys-tème juridique, c'est soit une entité socio-juridique, quand il s'agit d'une petite soci-été, soit la présence de plusieurs systèmes juridiques intégrés dans une structure d'ensemble, dans le cas d'une société plus large. C'est la combinaison de deux formes de droit opposées en une dichotomie ainsi que les combinaisons d'ensemble des trois dichotomies, variables en fonction des diverses entités socio-juridiques, mais intégrées dans une structure d'ensemble valable de par le 'postulat d'identité' respective de chaque culture juridique, qui maintiennent l'individualité/identité culturelle de l'entité concernée.

Je suggère en japonais une classification des droits ou cultures juridiques non-occidentaux selon trois objectifs[64]. Le premier est l'étude de la culture juridique en relation avec le droit étatique des pays non-occidentaux. La raison est claire: le droit étatique est une forme de droit typique du monde non-occidental comme du monde occidental. Au cours de mon argumentation, j'ai présenté, ici et là, quelques critiques du droit occidental, mais n'ai jamais eu l'intention de sous-estimer les mérites du droit occidental et de la doctrine qui l'accompagne. Je veux simplement traiter les droits non-occidentaux tels qu'ils existent, afin d'assurer une perspective équilibrée des droits occidentaux et non-occidentaux dans un but

Chapter 7. Une conclusion d'identité culturelles juridiques non-occidentales *129*

scientifique. Je présuppose l'existence essentielle du droit étatique quand je définis la culture juridique régionale au-delà des frontières nationales. La culture juridique entourant le droit étatique des pays non-occidentaux, bien que hors de la perspective directe de ce livre, peut constituer un premier objectif dans l'étude de la culture juridique non-occidentale, sous deux conditions. L'une est que l'on traite le droit étatique comme existant sous forme de pluralisme juridique à côté d'autres formes de droit officiel, du droit non-officiel et du droit mondial. L'autre est que l'on applique une autre méthodologie adéquate pour observer et analyser ce droit étatique ou la culture juridique.

Un deuxième objectif peut être l'étude du droit non-officiel, qui fournit à une culture juridique ses qualités essentielles et qui exerce une influence non seulement latente mais aussi manifeste sur la validité du droit étatique et des autres droits officiels. Les récents progrès en sociologie/anthropologie, pour remarquables qu'ils soient, montrent surtout qu'il y a encore beaucoup à faire de par le monde. Dans chacune des six cultures juridiques régionales et les autres précédemment mentionnées[65], il y a beaucoup de droits non-officiels restés non étudiés parmi une variété de groupes ethniques, locaux ou religieux et de classes ou stratifications sociales. Ces lacunes invitent les chercheurs intéressés à les explorer dans des conditions similaires à celles que l'on vient de mentionner: sous l'angle du pluralisme juridique et avec la méthodologie adéquate.

Le troisième objectif est l'étude de la culture juridique en relation avec le droit mondial, autrement dit, la culture juridique mondiale. Elle peut se diviser en culture régionale et universelle, selon la division précitée entre le droit régional et le droit universel. Des deux, c'est la culture juridique régionale qui été choisie comme sujet de cette Conclusion. La raison de ce choix est que les variations existantes exigent un examen précis préalable à une comparaison entre les unes et les autres, et avec la culture juridique du droit étatique et du droit non-officiel, alors que la culture juridique universelle est plus importante par son influence sur les niveaux inférieurs plutôt qu'en comparaison avec eux.

Toutefois, je ne voudrais pas terminer mon argumentation sans deux commentaires sur la carte des cultures juridiques régionales. Le premier est que plusieurs d'entre elles ont été exclues par manque des données nécessaires: Amérique latine, Asie du Nord et Asie centrale. Mon premier commentaire sera que je souhaite qu'elles soient étudiées par d'autres. Mon second commentaire concerne le problème du chevauchement desdites cultures juridiques avec celles du bouddhisme *Theravada*, d'Asie Centrale et quelques autres. Comme il s'agit, en fait, d'un problème dont l'examen suppose une perspective élargie, cela pourra se faire en conclusion.

Lumière nouvelle sur la culture juridique occidentale

En revoyant la description qui a été faite jusqu'ici de la cultrue juridique régionale non-occidentale, je sens une nouvelle lumière éclairer l'étude de la culture juridique dans son ensemble. Je note deux directions urgentes à suivre parmi d'autres: effectuer un examen plus poussé de la culture jurideque occidentale, brièvement mentionnée plus haut, et rechercher la signification profonde du chevauchement des cultures juridiques dans le monde.

Selon les théories reçues, le droit occidental est un système juridique particulier en tant qu'il est isolé des autres normes sociales et facteure socio-culturels, y compris la culture juridique. Le droit non-occidental représenté par les droits islamique, hindou et africain s'oppose, selon l'*Encyclopédie,* au droit occidental en ce qu'il est tout à fait hétérogène, et au droit socialiste comme partiellement hétérogène. Cela semble être une caractérisation trop simpliste du droit occidental par rapport à ces réalités.

Premièrement, parce que des tenants du pluralisme juridique ont rapporté que plusieurs cultures juridiques coexistent dans différente zones de droit occidental. Deuxièmement, parce que si l'on considère le 《droit dans la subjectivité》, chaque individu vivant dans un pluralisme est qualifié pour sélectionner un des droits opérant de manière plurielle, et décider comment mener sa vie quotidienne, en ne s'en remettant au droit étatique qu'en dernier ressort.

Quelques éléments peuvent être avancés — sur la foi des données limitées dont je dispose — permettant de définir la base de la culture juridique occidentale en matière de pluralisme. En Europe, le pluralisme juridique est formé dans chaque pays par diverses combinaisons de droit étatique, droit religieux officiels ou non-officiels, et d'autres droits non-officiels. Parmi eux, les droits religieux se divisent en droits des églises catholique, protestante, orthodoxe et en différentes religions non-chrétiennes. Le droit non-officiel se subdivise également en droits coutumiers,

Chapter 7. Une conclusion d'identité culturelles juridiques non-occidentales   **131**

droits locaux, droits populaires, ou ordonnances indigènes[66]. L'Amérique du Nord présente des combinaisons fondamentalement similaires de droit étatique, de droit religieux et de droit non-officiel, mais un peu différemment, en donnant plus de poids au droit indigène parmi les peuples natifs, comme c'est le cas aussi bien aux États-Unis qu'au Canada. En Australie et en Nouvelle-Zélande, cela se passe à peu près comme en Amérique du Nord.

Ces faits nous exhortent à recaractériser la culture juridique occidentale non seulement pour la saisir par comparaison avec la culture juridique non-occidentale, mais également pour avoir un aperçu précis des cultures juridique existantes, à la fois dans le monde occidental et dans le monde non-occidental. Sur deux points, au moins, la réalisation est perceptible. L'un concerne la classification, autant que cela s'avère possible, des différents types de cultures juridiques occidentales dans des sous-systèmes adéquats, tels que, comme c'est le cas dans l'*Encyclopédie*, celui d'Asie en sous-système hindou et sous-système d'Extrême-Orient, ou celui d'Extrême-Orient en sous-système chinois et sous-système japonais. L'autre consiste à donner plus de poids au droit religieux dans le pluralisme juridique occidental, en comparaison avec des droits religieux non-occidentaux assez significatifs tels que les droits islamique, hindou et confucéen, l'étude n'ayant guère été menée que sur le droit canonique.

C'est pour cette raison que quatre titres liés à ces aspects de la culture juridique occidentale furent adoptés dans la nouvelle édition du *Dictionnaire Encyclopédique de Théorie et de Sociologie du Droit*, 1993, après sa redéfinition: 《Tradition juridique occidentale》[67] en tant que produit de la 《commune allégeance à une autorité spirituelle unique, l'Église de Rome》[68], 《Réception du droit (en Occident)》[69], 《Culture juridique catholique》[70] et 《Culture juridique protestante》[71]. Ces titres sont parus pour la première fois au forum de la science juridique, comme composantes de la culture juridique occidentale comparables avec la culture juridique non-occidentale — à supposer que la portée de 《réception du droit》 soit étendue à celle de toute l'histoire, incluant la formation du droit de l'Union européenne aujourd'hui. Leur apparition doit être saluée. Mais le caractère inédit de ces études ne permet pas de dresser une carte satisfaisante de l'ensemble, et il s'avère nécessaire que des compléments y soient apportés par des chercheurs natifs de l'Occident et qualifiés pour cette tâche.

Chapter 7. Une conclusion d'identité culturelles juridiques non-occidentales

Quand on essaie de classer la culture juridique occidentale en quelques sous-systèmes, on se trouve face à d'indéniables chevauchements de cultures juridiques différentes, non seulement des droits des tribus d'origine, droits locaux, droit chrétien, droits nationaux, mais aussi des droits indigènes étrangers et des droits religieux en usage chez des portions de la population discriminées, immigrante et réfugiés, à quelque minorité qu'ils appartiennent. Le chevauchement de telles cultures juridiques est plus important dans le monde non-occidental contemporain, où les cultures juridiques traditionnelles sont fermement ancrées dans les identités culturelles.

Nous avons retenu six principales cultures juridiques régionales non-occidentales, reconnues pour leur importance dans le monde contemporain, et sur lesquelles on dispose de données satisfaisantes. Chacune d'entre elles est caractérisée par son indubitable empire sur toute la région. En fait, comme tout le monde le sait, chacune se compose non pas d'une seule culture juridique, mais d'un mélange de cultures se recoupant, et le mode de chevauchement varie selon les sous-régions et les divers lieux, principalement en raison de la différence entre les droits indigènes d'origine et les droits étrangers transplantés. L'énumération des cultures juridiques régionales dans ce livre est ainsi faite pour assigner des tâches urgentes, tenter, entre autres, une classification des différentes cultures juridiques des sous-systèmes de chaque culture juridique régionale majeure énumérée. Quand cette tâche sera achevée avec succès, sans oublier la culture latino-américaine et d'autres encore, ni la culture juridique occidentale parallèle, une carte générale approximative de toutes les cultures juridiques existant dans le monde pourra être tracée, qui mentionnera leurs particularités.

Nouvel éclairage sur le chevauchement des cultures juridiques

Il faut rappeler au lecteur qu'on a exclu certaines cultures juridiques régionales. Il s'agit de cultures juridiques qui paraissent ne pas présenter de caractéristiques dominantes. On entend, par là, qu'elles ne sont pas représentées par une culture juridique dominante parmi les nombreuses autres de la région concernée. Ce sont, comme on l'a dit, la région de l'Asie du sud-est, autour de la Mer de Chine méridionale, la région d'Asie centrale et la région du Nord. Elles n'ont

Chapter 7. Une conclusion d'identité culturelles juridiques non-occidentales   *133*

pas été prises en considération, ici, en raison de la difficulté qu'il y a à identifier leur caractère régional, sans compter l'absence de données fiables. D'un autre point de vue, qui est celui du mode de chevauchement de différentes cultures juridiques dans une région, je pense que chaque culture retenue doit présenter une spécificité importante de la culture juridique contemporaine. En fait, les cultures juridiques principales énumérées sont chacune un mélange de nombreuses cultures juridiques exclues, mais assez similaires aux cultures dominantes pour être représentées par elles. Le mélange — notamment le chevauchement — de cultures juridiques est ainsi un attribut fondamental de la culture juridique humaine.

Dans la région d'Asie du sud-est, toutes les cultures juridiques civilisées majeures créées par l'homme ont été transplantée en se chevauchant sur une variété de droits indigènes d'origine: il en va ainsi, par exemple, d'abord, du droit indien et du droit bouddhiste *Theravada* venus de l'ouest, puis du droit chinois du nord et du droit islamique de l'ouest, et enfin du droit occidental accompagné du droit chrétien sous différentes formes également de l'ouest, l'ensemble présentant ainsi un croisement contemporain confus de cultures juridiques humaines. Le résultat de la diffusion et de l'acculturation des droits transplantés avec les droits indigènes s'est tellement diversifié d'une sous-région à l'autre que nous avons bon droit de nous plaindre de la difficulté qu'il y a à discerner une culture juridique dominante. La culture juridique d'Asie centrale est supposée être caractérisée par un trait similaire, à savoir le chevauchement des droits oriental et chrétien catholique, du droit chinois et du droit islamique, et enfin du droit chrétien protestant et du droit occidental moderne, qui, de provenance multiple, s'y sont transplantés en suivant la route de la soie. Il s'agit d'un croisement historique typique — et contemporain — de cultures juridiques humaines avec des résultats divers par sous-région. La vérification de ces affirmations constitue une autre tâche pour nous. Nous y apprendrons les différentes formes des transplantations répétées de droits dans l'histoire humaine.

Une telle considération nous mène à notre dernier objectif: confirmer l'existence d'une transplantation des cultures juridiques parmi les sociétés humaines. Enraciné dans la culture, chaque système juridique s'est développé à travers une entité socio-juridique particulière fondée sur un postulat d'identité de culture juridique propre, d'une part; par ailleurs, chaque système juridique échange plus ou moins d'influences avec d'autres droits étrangers, que ce soit intentionnellement ou non, le résultat étant la diffusion de systèmes juridiques différents. La problématique de la culture juridique peut ainsi suivre deux directions: la recherche des particularités de chaque culture juridique, comme cela a été fait pour les cultures juridiques régionales dominantes, et la recherche de leur diffusion, manifeste ou latente, dans les cultures environnantes. Et j'en finirai, ainsi, avec un commentaire sur la diffusion, autrement dit le chevauchement, du droit ou de la culture juridique.

La diffusion du droit est bien connue des chercheurs juristes comme thème de la 〈réception〉, en particulier de la part des juristes qui pratiquent l'étude comparative. Leur intérêt est, bien sûr, probablement soutenu par des *vérités* sous-jacentes, mais la conception qu'ils expriment par le mot 〈réception〉 laisse planer un doute dans la mesure où elle implique une déformation occidentale, contraire à la *vérité* totale. En effet, le modèle de 〈réception〉 est, généralement, celui de la réception droit romain par les royaumes européens au Moyen-Age, et du droit occidental par les pays non-occidentaux au cours des temps modernes. Cela présuppose donc la supériorité du droit d'origine occidentale. Je respecte parfaitement la valeur du droit occidental et du génie occidental qui l'a créé, mais je voudrais demander en même temps un respect équivalent à l'égard du droit non-occidental.

Considérée du point de vue du droit dans sa subjectivité, la transplantation du droit a eu lieu de manières variées. Beaucoup d'entités socio-juridiques mineures non-occidentales ont accepté des droits étrangers sans intention manifeste de les 〈recevoir〉 comme par ce qui pourrait être appelé avec justesse une 〈diffusion〉 culturelle; ou bien, quelques entités majeures, parmi d'autres pays, ont importé des droits étrangers, manifestement et volontairement, par ce qui pourrait avec justesse être appelé 〈réception〉; ou bien, encore, beaucoup d'autres ont dû accepter des droits étrangers, manifestement mais involontairement, ce qui pourrait être appelé 〈imposition〉[72]. Ces différents processus peuvent être exprimés par un jeu de termes neutres, sauf déformation occidentale. C'est pour cette raison que j'ai proposé d'utiliser le terme 〈réception〉 dans le cas d'une acceptation volontaire, par opposition à 〈imposition〉 dans l'hypothèse contraire, et 〈transplantation〉 pour le terme général incluant les deux. Bien entendu, le droit reçu autant que le droit imposé peuvent être acculturés dans un droit transplanté sur une

Chapter 7. Une conclusion d'identité culturelles juridiques non-occidentales *135*

longue histoire, de différentes manières et à différents degrés, le résultat étant un droit rendu indigène, qui s'oppose au droit transplanté par la suite[73].

Une telle transplantation de droit s'est produite non seulement entre les mondes occidental et non-occidental, mais aussi parmi toutes les entités socio-juridiques appartenant à ces deux mondes. En faire une étude précise et corriger, en fonction de la réalité, la théorie générale qui prévaut, doit être le but final assigné aux chercheurs qui travaillent sur le pluralisme juridique.

Notes

(*) Ainsi que le chapitre 5, les pages qui suivent constituent une version remaniée d'un texte paru au Arnaud 1993. La traduction en a été intégralement reprise par André-Jean Arnaud.

(1) Dans cette Conclusion, le terme 'droit' est utilisé dans un sens large, allant du droit d'État, incluant par extension le droit international, le droit coutumier et le droit naturel, à la 'culture juridique'. 'Droit' et 'culture juridique' peuvent ainsi être utilisés de manière indifférente ou interchangeable. Sauf mention expresse, la signification spécifique de 'droit' ne sera pas indiquée dans la suite de ce chapitre.

(2) J'ai moi-même coopéré avec André-Jean Arnaud, éditeur en chef du *Dictionnaire Encyclopédique de Théorie et de Sociologie du Droit*, 2ᵉ éd., 1993 au travail de collecte, d'organisation, de vérification, voire de rédaction des articles originaux concernant l'aire non-occidentale. Pour être exact, le rapport sur la culture juridique africaine par Botiveau avait été inclus dans l'édition d'origine (Arnand 1988) à l'initiative de l'éditeur en chef, non par mes soins.

(3) Ma tentative (Chiba 1993) pourrait souffrir d'une imperfection dans la portée et la méthodologie de l'entreprise.

(4) *IECL*: vol. II, (David 1975). Du même auteur, *Les grands systèmes de droit contemporain*, Paris, Libraire Dalloz, 1964 (English edition: David & Brierley 1985).

(5) Cf. Berman 1983. Comp. avec Berman 1993.

(6) *IECL, op. cit.*

(7) Par ex. Podgorecki 1974; Macaulay 1989.

(8) Par ex. Blankenburg & Bruinsma 1994.

(9) Par ex. Friedman 1975: chap. 6, 9; Ehrmann 1976; Snyder 1985.

(10) En fait, j'ai écrit une série d'articles en japonais sur 《Droit et culture》 en 1977-78 pour passer en revue les résultats obtenus dans le domaine de la culture juridique dans le monde et pour indiquer les tâches à accomplir. D'autres résultats sont collectés séparément dans mes livres ultérieurs en japonais (1991) ou en

anglais (1989).
(11) Cf. Kidder 1973.
(12) Cf. Gilissen 1972.
(13) Cf. Hooker 1975; Sack & Minchein 1986; Griffiths 1986; Merry 1988.
(14) Voir Allott & Woodman 1985; Morse & Woodman 1988; von Benda-Beckmann et al. 1988; etc.
(15) Cf. chap. 10 de ce livre.
(16) Cf. Grahl-Madsen & Tomen 1984.
(17) Cf. Renteln & Dundes 1994: sect. 8.
(18) Cf. chap. 9 de ce livre.
(19) L'adoption du chapitre sur la conception du droit n'est pas considérée comme faite dans l'intention de traiter du droit non-occidental de manière spécifique, parce que les éditeurs ont inclus également le droit ocidental et le droit socialiste dans le même chapitre. Toutefois, je note que la conception non-occidentale a été décrite comme le mérite le mot《conception》, alors que les conceptions occidentale et socialiste tendaient à n'être pas plus que l'histoire bien connue, la théorie et/ou la philosophie de chaque droit.
(20) Leur quatre variables sont le droit dans les livres, l'infrastructure instrumentale du système juridique, les modèles de comportement juridiquement convenables, et la conscience juridique (Blankenburg & Verwoerd 1988; cf. aussi Blankenburg & Bruinsma 1994).
(21) Voir, pour plus de détails, Chiba 1989: chap. 12.
(22) Hoebel 1954: chap. 4. Je suis convaincu de la probabilité de succès d'une formulation d'un jeu de concepts outils opérationnels de *droit* et de *devoir* fondés sur celui de Hoebel; j'ai tenté de le faire en japonais, mais sans succès.
(23) Cf. Benedict 1934.
(24) J'ai suggéré des formulations hypothétiques sur quelques postulate d'identité majeurs. Par exemple, le pluralisme juridique chinois à la manière *Ciel,* le pluralisme juridique indien à la manière *Dahrma,* le pluralisme juridique islamique dans l'*Umma*, le symbolisme standard français de l'*esprit,* le caractère *raisonnable* à la manière des gentlemen anglais, la *systématique majestueuse* allemande, et la *primauté absolue de la 'rule of law'* des États-Unis. Je sais qu'on a adressé des critiques à l'égard de ces postulats d'identité. On dit, par exemple, qu'il ne s'agit là de rien de plus que d'une terminologie de remplacement pour désigner des tendances nationales bien connues. Je voudrais, pour ma part, que l'introduction que j'en fais constitue une invite à un dépassement.
(25) Voir chap. 5 de ce livre.
(26) Voir Woodman 1993: 105–115, pour une opposition absolue entre le droit africain et le droit occidental.
(27) Les droits à l'intérieur des frontières chinoises sont maintenus dans un état particulier. Du point de vue du droit considéré objectivement, ils peuvent être

Chapter 7. Une conclusion d'identité culturelles juridiques non-occidentales *137*

contenues dans le droit chinois représenté par le droit du gouvernement central. Dans la mesure où cela est interprété du point de vue du droit dans sa subjectivité, ils ont maintenu leurs propres systèmes indigènes de droit basés sur leurs postulats d'identité en conflit ou en harmonie avec le droit du gouvernement central. French 1995 nous éclaire sur le droit tibétain.

(28) Le droit socialiste constitue aussi une culture juridique importante à compter parmi les autres, même après le démembrement de l'URSS. J'ai omis de l'énumérer dans ce livre parce qu'il peut être examiné comme un droit ou une culture juridique universels plutôt que comme un droit ou une culture juridique régionaux.
(29) Cf. Sack 1982.
(30) Cf. Tamanaha 1993.
(31) Comparer Pérez Perdomo 1993 avec Capeller 1995, avec des éléments de bibliographie anthropologique en annexe.
(32) Cf. Gluckman 1955: chap. VIII.
(33) UNESCO Latin American Conference, 1981. Cf. Crawford 1988: 202.
(34) Cf. Rouland et al. 1996: 221-260.
(35) Cf. Hooker 1975: 427-446.
(36) Cf. M'baye 1975: 138-139.
(37) Cf. Cottran 1975: 168.
(38) Cf. Roberts 1998: 183.
(39) Cf. Kludze 1998: 187.
(40) Note de l'éditeur en chef: cf. Afchar 1975: 84.
(41) Ch. Chehata 1975: 138-142.
(42) Cf. Khadduri 1998: 192.
(43) Cf. Botiveau 1998: 197 et s.
(44) Voir Derrett & Iyer 1975: 110, 108, 117 etc.
(45) *Ibid.*: 108.
(46) *Ibid.*: 118.
(47) Voir French 1995.
(48) Cf. Ishii 1998.
(49) Par ex. Marasinghe 1993.
(50) Cf. Ishii 1998: 224.
(51) Par ex. Ji 1993.
(52) Voir Noda 1975. .
(53) Cf. Tay 1998.
(54) Cf. Sack 1998b: 225.
(55) *Ibid.*: 226.
(56) *Ibid.*: *eod. loc.*
(57) Cf. chap. 5 de ce livre.
(58) Cf. Kludze 1998: 185. .

(59) Cf. Sack 1998: 226 et s.
(60) Cf. 《Legal Concepts in Cross-Cultural Perspectives》, Numéro 41 du *Journal of Legal Pluralism and Unofficial Law*, 1998.
(61) Cf. Sack 1998: 46, 52.
(62) Cf. pp. 174-177, chap. 10 de ce livre.
(63) Détails dans Chiba 1989: chap. 12.
(64) Chiba, 《Pressing Tasks to Advance the Study of Asian Law》 (en japonais), *Journal of Social & Behavioral Sciences*, Tokai University (44), 1993: 17–29.
(65) Cf. pp. 113–121 de cette chapitre.
(66) Cf. Galanter 1981. Selon un jeune chercheur japonais, Masao Kotani, spécialisé dans les études socio-juridiques italiennes, le peuple italien est fondamentalement régi par trois systèmes juridiques principaux: droit étatique, droit canonique et droit non-officiel, les habitants pouvant choisir l'un d'entre eux comme standard juridique de leur comportement individuel quotidien — sous réserve de non prohibition par le droit étatique. Une telle observation peut être étendue aux autres pays occidentaux.
(67) Berman 1993.
(68) Cf, Berman 1983.
(69) Van den Bergh 1993.
(70) Gaudemet 1993.
(71) Ellul 1993.
(72) Burman & Harrell-Bond 1979.
(73) Chiba 1989.

Part III

HUMAN LAW

Chapter 8. Folk Law in Human History and Society*

1. The field of the anthropology of law has been growing, each stage of development marked by the opening of new areas of study, such as, ancient law, primitive law, tribal law, and folk law in legal pluralism. Outstanding achievements have also been made in researching the actual circumstances of people's law and the interaction of people's law with state law, thus clarifying the variations of legal pluralism.

Among the remarkable recent developments in this fiels have been the publication of encyclopedic works intended to offer a general view of legal pluralism. The most voluminous of these is the series on legal cultures in the International Library of Essays in Law and Legal Theory, under publication by Dartmouth Publishing Company since 1992 (a series unfortunately weakened by a methodology oriented to Western law alone except one volume, Sack & Aleck 1992). Another important contribution is Arnaud's dictionary (1993), which, by my count, contains thirty entries in the field of the anthropology of law, including, for the first time in a Western publication, eleven entries on non-Western legal cultures (among them, chapter 5 of this book). Four other entries (including Berman 1993) contain information indispensable for the comparison of Western and non-Western legal cultures. A further treatment of non-Western law is Chiba's small compilation (1993).

The volume under review represents yet another development in the field of folk law. This collection of preceding publications brings together fifty-seven essays in two volumes with a total of 1,037 pages. There is an introduction to the entire work, separate introductions to the eight sections that comprise the work, comments on and references to each essay, and forty-eight selected references. Below I give one-line summaries of each essay, along with the year of its original publication and the name and nationality (when known) of the author.

2. The first section, dealing with the definition of folk law, begins with the essay of G.C.J.J. Van den Bergh (1986, The Netherlands), which outlines variant

conceptions and treatments of unwritten law in European history and concludes that we have "to strive for a better operational definition of them". A. Arthur Schiller (1938, USA) next focuses on the Roman treatment of customary law. The four essays that follow discuss various forms of and approaches to folk law: M.P. Jain (1963, India) surveys Indian customs and the wide variations they show depending on locality, tribe, village, family, guild and caste; Gordon R. Woodman (1969, UK) stresses, on the basis of his Ghanaian and Nigerian data, the necessity of "sociological investigation"; J.P.B. Josselin de Jong (1948, The Netherlands) considers the "law-complex" as a phenomenon of culture; and A.W. B. Simpson (1973, USA) sees common law as "more like a muddle than a system". Finally, the modern jurisprudential doctrine of customary law is examined in an essay by Alan Watson (1984, USA).

The second section reviews trends in folk-law study in different countries. It opens with a wide-ranging overview of achievements in legal ethnology from eastern and western Europe first by Ernó Tárkány-Szücs (1967, Hungary). Following this we find contributions on pre-twentieth-century Russian studies of custom and customary law by Samuel Kucherov (1972, USSR); on "ethnological jurisprudents" and later ethnologists and historians among the German-speaking peoples by Rüdiger Schott (1982, Germany); on Dutch juridical ethnologists after C. van Vollenhoven (the founder of adat law studies) by A.K.J.M. Strijbosch (1977, The Netherlands); on the debate between those British who argued for the supremacy of British policy versus those who advocated "esteem for customary law" by Cornelis van Vollenhoven (1927, The Netherlands); and lastly on three Ghanaian scholars (J.M. Sarbah, J.B. Danquah, and N.M. Ollennu) by Irina Sinitsina (1981, USSR).

The third section on official ascertainment selects essays on English law as it was forced upon African peoples. First, A.N. Allott (1953 and 1957, UK) advises the adoption of careful practical techniques to counteract "the frequent attempts to force customary legal systems into an alien framework", while T.O. Elias (1958, Nigeria) pleads for caution, patience, nad care against "fossilization and fragmentation". There follow four essays analyzing the British restatement of native law: Simon Roberts (1971, UK) emphasizes "the discrepancy between the court records and everyday behavior" in Tswana; Muna Ndulo (1981, Zambia) argues

Chapter 8. Folk Law in Human History and Society *143*

that the dual system should be respected; Obeid Hag Ali (1971, Sudan) discusses E. Cotran's failed attempt to force English law on the Kenyan people; and Robert J. Gordon (1989, USA) attacks South African legislators for depriving the native population of indigenous law.

The fourth section collects various expressions of legal symbolism in the folklore and ritual of different cultures. An essay on a variety of "legally relevant" cultural forms among German-speaking peoples by Herrmann Baltl (1968, Austria) is followed by two sketches of children's games, one by Paul G. Brewster (1938, USA) on a German song about an old crime, and the other by A.F. Chamberlain (1903, USA) on a game called "law of finding" scatrered in six western European countries. These are followed by reports from various countries. John C. Messenger, Jr. (1959, USA) shows among the Anang in Nigeria how eleven legal proverbs are used in traditional subtribal courts even after their official invalidation. Harry L. Levy (1956, USA) reports on the Greek custom of distributing family property between brothers by lot. Durica Krstic (1981, Yugoslavia) lists numerous examples of legal symbols prevailing in the Balkan countries and certain other parts of the world. Clinton Bailey (1976, Israel) discusses the Bedouin image of justice as "well-balanced saddlebags" on a camel. John N. Hazard (1962, USA) compares proxemic relations in the courts of the USA with those in the courts of several European countries. Carl Bock (1884) reports a water ordeal used in Thailand to judge the ownership of a slave. Theodor Reik (1945, USA) argues that oral ordeal is disguised in the modern oath taken before a criminal court.

The fifth section considers different forms of legal codes. Two essays introduce ancient codes: Albrecht Goetze (1949, USA) discusses two pre-Hammurapi codes (the Sumerian Lipit-Ishtar and the Akkadian Eshnunna), and Raymond Westbrook (1985, Israel) takes up codes of Biblical and Cuneiform law. The next three contributors present rare data: Shih-Yü Yü Li (1950) discusses the Ch'ing penal law applied since 1733 in Tibet, with sixty-eight articles partly adopting Tibetan customs; Joseph Minattur (1964) considers poetic adat law in rhythmic form among matrilineal and exogamic Malaysians; and Edward Westermarck (1947, Finland) reports on well-organized customs concerning homicide among eleven Berber tribes in Morocco.

The sixth section contains case studies of folk law, preceded by two essays that take opposite sides in a debate on case method: one, by J.F. Holleman (1973, Holland), advocating the trouble-less case method, and the other, by A.L. Epstein (1969), promoting the trouble case method. Roger Howman (1948) tells of a midwife in Zimbabwe accused of practicing witchcraft (*muroyi*) but finally discharged by a native magistrate, who found that *muroyi* is used in twelve different meanings, including one approved of as lawful. R.F. Barton (1930, USA) reports homicide cases among Philippine tribes that could not be duly understood by the white man's law. R.S. Freed (1971, USA) surveys an Indian homicide case in which a Brahman daughter, who allegedly died of cholera just before marriage, was in fact killed by her father, who, realizing her infidelity, wished to give her a "merciful" death to ensure her rebirth. Beatrice Farnsworth (1986) analyzes late nineteenth-century records from four town courts in agricultural Russia that reveal customary law, as symbolized by the peasants' "right to beat their wives". Finally, Hendrick Hartog (1985, USA) records the development of "the judicial denial of the right to keep pigs in the street" in New York that was finalized in 1849 after thirty years of discussions.

The seventh section contains fascinating essays on the conflict of folk law with official law. L.C. Green (1975, Canada) cites cases from former British colonies in which tribal or primitive law was accommodated with "civilized" law in accordance with British standards. R.D. Kollewijn (1951, The Netherlands) shows the different attitudes taken by Holland, France, and England in their official recognition of non-Western marriage law that mitigated the Western "barbarous attitudes to alleged barbarians". E.G. Unsworth (1944, South Africa) analyzes the standards used by the British to discriminate "applicable" from "inapplicable" native law in their African colonies. Alec Samuels (1981, UK) looks into English cases in which immigrants' religious, polygamic, and other customs were adopted. Robert B. Seidman (1965, USA) reduces possible opinions in a hypothetical case on how to apply customary law in an African court to three: "not at all", "wholly", and "between". Roy Carleton Howell (1989) reports on a well-known Kenyan case concerning burial rights, in which the Luo tradition of the deceased Otieno won over his Kikuyu widow's invocation of official law. Alison Dundes Renteln (1988, USA), one of the editors, claims at first that there is no particular

Chapter 8. Folk Law in Human History and Society **145**

need for a cultural defense of the native practices of immigrants or refugees in the USA, since the existing legal mechanisms have been sufficient: an opinion the author later altered (Renteln 1994b).

The final section brings together essays that discuss the legal nature of international custom. Following Peter E. Benson (1982), who criticizes the opinion of François Gény as static; Nirmala Nagarathan (1971, Sri Lanka) analyzes certain recent trends, like the legal protection of the continental shelf and outer space. Rudolf Bernhardt (1977, Germany) encourages further scientific research into unwritten law for its "inseparable connection with written law". Two essays then maintain that official authorization by sovereign states is needed for internationalization to have legality: Richard J. Erickson (1975, USA) introduces certain Soviet opinions, while N.C.H. Dunber (1983, Australia) supports an English Court of Appeal decision to regard customary international law as "myth" when it comes to international conflict. Steven M. Schneebaum (1982, USA) insists on the need to protect existing individual rights internationally. Vladlen S. Vereshchetin and Gennady M. Danilenko (1985, USSR) promote the legality of international practices as applied to outer space. Allan Rosas (1984, Finland) finds customary international law applicable both regionally and universally.

3. Perfectionists might find it easy to point out shortcomings in this collection. For example, there are no essays in non-English languages, and only a few of the articles were written in the present decade. The quality of the section introductions is uneven, as is that of the respective bibliographies. Readers might also wish for indexes and bibliographical information on the authors.

And yet in spite of such apparent shortcomings, the book must be recognized as an invaluable contribution to the anthropology of law, providing as it does so many important essays, many of which had been overlooked, forgotten, or difficult of access. Its essays on folk law inform the scholars of historical variations in terminology and concepts (secs. 1, 2) and of the problems standing in the way of its official recognition by governments and scientific recognition by scholars (secs. 3, 5). It highlights the seriousness of folk law as an issue outside of or in conflict with state law (secs. 6, 7). And it reminds us of the two neglected fields of folk legal symbolism and international customary law (secs. 4, 8).

This said, I am nevertheless concerned that the book lacks any discussion of basic tool concepts that would enable us to grasp the dynamic realities of folk law as it actually exists. For example, if the data in the book is reformulated in accordance with the seven tool concepts I have discussed elsewhere (Chiba 1989: 177-180; pp. 14-20 of this book), a much different reality may be revealed, one more vivid than the simple view delineated by the book's static contrast between folk law and state law.

Folk law is an "indigenous" or "unofficial" form of law that is often regarded as inauthentic by the "official" law of a state, but that nevertheless forms a system under the central authority of a social organization, be it based on kinship, locality, tribe, occupation, religion, or voluntary association. Indigenous law evolves through history, impelled by its own potentials and by positive or negative interaction with pressures from outside, especially those of state law. And it may eventually even modify state law to some degree. We find cases in which it reshapes itself to better coexist with other forms of law, and cases where it disguises certain of its elements in "official" law (an example being the reformulation of certain types of Western folk law into modern state law). It may be imposed on or received by other peoples in the form of "transplanted" law, similarly when the Roman legal system was adopted by Western peoples. The transplantation of Western law to non-Western cultures has led to acculturation in some cases and to conflict in others (as in Trinidad, where the transplanted Western law of the colonizers clashed with the Asian indigenous law of the Indian immigrant laborers, see Haraksingh 1993).

Whether indigenous or transplanted, whether unofficial or official, law represents itself not only in the guise of "legal rules" (typical of state law, canon law, and sports law), but also in the form of "legal postulates" (prominent in religious law and international "social norms"). Law also works in various symbolic forms as in Tárkány-Szücs (above sec. 2) and synbolic functions as by Gusfield (1967, 1981). The different forms of law of a people may first be accurately observed and analyzed applying the above six dychotomic concepts and then all the forms may be synthetically put together by the seventh one, "identity postulate of a legal culture".

The more our analytical concepts are sharpened, the more accurately folk law can be observed and analyzed. However, the responsibility to promote such theoretical and／or methodolgical work must be borne not by editors who aim to be *anthropologists* of law but those of us who aspire to be anthropologists of *law*.

Notes

(*)　This chapter was originally my review essay of a book in English, *Folk Law: Essays in the Theory and Practice of Lex Non Scripta*, 2 vols., Garland Folklore Casebook 7, edited by Alison Dundes Renteln & Alan Dundes, publishied by Garland Publishing Inc., 1994.

Chapter 9. Legal Culture of Sports*

It may be wondered how relevant the topic 'sports law' is to nation building, the main theme of our Symposium. Truly, I have never heard that sports law has ever been discussed at any international meeting on legal theory, in which I am mainly interested, and I also suppose that the same applies to political science, the pertinent discipline of the main theme[1]. However, having been engaged in international collaboration to promote the study of legal pluralism (cf. Chiba 1989), I have come to be convinced of the importance of sports law as one which coexists with state law. If it is true, sports law must have a significant influence as a sub-culture upon the nation building of a people through law. I shall try to examine this hypothesis below, however preliminarily that may be.

1 What is sports law?

1. No one would deny that sport has been remarkably characteristic of cultures throughout human history (see Mandell 1984), nor that sports have grown into one of the major industries in the contemporary world (see Grayson 1988; Johnson & Frey 1985). Still, leading legal science has never bestowed adequate consideration on the relevance of sports to law. Some theoretical grounds are to be found in support of this indifference of the legal science toward sports[2].

First, separating the private world from the public world, the basic theory of modern jurisprudence leaves the former, including sports, to the freedom of private persons. Second, it adopts in particular the legal principle of not interfering with sports as it does with religion and morality. Third, this principle is embodied in the legal doctrine that the player who causes injury in sporting activities is exempted from both civil and criminal liability on the grounds of justifiable cause.

At the end of the nineteenth century, however, the established theory of modern law faced sharp criticism, as exemplified by the movements of critical legal studies and post-modern jurisprudence. To briefly review the development of modern law in this century, contemporary law in the world had in fact been shifting from its original ideals in two essential ways. The first occurred when modern law that had been created by Western thought to construct the capitalist society was transformed into another one, flexible enough to adopt somewhat different factors especially through confrontation with socialist law. The second became apparent when legal pluralism, comprising laws of different cultures, was found conspicuously in independent new non-Western countries, while in fact modern law is still believed, according to the original theory, to be the only standard law of universal prevalence. Legal science today is required under these circumstances to re-create itself, to theorize on the system of the shifting law in the world and furthermore to accelerate the shift toward a favourable one tomorrow.

One of the chief targets of such a re-creation must be, in a phrase, how legal theory can introduce culturally different factors into its system[3]. Sports law may be one of those factors as far as it works as the normative framework for sports, popular as they are in contemporary society, however leading jurisprudence might object.

2. In reality, the study of sports law began to be pursued around 1980 by some interested scholars scattered around a few Western countries and has developed in this decade to a collective activity in a greater number of countries. I will first make a brief review of its development based on the information I have collected.

Britain is distinguished in having accumulated many works related to both sports in socio-historical and political settings (for instance, Hargreaves 1986; Brailsford 1991) and sports law in particular (see Grayson 1988). In contrast, USA has accomplished an extensive study of working sports law. This is easily seen by a variety of references and bibliographies (Uberstine 1985; Hladczuk et al. 1991), introductory books (Weistart & Lowell 1979; Berry 1984; Berry & Wong 1985), case books and reports (*Sports and the Courts*), in addition to many articles and books on various related topics such as human rights, discrimination, contract, liability, school sports, professional sports, enterprises, broadcasting, television, antitrust law, damage, crimes, and many others (cf. Johnson &

Frey 1985; Champion 1990). Among European countries, Germany and France appear to be remarkable. After having produced an introductory book a decade ago (Weisemann 1983), German scholars have extended their perspective to various problems related sports by way of meetings and a continuing serial publication (*Recht und Sport*). France is the country that has made the most efforts at reasonable government regulation of sports in respect for personal freedom (*Droit et Sport* 1984; Alaphilippe & Karaqillo 1985; Collomb 1988). As for other European contries such as Spain, Italy, Switzerland, Holland and Belgium, it will suffice to mention that a bibliography is presented in a book (Will 1988: 89–103), because their achievements seem to be more limited than in the above-mentioned four countries.

Canada is also to be remarked upon, not only because of their works on sports law but also for the international relevance of their problems. They have been much influenced by American precedents as, for instance, offering a franchise to a professional baseball team owned by an American (see generally Barnes 1983; Harvey & Cantelon 1988). The international relevance of sports law is also clear in European countries, as evidenced by discussion about the cases on borders (Krähe 1987) and the comparison between some countries (Will 1988, 1993; Malatos 1988). Needless to say, international problems are often provoked by the exchange of players or by the feverish excitement at some world class competitions, including the Olympic Games.

As for non-Western countries, I have little available information on their sports law and studies thereof, except for my own country, where the new Japanese Association of Sports Law was instituted in December, 1992, to catch up with the more advanced studies made abroad. It is well-known, however, that sports are, or were, specifically encouraged in some Latin American and African countries as well as former socialist countries in Middle/East Europe, whether in accordance with legal regulation or national policy (Arbena 1988; Baker & Mangan 1987, cited in Vinokur 1988).

3. What, then, is sports law? Without doubt, it is the law of sports in society. Confusingly, however, the phrase bears different meanings.

The meaning of sport may first be questioned in order to delimit the objective of legal regulation. As a matter of fact, there are too many varied arguments among specialists about the concept of sports for an outsider like me to follow up. However, I would like to draw attention to two arguments noteworthy for their valuable suggestions. One analyzes the nature of sport as a complex of six factors: an embodiment of play; rule-structured, high formalization; contest within neutral rules; intrinsically dramatic means of expression; character of ritual practices often political; and symbolization through elaborate pageantry and ceremonials (Hargreaves 1986: 11-12). The other defines sports, as if to sum up the former analysis, as the "competitive activity of the whole human body according to sets of rules for purposes ostensibly or symbolically set apart from the serious, essential aspects of life" (Mandell 1984: xvii).

According to these suggestions, the nature of sports law may be abridged, insofar as my purpose of exploring its relevance to legal theory, in the following three particular essential factors: bodily competition, sets of rules, and symbolic formalization, each of which has appeared as belonging to the realm of personal freedom. It may be natural for this reason that the leading legal theory has kept sports separated from direct regulation by state law, unless sporting behaviour disturbs the social order or public policy. It may also be reasonable that sports law could find a rare position in the legal system of a nation. Still, the innate sets of rules for sports pose the problem of their relevance to law, as discussed below.

On the other hand, law has been limited by leading jurisprudence to the legal system of a sovereign state as most of the above-mentioned references presuppose. This state law is in reality not of a monolithic but of a plural structure. Because, in addition to its standard form as the law of the central government, it may firstly contain the law of the semi-independent governments within a bigger country called 'state,' republics, self-governing dominions, autonomous territories, or the like, and secondly extend both inward to the law of local organizations under the control of the central government and outward to international law as approved by the nation state.

I use the expression 'state law' for both the standard form and its two extensions, and 'national law' for the standard form alone. In this usage, state law schematically comprises three levels: sub-national law, national law, and supra-national law. Then, the state law of sports may be formed also at each of the three levels, while demanding basic accommodation of the different levels.

Yet, the recent explosion of sports in society after World War II has urged the development of a new type of state law, whether in legislation or in judicial precedents, to reasonably decide legal issues and regulate activities of sporting persons and related organizations, and, at the same time, it has necessitated a special study of this developing law. A rough picture may be gained from the above-mentioned American and German references (among others, Uberstine 1985; *Recht und Sport*). 'State sports law' has thus come to the foreground of legal science.

One noticeable feature is that sports activity is also regulated by another system of law, that is nothing but what was analyzed above as sets of rules. According to a British specialist, working sports law is first domestically categorised at four levels: "1. Playing laws for players and participants to play, 2. Playing penal laws for referees, umpires to control and discipline play, 3. Administrative laws for fair and sensible organisation and control, 4. National laws for the overriding control for justice and fair play at all the above three levels" (Grayson 1988: 11). It is then internationally extended to two other areas, that is, "law of international governing bodies and overseas national laws" (ibid.: 200) The four sports laws among the total six belong not to state law but to unofficial specific regulations formulated for that purpose alone. I will distinguish them from state sports law by calling them 'specific sports law'.

Specific law is essential in sport. No sport could exist if the specific rules for it were not firmly formulated; and no sporting event could take place without collective agreements to play and promote it amongst the people concerned. In addition, as my analysis shows, those rules and agreements are presupposed to be guided by some ideal postulates for sporting behaviour just as state law is supported by legal ideas such as justice or natural law. For these reasons, I would classify specific sports law into three:

1. 'Sports rules' to provide sporting players, referees, and sometimes spectators with specific rights and duties, including penalties and sanctions.
2. 'Sports legal postulates' as the ideal foundation and guide for the rules of sport, such as fair play or sportsmanship.
3. 'Sports organization agreements' to organize associations, federations, or unions devoted to sports as well as to promote their activities, whether domestically or internationally[4].

2 Sports law as a sub-culture

1. Before arguing sports law as a sub-culture, I would like to present my concepts of our key words to preclude misunderstanding. As for the concept of nation building, I would provisionally adopt the definition of Carl Friedrich, following a specialist of sports law, of "a matter of group cohesion and group loyalty for international representation and domestic planning" (Vinokur 1988: 16), in a word, national integration. Then, an integrating power must efficiently work to achieve nation building in the light of factors militating against it. The integrating power must be political because it has to predominate over resistance. We can thus first schematically classify the total powers functioning in nation building into the integrating political power and others that coexist, whether in support of or resistance to the former. This aspect of power in relation to nation building may be applicable to the total structure of law in a country. That is, national law is obliged to integrate sub-national laws of semi-independent governments, local governments or others, not to mention the components of its own system.

I give here a useful suggestion of a sociologist of law, Adam Podgorecki, to classify the legal sub-culture versus national law into three: "positive, neutral or negative" (1974: 228-229). According to this classification, laws ordinarily work positively to support national law under the latter's overwhelming legitimacy. There are extraordinary cases, however, where sub-national laws work against national law to be characterized as negative, when their governments raise objections or even demand independence. Except apparently supporting or resisting cases, sub-national laws might be regarded as keeping neutral; but we should

Chapter 9. Legal Culture of Sports *155*

pay due attention to the fact that neutrality in appearance often signifies resistance in reality[5].

Such a classification of state law must schematically hold true of state sports law. That is, state sports law works under the control of integral national law and is assisted by positive and neutral sub-national laws. In reality, however, its total structure is somewhat different from that of state law in general due to the specific nature of sports. First, in sports law, more importance has long been attached to the neutral freedom of citizens than to the direct regulation of legitimate state law. Although the recent development of state sports law has been truly rapid and broad enough to be observed as integrational, it apparently retains, generally in Western countries, its limitation not to interfere with private freedom in sport. Second, negative state sports law cannot be possible in practice under the legitimacy of the integrating national law and by the nature of sport.

Specific sports law is accorded particular status remarkably different from state sports law. It may be simply characterized as neutral from the jurisprudential perspective, for its substantial contents, sports rules and sports organization agreements, are left uninterfered with by state law, as codified in the constitutional freedom of privacy and contract (see note 5). In reality, those rules and agreements are essential for the existence of sport. People can enjoy sports in accordance with sports rules and organizational agreements even when no state law is furnished; and no sport can take place without such specific rules and agreements, while people may live in society without state law even though with some difficulty. In this, specific sports law is, from the sociological perspective, a genuine, valid law working as a sub-culture, however unofficial and however removed from official state law[6]. Its problem to be asked here must be how its seeming neutrality functions in reality against national law.

As to the concept of sub-culture, the issue is that of its elementary word 'culture', for that of 'sub' leaves no doubt as to its meaning 'smaller-scale' within a nation. According to the anthropological usage, the essence of culture is the integrated system of learned behaviour of a spatially identifiable population in a society (cf. Hoebel 1972: 6, 33-34). This definition is a variation of the lexical meaning of sub-culture respecting a group of same distinctive traits within the same society. It is too narrow, however, to use in treating our main topic and my own special one. Another lexical meaning must be appropriate for our purpose, that is, "the cultural values and behavioral patterns distinctive of a particular group in a society" (Random House Dictionary 1973). 'A particular group' may mean, as used in relation to sports, not only a permanent organization for sports activities or a transient grouping for a sports match or training but also a collection of people including spectators and fans as the case may be.

Most noticeable is the fact that sports presuppose specific sports law by its very nature and in addition to its original concept centerd on physical activity. I use the term 'sports' hereafter as also implying 'specific sports law' in its conception even when not specifically mentioned.

2. I am convinced, from the above analysis of the related key words, that the main problem of sports law as a sub-culture may lie in the relation, whether positive or not, between official national law and unofficial specific sports law as an essential constituent of sport.

From the jurisprudential perspective, possible conflict between both official and unofficial laws of sports appears to have been adequately accommodated. In fact, there may take place many violations of state law in sporting activities. The most frequent of them have been physical injury or damage caused by accidents, which should bring forth the problem of legal liability, whether civil or criminal. In most actual cases, however, the inflictor of the injury or damage is legally immune by virtue of his/her justifiable act or by the prior acceptance of its possibility by the parties, except in some few special cases where ordinary civil damages or criminal punishments are applied in accordance with the prescriptions of state law. This immunity doctrine enables jurisprudence to be satisfied without having to regard sporting accidents as a serious legal issue worthy of special notice.

From the sociological perspective, however, this evidences a latent conflict between state law and specific sports law. As stated before, sports are based on and armed by their own unique laws — specific rules of each sport. The specific rules enable people, to enjoy the sport self-sufficiently with no interference nor

Chapter 9. Legal Culture of Sports *157*

assistance from other norms and powers. In addition, the specific rules are so efficient that they are almost always satistactorily observed by the persons concerned, for any sporting activity would disappear if a specific rule were left unobserved. Such efficient regulation cannot be rivalled by state law, which is likely to be faced with many cases of violation and evasion in reality. Theoretically, sports rules of such validity must have ample possibility to fall into conflict with, or evoke positive resistance to, state law. In practice, however, most of such conflicts are adequately accommodated by the device of 'immunity doctrine' afforded by a jutisprudential doctrine. The rules in sports are thus known to be furnished with such an intrinsic power as to make state law yield to themselves.

This relation of sports and specific sports law to state law is similar to the status of religion and religious law as another sub-culture. It is a common sense approach to jurisprudence that religious freedom is respected as an inviolable human right never to be interfered with by state law, except for some legislation limited to protecting religious activity in society. This gives its first similarity to sport. Then, each religious denomination is furnished with the elaborate system of their own law as exemplified by Canon law, Islamic law, and others, which I would call 'specific religious law'. This attribute of innate specific law forms a second similarity of religion to sports. There are still other remarkable sub-cultures, in which freedom is protected as a human right by the constitution, such as freedom of thought, opinion, and others. However, there are none among them with such elaborate specific law as religion and sports.

For these reasons[7], we may duly conclude that the attitude of state law toward sports is to refrain from direct control and is, as toward religion, based on two factors derived from the essential nature of sport: that sports originally belong to the realm of personal freedom and that they are independently regulated by their own specific law. Here, it should be noted that the differences between sports and religion lie in at least three phases. First, in its basic form, the autonomy of religion is without fail made manifest in every democratic constitution — so much so that it rarely needs reinforcement from jurisprudential interpretation, while that of sports is rarely declared manifestly but is efficiently protected by the aforementioned jurisprudential principle and doctrine. Second, in its positive form, religion and sports appear to be differently regulated by the laws and ordinances concerned; in Japan, for instance, the main law affecting religion is the Religious Corporation Law, 1951, to regulate the activities of religious bodies, while that of sports is the Sports Promotion Law, 1961, declaring the duty of the government to assist sporting activities. Third, it is likely that religion actually to oppose national policy, whereas this is rarely possible for sporting activities. It is beyond the scope of my topic, however, to discuss such a comparison further. I shall confine myself to examining the function of sports for or against national policy.

3. Beside the immunity doctrine in jurisprudence, defending cases of specific sports law against state law are not conspicuous by their presence. I have never heard in Japan of any sport that was suppressed or prohibited for its resistance to state law. At the same time, I hesitate to deny that it could happen. Because we sometimes hear from foreign countries of some legal issues where sportsmen moved or fled from their own countries due to government oppression, and where they expressed their opposition to the government policy as typically exemplified by boycotted Olympic Games. I feel required to further examine those cases and others to confirm the possibility of resistance to state sports law. Still, we could safely regard this possibility as outweighed by the possibility of support, for there is a wealth of information about the contribution of sports to the national identity, its prestige and integration.

The British are distinguished in having developed sports with a national philosophy and in having produced socio-political discussions about sport. A brief summary comes from a specialist (Hargreaves 1986) and is supplemented by some others. The specialist analyzes modern and recent development of sports in its politicization by socio-political powers, while he regards the original nature of sports as a leisure to enjoy personal freedom (ibid.: 8, 222–223). This politicization emerged with industrial capitalism, because the hegemonic bourgeois wanted to develop sport into a rational recreation in gentlemanly amateurism (ibid.: 205–206) on the one hand, and on the other, the increasing free time of labourers was directed into sports activities through the Catholic and Protestant Churches, public schools, and voluntary associations (ibid.: 206–207; see also Coghlan 1990: 1

Chapter 9. Legal Culture of Sports *159*

-5; Brailsford 1991: 22). The trend developed rapidly in the twentieth century with increasing commercialization and mass society, because the dominant class succeeded through sports with intention but by a hidden agenda, first to divide subordinate classes into upper or lower, skilled or unskilled, man or woman, central or local, young or old, and different races, and then to integrate them into a non-class national identity (ibid.: 207-208). Sports are thus a 'discourse of national integration' (Jones 1988: 219-220)

The political function of sports is also seen among other peoples to a greater or lesser extent. For instance, Germany, France and some others had resistance movements comprising laborers active in sports organizations during World War II, while Britain did not (Hargreaves 1986: 212-213). In USA, the symbolic value of sports has been undoubtedly believed, according to two co-authors, as identical with the national spirit, that is, "democratic values of justice, equality and rule obedience" (Johnson & Frey 1985: 261-262). In consideration of such a significant function of sports for national integration, these authors advise against disturbing the balance between "the imperfections of the free market (for sports) and the imperfection of government regulation,"however the spirit may be identical between sports and nation (ibid.: 263-264). The situation does not differ greatly among other capitalist countries.

In contrast, it differed greatly in the former socialist countries in Europe and in some other continents. We know well that players from those countries achieved astonishingly brilliant records in Olympic Games and various world championship competitions, and that they were privileged, enjoying a special status under the control of their governments. No one would deny that "sports are an essential instrument serving the national and political integration of a country" in socialist USSR, East Germany, Rumania, Czechoslovakia, Hungary, and China (Vinokur 1988: 18-19, cf. 433-436). Such a contribution of sport to national integration is similarly found among many non-Western countries for somewhat different reasons and function. National sports noted among Latin American countries such as soccer, baseball or cycling, are "intrinsically linked to the complex of cultural patterns and values associated with urban-industrial institutions and their spheres of influence," thus contributing to their national rebuilding under the influence of

Western civilization, while accompanied by a negative function to sharpen "class and/or racial cleavages" (Arbena et al. 1988: 2, 5). It is also well noted that many Third World countries, including some African ones like Ethiopia and Kenya, confer high honours on their players who have distinguished themselves in international competitions. Such privileges go to "national heroes as opposed to local or tribal ones" (Mandell 1984: 268).

How, then, is the contribution of specific sports law to such a positive function of sports for national integration? First, sports organization agreements, among three components of specific sports law, must be directly contributory, because the cooperation of sportsmen in line with national sports policy, whether intentional or not, cannot be exercised without the organizations' intentional cooperation with their governments. Next, sports rules seem, in contrast, to be indifferent to such a contribution due to their intrinsic neutrality. However, those of some sports — specifically those popularized as national sports, whether transplanted from other nations or indigenous to the nation[8] — may be contributory indirectly when encouraged by nationalistic spirit and directly when officially supported by national policy. Last, the contribution of the sports legal postulates is not easy to exactly assess before we examine more data on both possibilities, supporting and opposing[9]. However, we could safely say there is undoubted evidence of the underlying possibility. As far as sports legal postulates are likely to play the role of national spirit in their symbolic formalization, this is one of three factors of sports I pointed out (in p. 152), as seen in USA and, though in a different way, former socialist countries. In sum, specific sports law proves the possibility of contributing to national integration, directly or indirectly, though leaving some problems to be examined.

It is clear that such a contribution of specific sports law cannot be spoken of without referring to the international function of sports. We are here reminded of another important characteristic of specific sports law, which is its international relevance beyond national boundaries.

3 Sports law as a supra-culture

1. Jurisprudence has paid scant interest in the international significance of

Chapter 9. Legal Culture of Sports *161*

sports law, as far as I have been able to ascertain from Japanese scholarship. Do sports, then, have no international nature at all? No one could ever deny that they have. More than that, sports must be one of the human activities where international exchange is most frequently made among many others. Remarkably enough, such an exchange is facilitated by international agreements of sports organizations from different countries in accordance with the same rules of each particular sporting event which goes beyond national boundaries under the guidance of sports rules and legal postulates, in brief, 'international specific sports law'. There is ample reason to advocate the internationality of specific sports law, while some public international law of sports may be formulated between national governments.

Before discussing it, I would refer to the concept of international sports law by James Nafziger revealed in the only book I know on this topic (1988). According to the author, an especially important role in international sports law is performed by general principles of public international law and supplemented by international custom. Supported by them and embodying related specific international customs and internal regulations, the Olympic Charter is of particular significance, for it provides the rules for the Olympic Games and organizes the world federation of the National Olympic Committees governed by the International Olympic Committee. In addition, regional and other organizations provide such rules that "are often well-defined and effective transmitters of shared values in international sports, though not 'law' in themselves" (ibid.: 32–38). Thus he reaches the concept of 'international sports law' as "a more or less distinctive body of rules, principles and procedures that govern the political and social consequences of transnational sports activity" (ibid.: 1). I support the thrust of his argument on the legal framework, for it basically coincides with my scheme of sports law; that is, state sports law extending to international sports law and specific sports law sub-divided into sports rules, sports legal postulates, and sports organization agreements.

I further take notice of his two other points. One is the flexible and dynamic nature of international sports law. It may be "hard" as is the practice of boycotting to discourage racism, or "soft and rather difficult" to enforce as are anti-commercialization rules against advertising, or else "developing" as are rules against gender discrimination, and "passing into desuetude" as are rules that attempted to restrict some sports (ibid.: 215). The other is that "in the face of politics, international sports law works surprisingly well" (ibid.: 217). It is the issue that is examined below.

2. The extraordinary encouragement of sports in former socialist countries mentioned above was founded on the constitutional duty of governments like East Germany (Vinokur 1988: 60) or on national policy incorporating sports legal postulates. The reason was to achieve their aim of national integration on the one hand, and on the other, to obtain international recognition in sports, especially from capitalist countries in place of normal political recognition (cf. ibid.: 16, 59). A somewhat similar circumstance may be found in some African countries distinguished in some sporting events, such as Ethiopia and Kenya. Sports are an efficient measure by which people may secure international prestige and diplomatic standing in addition to domestic political stability (Mandell 1984: 269). Similarly, there are some non-Western countries with distinguished national sports, such as Latin American countries (cf. Arbena 1988), China and others.

In contrast, advanced capitalist countries appear to be restrained in governmental interference in sports in obedience to leading legal doctrines. Still, their competitive spirit in international sports seems not so much different from the socialist and non-western countries noted above. Thus, international sports are a forum of competition among countries with different ideological policies, and international sports law is trusted, though within certain limits, to accommodate conflicts that may arise out of those differences. We have truly had sad events at Olympic Games such as the "Black September" action at the 1972 Munich Games where Arab terrorists attacked Israeli players, killing two and seizing nine, and the boycott of the 1980 Moscow Games by USA and retaliation by USSR at the 1984 Los Angeles Games. The *raison d'être* of international sports law might be questioned by these unhappy events.

Regretting those events, the above mentioned author realizes that possible conflicts can be caused by governmental intervention through boycotting international sporting events, refusal of visas, etc.(Nafziger 1988: 51). Still, he argues that the use of sports in an official sense to provoke conflict is fortunately rare, whereas its use to promote cooperation is commendable (ibid.: 99). *Inter alia*, he identifies its contribution in "enhancing human rights" by rejecting discrimination and "help(ing) establish diplomatic relations or recognize states" as typically exemplified by ping-pong diplomacy between USA and China, which enabled them to initiate official interaction in the early 1970's (ibid.: 74). I would again support his opinion.

Then, an important proposition is suggested on the manifest function of international sports law, that public international law may need to be assisted by various unofficial laws in order for it to work and develop in dynamic international relations. International sports law is without doubt at the forefront. In other words, it forms a sub-culture against public international law with its unofficial and specific nature. Thus in conclusion, specific sports law that acts as a framework for sport is a sub-culture not only against state law but also against international law.

The international nature of specific sports law is thus never doubted. I think it wise to entrust it to specialists to discuss this topic in further details except for this comment, because it is too big a problem for cursory treatment. As a matter of course, sports work internationally by way of their rules. The players and spectators, and the fans, who are excited by means of mass communication, of a particular sporting event can enjoy one and the same rules of the sport which prevail beyond the bounds of national territories, even when related persons are themselves not aware of the fact. Sporting organisation agreements similarly share internationality in a manifest way when they are concluded between different countries, and in a latent way by adopting internationally prevailing rules even when made between domestic organizations. Specific sports law is thus evidently found to be a sub-culture against international law, manifestly or latently.

3. The significance of sports law clarified above as an international sub-culture may need, I am convinced, further examination of its function in relation to domestic sports law. Because our main theme is limited to domestic problems

with the emphasis on nation building, on the one hand, and I am treating sports in an international forum, on the other, where different nations compete against one another for their own national identity and prestige.

The above arguments show in brief that international sports law, be it public or private, may be regarded as a 'supra-culture' of domestic sports law, whether state one or specific one. It truly contains some aspects of public law. In the main, however, its structure remains outside official regulation, formulated and prevalent in a realm left untouched by the sovereign power of the state, like the case of religious law. In any case, international sports law must be not 'inter-national' law. Rather, it is a legal system worthy of being called 'transnational' law (by Nafziger), or as I put it, a 'common law of world citizens'. It is thus concluded that international sports law is a valid legal system working as a supra-culture outside the alledged official realm of international law.

A comment may be added regarding the universality of sports law. Many different sports are truly transnational with their particular specific laws. At the same time, sports are not to be found in equal distribution all over the world but are in fact more diversed. Applying my dichotomic concepts of 'indigenous and transplanted' (see note 8), every sport is, or was, originally indigenous in a tribal or national culture but many of them are very likely to be transplanted to foreign nations. Contemporary transnational sports are an outcome of repeated transplantation among nations. Two tendencies are noticeable in this process. First, every nation tends to select to a lesser or greater extent some particular sports out of all the foreign sports that are available when it transplants some of them, thus resulting in an uneven distribution of the world of transplanted sports. Some transplanted sports may become so popular as to be called 'modern national sports' of a transplanting country: for instance, soccer in Latin American countries or baseball in Japan, while transplanting people may be obliged to revise some of the original but unessential rules of the sports to be able to adapt to different cultures. In contrast, some indigenous sports have been preserved with no or little possibility of transplantation, thus forming 'traditional (national) sports' like *pelota* in the Basque region of Spain or *sumo* in Japan, while they are also obliged to adapt to changing circumstances in their own cultures.

Chapter 9. Legal Culture of Sports *165*

These facts present us with a conspicuous relevance of culture to sports. In brief, it depends upon the culture of the nation what kinds of foreign sports a nation transplants and how the nation acculturates them in the process of transplantation, on the one hand, and what indigenous sports the nation preserves and how the nation adapts them to changing circumstances, including internationalization, on the other. The acculturated sports may be regarded as a supra-culture, and the preserved sports as a sub-culture. Here is found an essential nature of sports structured by specific sports law as 'a sub-culture and supra-culture'.

Notes

(*) This chapter was originally my paper presented before the Symposium on "Nation Building and Sub-Cultures" held by and at the Tokai University European Center, Vedbæk, Denmark, on 28-29, March, 1993.

(1) There might have been some international meetings that adopted sports law among their topics. I would be happy to receive information from readers about those precedents, while I have heard after having sent the final manuscript to the editor that an international association of sports law had started up in 1992. See also note 4 below.

(2) The contents of this and the next sections are a summary of my two preceding articles in Japanese.

(3) Another target is, as I am convinced, to establish the subjective viewpoint of law from the addressee to correctly understand the standing of those people who transplanted foreign law to form legal pluralism (see Chapter 10 of this book).

(4) Recently, I found a precedent to recognize specific sports law in an international forum. The International Institute for the Sociology of Law in Oñati, Spain, adopted in their survey in 1992 three words, 'indigenous sports law, sports organization law, and sports rules,' among a total of 273 key words for their sociology of law. The latter two of these three key words correspond to my words, sports organization agreements and sports rules, respectively. The first one is however confusing, for the word 'indigenous' may denote two different meanings: 'not elaborated into official system' like specific sports law and 'originating in a particular culture,' like traditional sports. I distinguish both by using the different words 'specific' and 'indigenous' respectively (see Note 8 below).

(5) Human rights to protect private freedom may in appearance be characterized as neutral to national law. It is noteworthy that such neutrality may in reality signify assistance insofar as active resistance is not shown. Being included in one of them, the right to sports bears the same character.

(6) 'Official law' and 'unofficial law' form a dichotomy in my conceptual scheme of law with the calling of 'three dichotomies of law under the identity postulate of a legal culture'. The former is "the legal system and its components authorized by the legitimate authority of a country," that is, state law and others officially authorized by the state. The latter is "the legal system and its components not officially authorized by any legitimate authority, but authorized in practice by the general consensus of a certain circle of people, whether within or beyond the bounds of a country, when they cause distinct influences upon the effectiveness of official law, supplementing, opposing, modifying or even undermining any of the official laws, especially state law" (Chiba 1989: 177). For the other dichotomies, see notes 8 and 9 below.

(7) There is another similarity between sports and religion, that is, internationality. It is discussed in the following section.

(8) The dichotomic words, 'indigenous' and 'transplanted,' are applied here after my conceptual scheme of law (cf. note 6). Indigenous law is broadly "law originated in the native culture of a people" and narrowly "the law existing in the indigenous culture of a non-Western people prior to their transplantation of modern Western law." Transplanted law is broadly "law transplanted by a people from a foreign culture" and narrowly "the state law of a non-Western country transplanted from modern Western countries."Notice the fact that transplanted law may be more or less indigenized through acculturation during a long period. (Chiba 1989: 178-179) This dichotomy is applicable, I believe, to sports law in international relations.

(9) The legal postulate of unofficial law is more serious than the ideas of official state law. Because unofficial law is generally not so elaborately furnished with distinct legal rules as state law is and, for this reason, needs a more influential function of legal postulates to supplement these deficiencies. My last dichotomy is thus formulated: 'legal rules' meaning "the formalized verbal expressions of particular legal regulations to designate specified patterns of behaviour" and 'legal postulates' meaning "the particular values and ideas and their systems specifically connected with a particular law to ideally found, justify and orient, or else supplement, criticize and revise the existing legal rules" (Chiba 1989: 178).

Chapter 10. Legal Pluralism in Mind

1

Every social norm designates a certain behavioural standard as a rule or principle for the relevant addressee, while in reality there may be great differences of his/her observance of it. Among the other social norms, the behavioural standard ordered by law is, however, presupposed to be observed with no exception. 'No exception,' according to authentic jurisprudence, because the behaviour deviant from law and consequent social conflict taking place now and then are to be corrected by any measure of compensation or punishment laid down by law, since law is the last resort to peaceful social order that is, in a total society, regulated by coexisting, often competing, other social norms, too. It is thus reasonable to say that jurisprudence has premised on the observance of the addressee and, as a result, exclusively focused on justification of the legitimacy and enforceability of the law.

It is true that the legal system is furnished with the capacity to afford such an inclusive and exclusive applicability in face of recurring deviances and conflicts. Identification of anticipation complex, a main point advanced by Niklas Luhmann in his system theory of law, may be one of the significant mechanisms of the capacity[1]. Two other mechanisms can be added to the capacity according to my legal theory.

One is the 'challenge-absorbing mechanism,' which includes the specified but abstract concept of particular right and duty, broader concept of legal ideas such as justice and natural law to supplement the specified concept of right and duty, and a set of measures to reform the existing legal system like legal fiction, equity and legislation as formulated by Maine[2] (cf. Chiba 1989: 45-46). The other is the 'challenge-rejecting mechanism' to restrain the law from interfering in such a type of social conflicts threatening its own proper foundation, as exemplified by the principles of 'separation of law from fact' and 'separation of law from ethics and religion' (Chiba 1989: 46-48).

Thus, law can maintain its self-sufficiency in its world indifferent to deviances and conflicts taking place in reality, whose capacity the authentic jurisprudence is proud of. In the Western countries, generally speaking, the said self-sufficiency of law appears to have been established in both practice and theory. Actually, unification of customary law into the centralized legal system of a state since early modern times has been so successfully achieved that people believe in state law monism. Theoretically, jurisprudence has limited the concept of law to state law alone, outlawing every kind of social norms with some exceptions when designated with a label of law like customary law, primitive law, local law, divine law, and others. Jurisprudence has been enabled to do without serious regard to deviances and conflicts as well as the other kinds of particular law.

On the other hand, there are multifarious facts, when observed from the viewpoint of social sciences, which leave us in reasonable doubts about the jurisprudential view of law, as seen by the proliferating achievements in the sociology and anthropology of law. As this is not the appropriate place to go into a deep exploration, I will just refer to two illuminating approaches to the problem they provoke, that is, 'conflict theory' and 'legal culture'.

'Conflict theory' regards conflict as essential to society and not necessarily antisocial to be utterly removed (Coser 1956) as I reformulated the idea into 'continuum theory of law and conflict,' meaning the coexistence in society of the tendencies of both law and conflict, based on the fact 'Where society is, there is law as well as conflict' (Chiba 1980). The doctrine of jurisprudence intentionally disregards this fact and social theory. For instance, it assumes adjudication as the final means of conflict resolution, while adjudication itself forms in fact a process of social conflict, though with the function to modify some phases of a social conflict in some way or other as an attempt to settle it but so often leaving other phases in conflict after the alleged final resolution by the law. The conflict theory thus suggests us to reformulate the relationship between law and conflict in society. To add a comment before the following argument, it is clear that this reformulation is more complicated and serious under legal pluralism than legal monism.

Still, concentrating on the social reality in objectivity, the conflict theory disregards another essential reality of law and conflict in subjectivity just like authentic jurisprudence. A social conflict observed in objectivity is usually accompanied by another conflict taking place in the mind of the persons involved in it. Such a subjective conflict may also occur when he/she finally chooses a behavioural standard designated by the law after a psychological struggle for choice between competing behavioural standards. Of course, the sociology of law has been aware of such a subjective problem though indirectly and from different angles. For instance, the survey of 'attitude towards law' is one of them, because the attitudes are produced from personal disposition (cf. Podgorecki et al. 1973). The voice of 'symbolic function of law' is another one, because it treats the influence of law upon the psychology of the addressee (cf. Gusfield 1967, 1981).

Recent extensive interest in 'legal culture,' in contrast, suggests that we may take a further and more thorough approach to the subjective problem. Truly, the prevailing concept appears to be so different which can be seen in the usages such as 'attitudes and values concerning law' (Podgorecki, 1974: 227-229; Friedman 1975: 15), 'legal tradition' (Ehrmann 1976: 8; Berman 1983: 11), 'interplay of four levels of legal phenomena from the law to consciousness' (Blankenburg & Bruinsma 1991: 8-9), 'popular legal practice formed from direct personal experience' (Macaulay 1989), and 'cultural configuration in law' (Chiba 1989: 203). Without doubt, however, no conception of legal culture could be produced if psychological and axiological factors in the mind of the addressee in respect of the law were not seriously considered. The problem of legal culture must urge us to treat the subjective problem of law directly and squarely.

The subjective problem is to be found wherever man lives with law. However, it must be more complicated and more serious under legal pluralism than legal monism, roughly in other words, in non-Western countries than Western countries. It is the theme of what I want to present here.

2

Legal pluralism is a social phenomenon in objectivity. An empirical variety of its circumstances has been reported and discussed in accordance with the diversified features of individual cases. At the moment, the reality seems inviting too many complicated findings to enable us to attempt to formulate the common understanding of the empirical legal pluralism. Legal pluralism, as found initially, was limited to non-Western countries. It has been extended in two ways. First, various types of normative orders that had been outlawed have been found to comprise pluralism with state law. The data concerned were presented from Africa, North America, South Asia, and Australia; we therefore expect different data to be presented from Latin America, inland Asia, Oceanic islands, and other areas in the world. Then, it has been sought in Western countries, too. Legal pluralism in Western countries, to which minor significance was attributed even when perceived, seems to have acquired greater importance since the development of the European Community and the recent disorganization of socialist regimes.

Still, we can find a common understanding presupposedly underlying the complicated data and discussions presented in respect of legal pluralism. It is that legal pluralism means a dual structure of state law and minor laws under the state law, while the nature and conception of the minor laws are variant (cf. Hooker 1975; Allott & Woodman 1985; Sack & Minchin 1986; Griffiths 1986; Merry 1988; Morse & Woodman 1988). There is no doubt that the advocates have found other systems of law, however minor, coexisting with state law of alleged monistic authority. 'Legal pluralism in double structure' is a reasonable aspect to be further explored in reality and theory.

At the same time, there is another phenomenon and accordingly meaning of legal pluralism to be added for further empirical study: 'legal pluralism in triple structure.' The triple structure comprises, schematically formulated in brief, minor systems of law under state law, state law, and law across and beyond state laws. When law across and beyond state laws is represented by international law, no one would deny the triple structure operating in a contemporary world. I would like to mention its essentiality to the idea of legal pluralism by expanding the prevailing concept of international law much more. First, the concept of law must be expanded enough to include any international norms that cause distinct positive or negative influences upon established international law.[3] Then, the addressee of the law may include, other than the sovereign state, also individuals and organizations with no direct relation to the state authority. Finally, the arenas of the law may be found in regional areas where not only states but also individuals and organizations interact with one another under their own particular laws. I would tentatively call such an expanded international law 'world law' replacing 'international law' I used before (Chiba 1989: 206-207).

I know the concept of 'world law' has not been elaborated enough. Supposing that its utility is accepted, on the other hand, I would advance my argument of legal pluralism by use of this concept, that is, legal pluralism in triple structure, comprising minor law, state law, and world law. In other words, legal pluralism in a particular arena in the world is nothing but a coexistence of the above three different levels of law, in each of which different sub-systems may be similarly coexisting. The coexistence never means complete harmony between the concerned levels or sub-systems. As a rule, on the contrary, it may be true to say that there is no society without more or less conflict between them. If a conflict between them is so intense that it may bring a societal legal order to dysfunction, there would be no legal pluralism but a struggle between the independent levels or sub-systems that has to go out of our focus. As far as legal pluralism is concerned, it is still difficult at present to clearly discern the different degrees of harmony between levels or sub-systems in a legal pluralism. For a practical heuristic purpose, however, it may be convenient to roughly differentiate them into two types. One is a 'conflicting situation' of competing plural levels or sub-systems, not so grave as to break off the societal order. The other is a 'complementing situation' between them indicating whether they are officially authorized by the state law or unofficially working as valid in reality.

A conflict situation in non-Western societies was first perceived as a conflict between transplanted state law and indigenous unofficial law. Then, the complementing situation was noticed when some factors of indigenous law were known to have been adopted in the official system of the state law or unofficially validated in reality with the function to supplement the overall prevalence of the latter. The legal pluralism comprising a double structure may be said to be an inevitable destiny of non-Western law. Legal pluralism in double structure later identified by Western societies was generally observed as a complementing situation under the supreme authority of state law. However, it also contains conflict situation in reality. To take a few examples, Western national states have often faced such struggles that are used to result in a compromise with or between minority groups who demand their legal autonomy, whether ethnically, religiously or politically. Western state law is in many countries apparently also competing with some of the world law, for instance in case of divorce and abortion with Canon law, and in case of conscientious objection to military service with religious conviction. Most striking is the formation and development of the European Community across and beyond individual sovereign states.

To sum up, the difference in legal pluralism between Western and non-Western societies may not be that of quality but of quantity in triple structure. There is a good reason, I am convinced, to focus my theme on non-Western legal pluralism, for the problem may be more serious in the conflicting situation than in the complementing situation.

3

My theme is thus identified as a subjective problem of the behavioural standard under legal pluralism in non-Western societies. Before going on to argument on its core, I would like to comment on the circumstantial process that kindled my aspiration for it.[4]

It sprang from my interest in the cultural feature of Japanese law. The Japanese legal system was alleged to have been completely modernized by transplantation of Western law since more than a century ago. In reality, however, it was an amalgamation of transplanted law with indigenous law as clearly exemplified by the absolutistic Tenno regime and patriarchal family system authorized in the allegedly modernized 1889 Constitution. Its total revision after World War II was aimed to advance the democratization of Japanese law and society abolishing the

Chapter 10. Legal Pluralism in Mind **173**

Tenno regime and the family system. Still, contemporary Japanese law contains a variety of indigenous practices such as a symbolical Tenno system with some latent political function, a more individualized family system with some collective function, and many others. Japan's modernization of law is distinctively different from the Western model (cf. Chiba 1986: chap. 7; chap. 2 of this book).

Such indigenous practices have rarely been discussed as a problem of legal pluralism but attracted the attention of, first, American Japanologists and, then, Japanese sociologists of law as a peculiar type of attitudes toward law. Their view may be abridged in such expressions as a too flexible conception of property and contract, preference of reconciliation and mediation to struggle and adjudication, disliking or alienating law. Noticeable of these expressions is that such seemingly peculiar attitudes are not always prevailing among all the members of a particular social group or under a specified circumstance, but rather perceived as a general tendency among some members under a particular circumstance, while they may allow him/her to adopt the alternative behavioral standard of modern type as prescribed in the state law.[5]

My first hypothetical theory to elucidate this type of attitudes was formulated using the concept of 'functional complement' in each culture (for details, see Appendix 2). In brief, every legal culture is furnished with its proper legal frame of reference, which is, generally speaking as far as non-Western culture is concerned, different from the modern Western culture. The basic one among the Africans is the social status of the parties in their kinship system which works to fix their alleged elastic concept of right and duty in a clear and distinct pattern according to varying circumstances. The similar one among the Japanese is the particular personal relationship between the parties which works to fix their alleged indefinite concept in a definite way like kinship status among the Africans. I called such a cultural variable 'functional complement', because it functions to complement the apparently insufficient legal concepts.[6] The concept might be naive to be further verified and elaborated for an efficient analytical tool. Convinced of its essentiality for our analysis of legal pluralism, however, I wish interested scholars to attempt to develop this idea further. At least, I have a special request to European scholars to identify the Western functional complement.[7]

Then, I would like to mention an advanced theoretical scheme, which was formulated to operationalize the concept of functional complement for empirical observation and analysis. The scheme called 'analytical variables of pluralistic attitude towards law' was obtained mainly based on my data on Japanese legal pluralism and the Sri Lankan one which was the result of a joint research organized by me (cf. chap. 3 of this book). It aims to provide analysis with a set of conceptual tools to observe and analyze a person's decision or choice of his/her particular behavioural standard among plural possibilities under a certain social circumstance. The main normative variables working there competingly were enumerated as follows (cf. Chiba 1989: chap. 8).

First, 'official law' which is usually represented by state law but in reality includes some other systems of law in so far they are officially authorized by state law, such as religious law, minority law, local law, specified customary law, and others. Second, 'competing norms' with official law, that may allow a person to be motivated for a certain behaviour deviant from official law. The last, 'a complex of the other relevant normative orders,' that urges or enables a person to choose between official law and competing norms. The main sub-variables of the complex are the 'particular relationship between the parties concerned' requiring the parties to maintain an established particular type of mutual behaviour, 'social appraisal by the surrounding circle' that is more effective for the other-oriented person rather than the self-oriented, and 'personal preference' that works in choosing a normative standard among competing variables and sub-variables. I do not necessarily believe the set of the variables including sub-variables to have been completed by the above enumeration. On the contrary, I wish interested scholars to try to validate or invalidate the set to reach a proposition with overall applicability by revising it again and again.

No more variables than just one for a person to choose a behavioural standard under a certain circumstance would be needed, if the person is so stubborn in his /her conviction of the exclusive authority of a particular social norm, whether state law, religious law, or other, irrespective of the negative sanction to be applied in accordance with the other norms. In reality, the overwhelming majority of people are otherwise or rather tend to waive in choosing his/her behavioural

Chapter 10. Legal Pluralism in Mind **175**

standard among competing ones. Such a bewilderment and resulting probable violation of the legitimate norm are more remarkable of the conflicting situation as usually seen in non-Western societies while they are also found in the complementing situation in Western societies.

Personal preference, for instance, of a particular relationship between the parties, as a result of the choice of the party, may cause a legal agent to refrain from rigidly applying punishment prescribed by state law, as in the case of gift-exchange bound by the socially obligatory *giri* relationship in Japan (cf. note 5), or motivate politicians and high officials to commit corruption as seen in both Western and non-Western societies. Personal preference of social appraisal may socially justify the behavioural standard against the state law as is usual among group-minded Japanese and caste-bound Hindus. Islamic legal rules may work in competition with the transplanted rules of state law. A group of people labelled as a minority in an independent country and an individual person so conscientious toward humanity may be convinced and in reality justified to resist the authority of the state law.

Generally speaking, ordinary people under legal pluralism, except a limited number of stubborn persons, may at least feel some different behavioural standards competing with the authoritative one, when he/she has to make a particular pattern of behaviour; and they may in reality consider which one should be chosen among them, and as a result may prefer a behavioural standard not officially authorized, often violating state law. The number of such people and the degree of their consideration and violation have not been empirically evidenced nor will it be done in the near future. Still, we can safely assert the existence and bewilderment of such people under legal pluralism, in so far as legal pluralism is empirically evidenced — in other words, 'normative ambivalence', among others, legal ambivalence under legal pluralism, that is caused by the clash between 'law in objectivity' and 'law in subjectivity' (cf. chap. 11, pp. 191–193).

'Normative ambivalence' may be found in the inmost mind of every person. If it is under legal monism, it is to be annihilated or else to be corrected in accordance with the monistic standard. In contrast, 'legal ambivalence' is typically found in a person living under legal pluralism, overtly in the conflicting situation and covertly in the complementing situation, remarkably in non-Western societies. Its circumstance is quite different from normative ambivalence under legal monism. Legal ambivalence here is never to be annihilated nor utterly corrected, but rather to be justified by definition of legal pluralism, in so far as it is caused by the conflict between different plural systems of law, even when a party of the pluralism may be official law. As far as it is justified, the person is entitled in his/her final choice to reject the behavioural standard designated by official state law to accept another competing one. Moreover, not only being justified, it is what the person concerned may pride himself/herself on, because it originates in any indigenous law of cultural heritage, religious precept beyond the secular authority, humane requirement superior to national interests, or the similar.

If seen from the authentic jurisprudence founded on legal monism, legal ambivalence must form a source of query beyond its theoretical capacity. It is natural for this reason that legal ambivalence and the resulting choice of an addressee are explained as an exceptional variation of what the monistic law expects to result. Japanese are, for instance, usually understood as tending to dislike law; Muslims and Hindus are often seen not to have interest in respecting state law; mountain tribes and ocean islanders are reported as mostly living out of the jurisdiction of the state law; and so on. On the contrary, when legal pluralism is respected for its existence in objectivity, legal ambivalence may be rather a privilege in subjectivity of the person living under a justified legal pluralism. The person may exercise the privilege with pride; and the science of legal pluralism is demanded to treat it correct as it works in society.

In conclusion, legal pluralism in objectivity also function in subjectivity, that is, in the mind of the person living under it. Such a subjective function may be observed as a psychological phenomenon; and it may be disregarded by the absolutist who is convinced of legal monism, or respected by the relativist who is disposed to different cultural/ethical values. The essential problem of it, however, can never be approached in its real significance with objective observation alone; it needs full understanding of the subjective privilege and struggle, both behavioural and psychological, of the person concerned. Because the problem is pro-

Chapter 10. Legal Pluralism in Mind *177*

voked according of Clifford Geertz, by 'inward conceptual rhythm(s)' and 'legal sensibilit(ies)' (1983: 69, 175) and, therefore, it urges us to make a turnabout of the 'source of justification' (Renteln 1990: 9)

At the same time, the privilege may not be duly enjoyed without serious consideration of its accompanying pitfall and responsibility to take preventive measures against the possible pitfall. The subjective pride and privilege essential to a pluralistic minor system of law may be respected for their cultural origin but very often tend to be no more than self-satisfying or egoistic or at worst self-destroying among the coexisting fellow systems in a national system or the world system. In order to prevent a person from falling into this pitfall, the person concerned is demanded to be so wise that he/she may succeed, together with fellow persons, in revitalizing the minor system in its combination with the other systems by reforming it according to changing circumstances. The pitfall and responsibility may thus form a special burden for the people under legal pluralism, which is unrelated to the people depending on the serene mind under legal monism. However, it should be another pride for them to bear the burden to create their own way of enjoying given pluralism.

This is my conclusion at present of the subjective problem of non-Western legal pluralism. At the same time, I never intend to limit the problem to non-Western people. I am convinced of its prevalence among Western people, too, though with some different features from the non-Western. Finally, I hope Western scholars may explore the problem to obtain a sound theory of legal pluralism.

Notes

(1) Luhmann 1987: 80-93. The anticipation complex is, according to him, a system not of conforming behaviour alone excluding any deviant behaviour, but of both behaviors together.

(2) These three measures may be well-known with the name of Maine (1954: 15). We are required to further identify other measures in order to theoretically rearrange the total system of the suggestions by Maine and Luhmann. This and the following mechanisms are a result of my attempts.

(3) The international norm so defined by some specialists is nothing but an 'unofficial law' in my conceptual scheme of law, that is, 'the legal system and its com-

ponents not officially authorized by any legitimate authority, but authorized in practice by the general consensus of a certain circle of people, whether within or beyond the bounds of a country, when they cause distinct influences upon the effectivity of official law, supplementing, opposing, modifying or even undermining any of the official laws, among others, state law' (Chiba 1989: 77).

(4) Generally, it may not be necessary in a scientific paper to describe the circumstantial process which led a scholar to scientific findings, because too often it includes personal, superfluous comments. I believe, on the other hand, it may help readers understand the writer's scientific statement more easily especially if the statement is strange to them.

(5) Japanese are often said to be furnished with alternative behavioural standards to choose a particular pattern of behaviour unlike Westerners with the sole one. It is exemplified, for instance, by the dichotomous standards of *giri*, formal social duty, and *ninjo*, personal human affection (cf. Noda 1976: 174-182) and such an apparently curious attitude of a person as 'a democrat in public and a despot in home'.

(6) The argument is made not for empirical generalization but rather for theoretical formulation of ideal types to contribute to sound empirical study.

(7) Many legal pluralists who agree upon my concept of functional complement, however, tend to perceive none of this among Western people who are believed to be relying upon legal monism. I am convinced otherwise. If I am allowed to suggest an idea while I doubt my ample qualification to do so, I would like to present my idea of it as the 'freedom of each party to resort to or waive his/her right and duty' (Chiba 1989: 49, n. 5, see Appendix 2 for the original). I wish it to be verified, or correctly invalidated through the efforts of Western scholars for us to reach the final truth.

Chapter 11. Other Phases of Legal Pluralism in the Contemporary World

1. Questions about discussions on legal pluralism

The term "legal pluralism" has been used for many years in various ways without a widely accepted definition. For instance, legal philosophers have used it to describe the law's relation to ethics or philosophical ideas,[1] legal historians to describe the overlapping transplanted systems of law in European countries, and constitutionalists to describe the confederation of certain states. In contrast with these usages, a specific definition of legal pluralism has prevailed over the last few decades among legal scholars with a sociological/anthropological orientation, who found a vital problem in the post-colonial circumstances of law mainly in non-Western countries. The development of the discussion on this topic may well be informed by such works as Gilissen 1972, Vanderlinden 1972, Hooker 1975, and Friedman 1975 in the 1970s, followed by Marasinghe and Conklin 1984, Allott and Woodman 1985, Sack and Minchin 1986, Griffiths 1986, Merry 1988, Rouland 1988, Greenhouse 1989, and Chiba 1989 in the 1980s. Reviewing these achievements, I have noted the following reservations/questions about their discussions as a result from my non-Western perspective.

1) Many of the discussants appear manifestly or latently to have their own definitions of legal pluralism. However, a clear and distinct definition is still lacking. Is such a definition unnecessary? 2) Most legal pluralists have focused their discussions mainly on the search for customary law, tribal law, social law, or the like, in short *minor law*, as I call it, working with *state law* in a dual structure in non-Western countries. Are we not needed to search for other structures as well? 3) Among the other structures, there is one working within European/Western countries, which legal pluralists tend to disregard in contrast to some specialists from comparative law, legal philosophy or legal history. Is European/Western legal pluralism of no significance? 4) Another topic called "legal cul-

ture" has been discussed more frequently among some other specialists from various disciplines. However, they appear, together with legal pluralists, not to have been interested in examining the relationship between legal culture and legal pluralism. Is such a lack of interest reasonable ? 5) The discussion among legal pluralists seems recently to have disappeared from the forefront of scholarship after the proliferous 1980s. Does this suggest a shift of their interest or a change in the existing legal pluralism ? 6) Each system of law in a plural structure has been treated as if it is working in harmonious coexistence with another system or others in the structure. In practice, there are numerous conflicts between coexisting plural systems, however irregular they may be. Why is the conflicting coexistence excluded from the whole phase of legal pluralism ? 7) Most scholars have treated legal pluralism as an objective construct from the viewpoint of a third party, that is, the *objective perspective*, seldom paying attention to the attitudes of the recipients towards legal pluralism, which I call the *subjective perspective*. Is this tendency reasonable enough to grasp the true significance of legal pluralism ?

The first question concerns the scientific validity of the inquiry into legal pluralism, for it is a basic requisite of scientific inquiry to formulate the operational definition of its objective in order both to delineate its extension distinctly and to analyze its intension clearly. The various definitions of legl pluralism presented by discussants (for a review, see Griffiths 1986: 9-37; Merry 1988: 870-874) showed that they have indeed succeeded in the initial attempt to delineate their own objectives, thereby establishing a new scientific inquiry of a legal phenomenon called legal pluralism. However, their attempts seem to have stopped short of succeeding in making the definition operational, or even attempting to do so, as is similar to the situation of the inquiry into legal culture (cf. Nelken 1995). Any attempt may be made to attain the goal, provided the inquiry remains a science. Thus, the *definition of legal pluralism* will be my basic issue here. I shall deal with this in the last section, as it may be better formulated after examining the issues suggested by the other questions.

The second question suggests that we should search for all phases of legal pluralism in addition to the said dual structure of state law and minor law. The dual structure is truly an essential phase of legal pluralism to have provoked such important scientific interest in legal pluralism. Its two constituent parts and their working mechanisms have, however, not yet been satisfactorily investigated. In addition, the literal meaning of the word "pluralism" suggests even more phases of legal pluralism not limited to the dual structure.[2] Furthermore, some of the various functions of legal pluralism attract our attention due to their major influences upon recipients together with or apart from the structures. If we do not search for them, the discussion will fail to grasp legal pluralism as a whole. Legal pluralists should therefore identify *all the various phases of legal pluralism at work in the contemporary world*.

The fourth question is found to be closely connected with the second. The interest in legal culture, aiming to identify cultural differences among existing legal systems, has formed a different scientific inquiry from ours of legal pluralism. It has, nevertheless, provided valuable data which are useful for our inquiry as well and which gave me some answers to the third and fifth questions, too. In fact, many studies on legal culture were not only published individually before and after 1990 (Macaulay 1989; Blankenburg and Bruinsma 1991; and others), but also done collectively in the 1990s (Varga 1992; Gessner et al. 1996; Nelken 1997; Feest and Blankenburg 1997; Blanpain 1997). Their focus is mainly on the coexistence of different legal cultures in European/Western countries, though including those in some non-Western countries. Their works contain some answers to my fourth question presenting another phase of legal pluralism in the world since the 1980s, and to the third and fifth questions in clearing up my doubts.

The exclusion of conflicting coexistence from the scope of legal pluralism, as suspected by my sixth question, implies a basic problem on the concept of law. I know of no legal pluralists who have argued manifestly for the exclusion. They seem to have simply assumed it on the ground that the expression "law in conflic" is theoretically a conceptual contradiction, in so far as peace or stability is one of the essential features of law, and that it is in practice no more than an irregular phenomenon to be corrected even when found. I will not outright reject such a view of the nature of law, but I cannot help admitting frequent cases of the conflicting coexistence of plural legal systems. The *legal pluralism in conflict* thus forms another issue of mine.

The seventh question might sound strange to those who are convinced of the established methodology of legal science, which presupposes that we ovserve law as an objective normative system without needing to pay attention to the subjective psychology and/or situation of its recipient. Such an objective perspective may be justified by those who concentrate on the state law monism. However, it must fail to catch the essential nature of legal pluralism. As far as legal pluralism prevails in a society, people living under it may formally be allowed to choose one of different, or even competing, legal rules authorized by the plural systems of law. This may appear from the perspective of legal monists to be a peculiar, neglectable circumstance of law, but is rather an ordinary circumstance of legal pluralism, though often causing conflicts in the whole structure as a result of people's differing choices. Such a circumstance is not only found in non-Western societies, but also in Western societies, as evidenced by some of the above-mentioned recent studies of Western legal cultures. It forms my last issue to examine the *subjective perspective of legal pluralism*.

The answers I shall give to the questions raised are thus summarized here into four, while some other problems will be explored to advance the inquiry into legal pluralism further: in sum, the various structures of legal pluralism, the significance of legal pluralism in conflict, the subjective perspective of legal pluralism, and the definition of legal pluralism. My answers to the third and fifth questions will be mentioned among the arguments below, too.

2. Various structures of legal pluralism

The said *dual structure of state law and minor law* have aroused the main concern of legal pluralism. However, some legal pluralists have caught sight of other structures of legal pluralism apart from the dual structure. For instance, Jacques Vanderlinden earlier hypothesized legal pluralism broadly as the "existence in a certain society of different legal mechanisms to be applicable to an identical situation" (Vanderlinden 1972: 19). Peter Sack later defined legal plural-

Chapter 11. Other Phases of Legal Pluralism in the Contemporary World

ism as "a plurality of law ⋯ of an ideological commitment," which is "never integrated in a systematic fashion ⋯ but a conglomerate of (more or less diverse) phenomena" (Sack & Minchin 1986: 1-2). Those conceptions of legal pluralism await elaboration by accurately identifying all the other structures of legal pluralism working in the contemporary world in addition to the dual structure.

The *coexistence of modern law with traditional law* in a national legal system must be another remarkable structure of legal pluralism from the modernist viewpoint. This phase of coexistence seems to have in fact been known among legal scientists but disregarded based on their assumption of state law monism. The assumption produced two outcomes. One was the apparent disregard of the coexistence in European/Western countries on the ground that, as I see it, there was no traditional law contrary to state law. However, the recent trend of the above-mentioned discussions on European/Western legal cultures revealed that the disregard has been amended and thus that new data concerning *European/ Western legal pluralism* have been presented as a phase of the various structures of legal pluralism.

The other outcome was the tendency of Western legal pluralists to be indifferent to the coexistence of modern law and traditional law in individual non-Western countries. Non-Western legal pluralism may be seen in theory as one form of the dual structure of state law and minor law or coexistence of modern law with traditional law. Its reality is, however, never reduced to the simple structure or coexistence, but is built up with other systems of law. The different systems include, first, Christian law, Islamic law, Hindu law, Buddhist law, or other forms of religious law, each of which is administered mainly by its own authority but partially by the state authority; second, unofficially working various kinds of indigenous law among each people, often officially authorized by the state law, such as kinship law, tribal law, community law, local law, and many others including cosmological postulate; and third, transplanted foreign laws other than Western modern law including socialist law. As a result, the actual legal pluralism of a non-Western country is structured as a unique conglomeration of those various systems of law, which the people concerned have chosen among many possibilities, mostly on their own initiative, but not uncommonly by the manifest or latent imposition of foreign countries. A glance at a few countries such as Egypt, India, Thailand and China will clearly suggest the outcome of such a conglomeration. Non-Western legal pluralism has developed in individual countries in a manner too complex and unique to be grasped by the simple coexistence of state law with minor law or modern law with traditional law. Without basing the discussion on legal pluralism on the empirical data of those unique conglomerations of plural, or rather multiple, systems of law, it would end up being an empty theory. In short, our task is to investigate *complex structures of legal pluralism in each non-Western country*, another phase of the various structures of legal pluralism.

I have a good example of such a complex structure with regard to Asian Islamic law. The name and principles of Islamic law are well known, but its actual circumstances are surprisingly little known among legal scholars. According to my recent collective study on Islamic law in Asian countries (cf. chap. 4 of this book), Islamic law has formed a characteristic legal pluralism in individual Asian countries coexisting with modern state law and other indigenous and transplanted laws. Many Islamic countries have maintained their unique structures of legal pluralism built up mainly of modern law and Islamic law,[3] with the superiority of the latter in reality (cf. Nezami Talesh 1986, for example), supplemented by other indigenous and transplanted laws. It is clearly seen in Afghanistan, Pakistan, Bangladesh, Malaysia, and Indonesia, as well as the home countries of Islam in the Near and Middle East. In other countries such as India, Sri Lanka, Thailand, Philippines, and China, Islamic law is, though perhaps classified into minor law, found not only unofficially prevailing among people in different precentages in each country, but also often authorized by the state law as a minor but working official law, while there are still some countries left unmentioned like Japan and Korea on account of their small Muslim population. These results demonstrate that the countries mentioned have each maintained their own legal pluralism uniquely constructed by modern law and Islamic law plus other indigenous and transplanted laws. Such a complex structure may also be found in other non-Western countries.

My arguments above urge us, at the same time, to reinvestigate the validity of

Chapter 11. Other Phases of Legal Pluralism in the Contemporary World *185*

the said dual structure in both its internal mechanism and external circumstances. As to the internal mechanism, its two constituent parts, satate law and minor law, are each usually used as if distinctive with no further examination needed, often in different callings from mine. I have some doubts about the usage. Because the concept of state law includes, in addition to the law of a sovereign state, some other forms such as the hierarchial systems of a confederation in two or more levels (Williams 1997) on the one hand, and the officially authorized laws of local governments and such autonomous bodies as army and navy, imperial court, or the like, though usually neglected, on the other, many of which may be classified into minor law, too. The concept of minor law is simple but its reality is thus multiple, ranging from the above-mentioned law of local governments and autonomous bodies, through the "indigenous law" of modern organizations such as churches, universities, and trade unions (Galanter 1981), to the law of alleged "semiautonomous social fields" such as kinship groups, tribes, localities, and the like (Moore 1978). In addition, there are other situations whose relevance to legal pluralism may be examined: for instance, the "informal symbiosis of Islam and the Law" in a non-Western society (Boudahrain 1997), "symbiosis of indigenous and Western law in Africa and Asia" (von Benda-Beckmann 1992), the Hindu "caste system as practised in India" prevailing across believers of "even Islam, Christianity, and other religious denominations" (Verma 1997: 133), "litigiousness [differing between] insiders [and] outsiders in an American community" (Engel 1984), and so on. If the dual structure is to be fully disclosed, all of the above cases may be systematically arranged into a whole system of legal pluralism. In brief, state law and minor law, each being plural or rather multiple, urge us to reinvestigate the *multiple mechanism of the said dual structure*.

The external circumstances also need to be reinvestigated since the dual structure survives not in isolation from the surrounding circumstances, but rather are influenced usually to some extent and often vitally by various kinds of trans-state law.[4] Presupposing the doctrine of the inviolable sovereign state, modern jurisprudence tends to be disinterested in the actual influence of trans-state law upon state law. In fact, no state legal system can escape from the overt or covert influence of related trans-state law, whether by official treaty or unofficial agreements. There are three examples at hand. The most conspicuous are regional treaties as represented by EU law across European countries. Another is the indigenous law of minority peoples officially authorized by state law in response to international developments in protecting the proper rights of indigenous peoples. Last, albeit unofficially, is the change in sport rules administered by a domestic sport organization in response to the revision of the rules by an international organization (cf. Nafziger 1988). I know my suggestion of both trans-state law and the examples are not satisfactory, but I hope it will suffice for interested scholars to validate them. In sum, the *triple structure of minor law, state law, and trans-state law* may be added instead of the dual structure among the various structures of legal pluralism.

The problems suggested above are primarily of an empirical nature which legal philosophers might not be interested in. Secondarily but essentially, two theoretical problems may be found underlying these empirical problems. They are the concepts of law and legal pluralism. As my concepts might appear confused as a result of my mentioning various kinds of law besides typical state law, such as unofficial law, religious law, indigenous law, or even custom, morality and cosmology, I shall answer the problem in a later section before defining legal pluralism.

3. Legal pluralism in conflict

Most discussants appear to assume that legal pluralism will never be in conflict. For instance, Sack limits legal pluralism to "the coexistence of different forms of law" with their "alternative" function in a "not integrated" but "*organized*" way (Sack & Minchin 1986: 1-2, my emphasis), which may imply the exclusion of legal pluralism in conflict. Arnaud admits some "contradictions between several legal orders" but asserts that they "must be solved in a mutually satisfactory way" (Arnaud 1995: 152). I also admit them, for their concept of legal pluralism is based on some justifiable reasons. However, I suspect, another concept including conflicts is necessary in order to grasp the whole working structure of legal pluralism in reality. I shall demonstrate their existence and significance by some representative cases among Asian countries.

Chapter 11. Other Phases of Legal Pluralism in the Contemporary World *187*

First, my country, Japan. Japanese law has featured in a wide variation of legal pluralism throughout its history (for details, see chap. 2 of this book), apparently in peace but characterized by frequent conflicts. A first critical conflict took place between the Court Law of *Tenno*[5] and clan law, when the leader of a powerful clan attempted to usurp the throne. It was finally pacified through a new transplanted official legal system in the seventh to eighth centuries modelled on the Chinese system, exiling indigenous law into the unofficial world. However, the new Chinese-modelled law soon encountered the tenacious resistance of indigenous law and was almost replaced by a new indigenous system in a few centuries, the structure of which basically survived from the twelfth to the nineteenth century. The indigenous system was a coexistence of various systems of law. Among them, the fundamental was two national systems: Court Law on the nominal authority of *Tenno* and Shogunate law[6], or *Bakufu* Law, on the real power of the *Shogun*, both of which were in reality based on various forms of official or unofficial minor law such as local land law, warriors' discipline, kinship system, communal law, shrine and temple law, *iemoto* law,[7] and the like. Its whole structure could not be maintained, however, without conflicts within. Let me give some examples. First, the authority of Shogunate law was defied for nearly a century around 1500 in incessant civil wars between local lords struggling for the hegemony of the time on their land law. Second, against the new legal pluralism created by the Tokugawa *Shogun* after the civil wars, which included the Shogunate's policy for the eradication of transplanted Christianity, the tenacius resistance of the minor law was provoked by a few local lords for the protection of Christians until the lords were finally conquered in 1638. Third, the Tokugawa *Bakufu* Law struggled in fact for several decades against the allied power of the resistance relying on local land law and Court Law, until it was finally replaced by the modern legal system transplanted from Western countries in the late nineteenth century, which was in fact indigenized into the unique Japanese system (see chap. 2). In sum, Japanese legal pluralism has truly formed a dual structre of atate law and minor law. Nevertheless, it has been a unique development centering on the ups and downs of Court Law and the systematic transplantation but indigenization of foreign law twice,[8] involving many conflicts in the process. I am led to accept an interim proposition on those facts that *legal pluralism is never a stable phenomenon solely in peace, but rather functions dynamically punctuated with a variety of conflicts*.

Next, the neighbouring Korean Peninsula. Today, according to modern jurisprudence, two sovereign states, that is to say, two independent legal systems, exist there in antagonism rather than in friendship: the Republic of Korea (South Korea) and the People's Democratic Republic of Korea (North Korea). Throughout Korean history, the people have fostered a single Korean nation with all its divisions into three countries in ancient times and two countries today. I have two grounds for making this assertion. First, the Korean people have sought enthusiastically, though desperately in reality, to maintain a single nation in opposition to surrounding enemies. The three countries before were, unlike the modern sovereign states, in fact sub-structures struggling for the unification of the whole nation, which was realized later by Icho Korea from 1392 to 1910. Each of both North and South Korea today hold fast unification of the nation as their supreme political goal. Also in ideology, the whole Korean people have cherished the myth that the Creator named Hanunim sent their legitimate King of the entire nation to the Peninsula. This myth enabled them to have a unified nation represented by Icho Korea, but at the same time caused frequent struggles for national legitimacy between some rulers ambitious for the goal, the extreme example of which is the divided countries previously and today. Recently, the myth seems to have lost former prominent manifestation, but is latently alive in socio-cultural ideologies in South Korea and in a political ideology in North Korea as seen by the late Kim Il-Sung's erection of the magnificent Hanunim Shrine. The two Korean states today must form an unusual structure of legal pluralism in conflict with their declared aim to be an integrated nation. Of course, Korean law has shown us, apart from this extraordinary phase, the usual phases of legal pluralism, as reported of South Korea, structured by official national law and local law and unofficial minor laws of kinship groups, local groups, personal alliances and others as well as the conspicuous legal postulate of "traditional aversion" to official law or "alegalness" (Hahm 1969: 19). Korea also represents another phase of legal pluralism in conflict. While Korea was under the Japanese rule from 1910 to 1945,

Chapter 11. Other Phases of Legal Pluralism in the Contemporary World **189**

the Korean Interim Government worked in Shanghai from 1919 until independence after World War II. The Government must have been founded on its own legal system, however primitive it may have been, to resist the ruling Japanese law. In sum, Korean legal pluralism is featured, in addition to the common character, by a unique structure coloured by the Korean traditional way, including so frequent conflicts.

Then, the huge country, China. The term, Chinese law, is simple, but in fact exhibits, together with Indian law (see Baxi 1986b), a most complex legal pluralism. The first reason for this complexity is that its official law is structured in multiplicity rather than plurality by those of the central government and different levels of multiple autonomous regions and minorities, including large frontier nations such as Tibet, Mongolia, Muslim Hsinchiang and two others. The second is that the official law has coexisted with a variety of unofficial laws of diverse social organizations such as patrilineal kinship groups, local communities, guilds, and many others. The third is the unrivalled flexible coexistence of indigenous law with transplanted law as demonstrated by the fact that the present socialist government has systematically adopted capitalist law in recent years (for details, see Ji 1993). Among these seemingly peaceful structures of legal pluralism, some phases of conflict have occurred throughout. One such contemporary conflict is the confrontation between Mainland law and Taiwanese law, which has been divided from the former single Chinese law in a manner similar to the Korean case. Another is the struggle of Tibetan law against the law of the central government, in which indigenous Tibetan law of Buddhist heritage was working for its own government led by the Dalai Lama, who has been exiled to an Indian city by the central government since 1959 (cf. French 1995: 50-52), while the central government supports the Panchen Lama staying in Beijing as the religious leader of the whole Tibet in place of Dalai Lama. Yet another conflict is found in the new Chinese official policy of preserving "one country, two systems" in Hong Kong, which was returned to China in 1997 after more than a century of British rule. The last case appears to be a phase of legal pluralism in peace, but the new policy could not be devised without preceding conflicts between both parties; and the nature of conflict is basically nothing other than the clash between human rights and government control as represented by the Tienanmen Case in 1989. In consideration of these and other conflicts in Chinese law, another proposition may be accepted that *the more complex a legal pluralism is, the more dynamic the interactions will be between constituent multiple systems, including conflicts it contains.*

My emphasis on conflict is never to aim to encourage it, but rather to discourage it by devising a way to manage it wisely. According to the established sociological theory, social conflict functions negatively against social order, but it also works positively by revealing the defect of the existing order for improvement. The same applies to the case of conflict in law. We hope law will prevail without conflict, but in reality we cannot do without any conflict in law. What is expected of us living under law is never to try to simply disregard or hate conflicts, but to manage them wisely in response to their nature and our social ideals. Accurate observation of conflicts in law is indispensable to manage them wisely, without which legal pluralism could not survive in peace. Some individual cases of legal pluralism in conflict will be added below with a request that attempts be made to devise new ways of managing them wisely.

In India, a Brahman gave his infidel daughter a "merciful" death contrary to official penal law, but it was approved by his community under Hindu law (Freed 1994). In Papua New Guinea, four murderers of an alleged sorceress were ordered by a trial judge to pay damages based on their tribal law, but that outcome was reversed to criminal punishment by the Supreme Court (Narokobi 1986). In Kenya, the tribal burial right of a deceased lawyer was approved by the Court against the widow's invocation of official law (Howell 1994). And finally in the United States, a refugee Hmong youth who had followed the traditional procedure of marriage by capture was accused by the fiancée of abduction and rape and finally deported by a sentence (Renteln 1992: 488-489). Spurred by these examples, legal pluralists may feel obliged to investigate "the dynamics of change and transformation" as a result of "the interaction between legal orders, particularly between state law and non-state law" (Merry 1988: 879), which naturally contain legal pluralism in conflict.

4. Legal pluralism in subjectivity

The problem which I would raise here is one relevant to the dynamics of legal pluralism in peace and conflict, for it relates to the motive of the recipient of law who prompts the dynamics. It is to inquire into *law in subjectivity* through the subjective perspective, which has been excluded from the prevailing jurisprudence. The reason for the exclusion is that modern jurisprudence aiming to observe *law in objectivity* through the objective perspective is furnished with no room to consider such a seemingly personal factor. On the other hand, the problem of legal pluralism in subjectivity has been suggested by some legal pluralists since the 1980s. Inga Markovits warned in 1986 that EU law and the transplantation of Western law in Central and Eastern Europe will be "largely ineffective" without due consideration of different legal cultures on "the *actor's levels*" (as cited in Gessner et al, 1996: 251, my emphasis). Sally Merry counted "the micro-level processes of legal action," which may cause "*forms of resistance* to the penetration" of state law among various phases of dynamic legal pluralism (Merry 1988: 882, my emphasis). More pointedly, Vanderlinden stated in 1989 that he would abandon his former "rule-oriented approach (in 1972)" to redefine legal pluralism as follows:

> ··· from the standpoint of the individual ···· It is the condition of the *person who, in his daily life*, is confronted in his behavior with various, possibly conflicting, regulatory orders, be they legal or non-legal, emanating from the various social networks of which he is, voluntarily or not, a member. "Legal pluralism" is pluralism limited to the legal regulatory orders with which the "*sujet de droits*" can be confronted. (Vanderlinden 1989: 153-154, my emphasis)

The article was brief but important in manifestly turning the perspective of our topic from the prevailing objective one to the neglected subjective one, focusing on the will and decision of the recipient under legal pluralism, which I call *law in subjectivety*.

Since 1990, legal pluralists have begun to clarify the subjective perspective. The most remarkable is Hanne Petersen's attempt with collaborators to elaborate the concept of legal pluralism into "legal polycentricity" based on the nature of "law as being engendered in many centres" and to understand "*law from inside*" (Petersen & Zahle 1995: 8, my emphasis). The former point requires no further explanation since the new term, polycentricity, may in subatance be another one among the various structures of legal pluralism I identified in the preceding two sections, while she has her own reason for this new concept as seen from the latter point, which needs to be examined for its relevance to my topic. First, Petersen herself appears to find the essential factors of the "law from inside" in three phases: "everyday practices" instead of legal rules, "experiences of women" labouring with their "values of work (and) equality in different spheres of life," and particular "home-knitted law" in place of the general term, informal law (Petersen 1996: 13-18). The everyday perspective has been adopted by others including "popular legal culture" (Arnaud 1989; Macaulay 1989; Friedman 1989). The women's perspective may be a variation of the "subject of right" (Vanderlinden 1989) or "actor's perspectives" (See Gessner et al. 1996, quoting Markovits) to regard people as "*agents of change* rather than as victims of particular legal structures" by making their "choice of action" (Hellum 1995: 18-19, my emphasis). The perspective adopted by them may uncover a normative ground to enable an actor to choose a particular legal standard among plural, often competing, ones in his/her everyday life. In other words, an actor is motivated by "individual drives which can express themselves in productive and creative, but also *in highly destructive ways*," that is, "deviant behaviour and criminality" (Gessner et al. 1996: 408, 269, my emphasis).

The above arguments suggest the essential importance of the subjective perspective that a person under legal pluralism is not only a passive recipient of legal regulation but also an active agent for the law by his/her choice of an alternative legal rule among the plural. The choice is made to support one of the plural standards, i. e., to reject the other ones. The supporting choice may need no special mention, for it signifies the "productive and creative" function of the law. The rejective choice, on the contrary, needs special attention, for it may cause minor or major conflicts in the whole legal order, whether passively by evasive behaviour (see, e.g., Rosen 1992) or positively by "destructive" behaviour of personal criminality (Gessner et al. 1996). When those rejective choices are accumulated, they may result in collective resistance to or even revolution of the legal order in force.

I wish to add some comments on the above findings concerning the nature of a person's subjective cognition of legal pluralism from among my data on non-Western peoples. First, a person under legal pluralism may stand in the position of legal ambivalence between conflicting legal rules. Thus, he/she is aware of being legally entitled to choose one of them and reject the others. Further, he/she is encouraged to make that choice on the ground that it is culturally justified. Finally, he/she may be proud of the choice as a cultural privilege for its traditional value (cf. chap. 10, pp. 175-177). In sum, being accompanied by the cognition of cultural pride, *the recipient's choice may produce a considerable effect upon the working pluralism*, whether positive or negative and manifestly or latently.

5. Systematic arrangement of various concepts of law

Having explored various phases of legal pluralism, I believe I should arrange the various concepts of law, which I used in my preceding argument in a possibly bewildering way, systematically before finally defining legal pluralism. The key point to justify my position must be to devise a set of tool concepts sufficient to furnish my various concepts of law with a systematic arrangement of the whole. For such a conceptual scheme will, if adequately conceptualized and systematized, not only overcome any bewilderment, but also afford a conceptual apparatus for the demanded definition of legal pluralism.

As mentioned earlier, some leading legal pluralists have attempted to arrange the concept of legal pluralism. However, most of them focussed their attention on the kind of law which should be paired with state law in the pluralism, as abridged by Griffiths (1986) and Merry (1988), while others like Vanderlinden (1989) and some others had broader perspectives. No one has yet tried any systematic conceptual scheme of law in general nor legal pluralism in particular, while Marasinghe and Conklin appealed for adequate concepts (1984: vi). Hoping it may be helpful, I summarize my scheme below.[9]

Chapter 11. Other Phases of Legal Pluralism in the Contemporary World

At the outset, *law* may be delineated distinctly from other social norms by its definition as a particular type of social norms supported by a set of values/ideas under the legitimate authority/power of a certain social organization. The social organization may be called the *socio-legal entity* as far as it maintains its own system of law, ranging from a kinship group, tribe, locality, and other minor societies in a national society, through the sovereign state or a nation, to an international organization across national boundaries. The smallest socio-legal entity, such as kinship group or village community, must, to ensure its survival, maintain a close connection with its neighbours and overlapping larger organizations, and will eventually form a conglomerate structure of certain multiple laws that may be called legal pluralism, as typically seen in the dual system of state law and minor law. All the different kinds and levels of law related to legal pluralism may be classified into a systematic conceptual scheme of law as follows.

State law forms the standard concept to characterize the others as non-state law. In consideration, however, that the main problem here lies in the reclassification of such diverse non-state laws, a more useful dichotomic classification may be formulated between *official law*, including state law and those officially authorized by state law, and *unofficial law*, not officially authorized but valid outside the official law. It must be noted that unofficial law may frequently be adopted in official law like religious law or minority law but largely maintains its original nature outside official law, albeit with some possible transformation of its character in history. Then, in respect of the cultural identity of each socio-legal entity, another dichotomy may be divided between *indigenous law*, which originated from the indigenous culture, and *transplanted law*, which was received from foreign cultures or imposed by foreign countries. The two types of law encountered in a plural structure may be harmonized or conflict with each other, thus resulting in mutual assimilation, transformation or rejection. Yet another dichotomy may be useful between *legal rules*, clearly formulated legal standards, and *legal postulates*, in the form of ideas or ideology to base, orient and revise the legal rules. Legal postulates may be less useful in state law, which is furnished with clear and distinct legal rules under the principle of the rule of law, but more useful in other kinds and levels of law, such as religious law under

Chapter 11. Other Phases of Legal Pluralism in the Contemporary World *195*

God's omnipotence or customary law so often lacking in clearly formulated legal rules.

With the above six concepts in three dichotomies, the complex structure of any legal pluralism will be analyzed into its constituents. However, further questions may reasonably be raised. In theory, how can those individualized constituents be built up into a workable, arranged structure called legal pluralism ? And in practice, how can a socio-legal entity choose its own structure among many other possibilities ? Obviously we need to postulate an integrating principle to reorganize individualized constituents into a workable legal pluralism. Here appears the *identity postulate of a legal culture*. It guides a socio-legal entity to choose the particular combinations of three dichotomies of different laws and the conglomeration of them into a workable coexisting structure of legal pluralism.

The above conceptual scheme is called *three dichotomies of law under the identity postulate of a legal culture*. As the first attempt of its kind, it may leave much room for improvement. Still, I am convinced of its basic validity on two grounds.[10] On the one hand, I believe it has been verified by my attempts to apply it to Japan (chap. 2 of this book), Sri Lanka (chap. 3), and some other countries. On the other hand, most of legal scholars know that each state law and legal family working in the world features any postulate to guide its whole system constituted of so many factors of different origin. Such a postulate may, I expect, be elaborated into an identity postulate working for the legal system or legal culture.

Assuring the validity of the conceptual scheme for legal pluralism, the scheme may be applied to law in general, including those of Western countries, for law in society always exists and works in pluralism discernible by this conceptual scheme. The three dichotomies of law under the identity postulate are accordingly found not only to be the conceptual scheme for legal pluralism, but also for law itself. However, it is too big a problem to treat here. I think it wise to close my argument by answering my final issue raised.

6. Definition of legal pluralism

By using my conceptual scheme, I define legal pluralism as "the coexisting structure of different legal systems under the identity postulate of a legal culture in which three dichotomies of official law and unofficial law, indigenous law and transplanted law, and legal rules and legal postulates are conglomerated into a whole by the choice of a socio-legal entity." I am convinced of its merits in two respects. One is its nature as an operational definition. The reason is that it enables us to discern distinctly and analyze clearly any existing legal pluralism by six operational concepts, whereas previous definitions by other legal pluralists are not so well operationalized as to be used as a scientific tool by every scholar with all their utility as a first step definition to delineate the objective. The other is its utility to make comparison between existing legal pluralisms because the feature of each legal pluralism is sufficiently represented to enable analytical comparison between them as the different combinations of six dichotomic laws and their resulting conglomeration based on the identity postulate.

To add a comment, I believe it may be possible to use this definition to operationally define legal culture. This may be defined in another way, I know, when the purpose of inquiry differs from mine. However, according to my conceptual scheme, legal culture may be the "cultural feature of each existing legal pluralism." Hence, a legal pluralism featuring a unique combination and conglomeration is found to be the core of legal culture. This finding will positively support my treatment of legal culture in close connection with legal pluralism, leaving a request that interested scholars may elaborate this further.

Notes

(1) Legal philosophers have tended to discuss legal pluralism without using the word "legal pluralism." Jørgensen (1982) is one of rare exceptions to have used the word.
(2) For instsnce, Alice E.S. Tay and Poh-Ling Tan distinguish six forms of legal pluralism as follows: 1. The global perspective: many legal cultures; 2. the national perspective: legal pluralism within each society; 3. legal pluralism recognized by and within a legal system; 4. legal pluralism through recognition of personal law; 5. plurality of individuals, institutions and interests; 6. legal pluralism

Chapter 11. Other Phases of Legal Pluralism in the Contemporary World **197**

of open-ended concepts (Tan 1997: 396-403). I hope other attempts may be made to further our inquiry.

(3) Note, however, Saudi Arabia and Sultanate Oman form two exceptions upholding Quran as their fundamental law without transplanting the modern constitution.

(4) The word "trans-state law" is used here in place of "international law" or "world law" used in my preceding works.

(5) Court Law, or *Tenno* law, formed a legal system based on the authority of Emperor to rule the whole country initially assisted by Court nobles, but, after the warriors assumed real power in medieval times, was largely disguised in the law of nominal authority to give official ranks to ruling warriors, including the highest *Shogun*, with the Emperor retaining the limited jurisdiction to administer Court affairs. Such a nature of Court Law basically continues in the persent *Tenno* system.

(6) The Shogunate, *Bakufu* in Japanese, was the office of the *Shogun*, supreme commander of the warriors appointed by *Tenno*, thus meaning the real government over the whole of Japan with the Shogunate law.

(7) The *Iemoto system*, called the "heart of Japan" (Hsu 1975), formed and still forms a particular type of social organization for those who want to learn such traditional arts as the tea ceremony, flower arrangement, *No* play, martial arts, and the like. Its structure and function are characterized by the communal tie between the highest leader with the hereditary authority to monopolize the administration of both the art and organization and the members voluntarily joining but faithfully obedient to the leader in learning the art and maintaining the organization. Remarkably, the *Iemoto* structure has been fictitiously extended to other social organizations, ranging from conservative political parties or conglomerates of companies to *boryokudan*, organized gangs.

(8) The two Japanese experiences of transplantation of foreign law from ancient China and the modern West are often said to be one of the best examples of the systematic and successful transplantation of foreign law in the world. In fact, such an appearance is possible only from the formal perspective of official law, for a variety of indigenous law were not only adopted in the transplanted official systems, but also unofficially working outside the official law, too often undermining the latter. (See chap. 2 for details).

(9) Refer to Chiba 1989: 177-180, and chaps. 2 and 15 of this book, for the definitions and explanation of my terms introduced below.

(10) Tan (1997: 6-7, 392-393), demonstrates the usefulness of my scheme in observing and analyzing the complex legal plluralism of East Asian countries more accurately. I hope non-Western law and legal culture, which are of "diversity" (p. 90, chap. 5) with the "nonstate, unbounded, unsystematic" nature (Woodman

1993), and which are for this reason too often done with the concept of a "black box" (Kidder 1993), may be more clearly conceptualized by devising adequate tool concepts.

Chapter 12. World Peace through What Law?

No one except an anarchist would deny the ardent desire of humanity for World Peace through law. However, the variety of conflicts and struggles within society reveals an apparently insurmountable contradiction between the reality and the dream. I wish to present suggestions which are based on concepts of law and peace with the goal of freeing common sense from its conceptual prejudice.

I am not an experienced pacifist, but I feel responsible for presenting my opinion on these concepts based on my own studies. My initial question was to seek for another law besides enacted governmental law, which had, and in fact still has, control over the daily behavior of the Japanese people. The study branched into two directions. One was the study of legal pluralism existing in the world as evidenced in the IUAES Commission on Folk Law and Legal Pluralism organized in 1991. The other branch was the social theory of conflict. Conflict is generally seen as the main target which law is obliged to manage. Studies in these two areas have given me the following findings.

The prevailing theory of law presupposes that "Where society is, there is law". This theory regards conflict as an enemy to be eliminated from the world of law. In actuality, however, there is no society where conflict has been entirely eliminated. There are many major and enduring conflicts which not only threaten society, but could indeed destroy it. In addition, there are much more minor conflicts. Prudent persons must be cautious of all existing conflicts, whether major or minor, and attempt to manage them. The peaceful order of a society is in fact maintained not by non-existence of conflicts but by wise management of existing conflicts.

We must accept that where society is, there is conflict, and accordingly, where society is, there is law and conflict together. For this reason, it is unrealistic to aim for perfect peace. Rather, we must aim to make peace symbiotic with attempts to manage conflicts. Violent and enduring conflicts should, in general, be managed by legal mechanisms or political interventions. Management of minor conflicts may be entrusted to the involved people. Acting through all social means, their solutions must be sought within the framework of the groups of related people.

According to the above consideration, world peace cannot be without some conflicts. While the existence in a peaceful society with some conflicts is regrettable, it not only is unavoidable in the natural course of society, but must prove the fundamental importance of contlict management.

In sum, world peace to be realized through law must be a peace symbiotic with some conflicts instead of exterminating all the conflicts.

Generally speaking, two common sense attitudes of law have been established. The first is that formal law should be limited to the legal system of a national government, in other words, 'state law monism'. This is evidenced by the fact that the simple word, law, necessarily refers to 'state law alone'. Other types of law are expressed with specific adjectives to denote their differences from state law, such as natural law, customary law, tribal law, local law, or sports law.

The other attitude is that modern state law, Western law in nature, should be the only model to be applied as the valid legal system, in other words, 'Western law universalism'. The evidence for this is that modern Western state law has been transplanted into non-Western countries, whether forcibly or voluntarily.

This modern state law is truly an advanced system opening a new era of freeing Western peoples from their preceding legal and social chains as well as including some postulates universally applicable to non-Western peoples, too. Its essential ideas have been extended to municipal laws as well as international law. These achievements cannot be devaluated. Western people may be proud of their contribution to this unprecedented factor in human advancement. Non-Western peoples must be aware of its helpfulness in supplementing their indigenous laws.

However, some negative attributes of modern state law have been long disregarded due to eurocentricism of the state law monists. In fact, those convinced of the superiority of their law tend to stick to the particularities of their own legal system and remain ignorant not only of non-Western legal systems but of neighboring Western traditions as well. The differences in culture underlying each state's legal system tend to be ignored.

About two decades ago Western legal scholars began to recognize these cultural problems and to advocate 'legal pluralism'. Originally referring to the plural structure of law in non-Western countries which constituted transplanted state law and indigenous minor law, the concept expanded to embrace Western countries as well. Legal pluralism began to cast doubt upon the hitherto unquestioned values of state law monism and Western law universalism due to their ethnocentricity. Given various labels such as folk law, local law, religious law, customary law, native law, these minor laws were known to have sprung from a common origin and were reflective of their politically unofficial and culturally indigenous nature. Their importance for non-Westerners was not only that some had been adopted into state law, but also that they reflected the multifarious realities of each culture's world.

It is too simplistic to conceive of legal pluralism as merely a dual structure of state law and minor laws. In reality, state law is itself a complex of various laws. It extends to the law of autonomous municipalities, tribes, and other similar social units on the one hand and to international law on the other. While state law is composed primarily of transplanted factors, it additionally officializes indigenous factors. However, the real function of legal pluralism often depends on unofficial indigenous law rather than official law.

The totality of law embraces in reality a third structure, world law, valid across and beyond the boundaries of sovereign states. This includes alleged international law, both public and private, and is further extended, as has recently been advocated by some specialists, to international agreements and arrangements between regional or private organizations and persons. Legal pluralism is thus basically composed of three structures: world law, state law, and minor law. Each of these structures are in turn multi-tiered.

Another important attribute of law not regarded in prevailing theories of jurisprudence and legal pluralism is, as I dare to advocate, the perspective of law in subjectivity. Law is confined without exception to that which exists and functions irrespective of the subjective mentality and attitudes of its recipients. This is supported by the basic premise of objectivity in modern science. Modern science reflects transcendental reasoning apart from human individuals. Modern jurisprudence treats legal system as objectively valid norms to control human arbitrariness. Even though the recipients of law exist and function in reality, their subjective mentality and attitudes generally find rare place in the science of law.

While modern jurisprudence is reflected in state law monism, the situation is different under legal pluralism. Accepting the existence and function of plural legal standards, legal pluralism affords the recipients the possibility to choose one of the plural legal standards no matter how different from the official state law it may be. In effect, this leaves the final decision of valid law to the subjective choice of the recipient. This may be viewed as similar to the point of American legal realism in which valid law is given not by written legal rules but by the individual judicial decisions. Law in subjectivity is nothing but the final channel to implement law in objectivity, although the choice is limited among given plural standards.

Plural standards may be found first in state law and then among competing minor laws or world law. Each competing standard is supported as valid by its own system composed of particular legal rules and ideational postulates. As a result, it is a usual occurrence when the recipient is faced with conflicts among plural legal standards or different legal postulates. There are various examples of such conflicts, too many to enumerate.

The different concepts of human rights existing in the world is one of the best-known and serious conflicts between East and West as well as South and North. It reflects different basic principles of legal cultures which various peoples have cherished and without which they would feel a loss of their cultural identity.

Everyone accepts human rights as one of the most important legal ideals. Still, conflicts to the ideal may arise as a result of various factors such as poverty, violence, war, incompetent legal systems and political leadership. Also, differing cultures may attach various degrees of importance to human rights.

Western intellectuals and politicians tend to criticize apparent antihuman-rights realities in non-Western countries. This was illustrated by the stiff protest of the American government against the military oppression of the Chinese government at Tienanmen in Beijing in 1989. American protests were supported by many other Western governments and peoples, but not by many Third World countries. Such a contrast in attitudes may seem to be a reflection of international politics, but is actually, more than that, a reflection of the differing ideas of human rights between Western and non-Western cultures.

Human rights as expressed in the Universal Declaration of Human Rights must be seen as one of the legal postulates originated in Western culture. It certainly contains universal factors applicable to other peoples of the world. At the same time, however, it reveals a perspective unique to Western culture which is rooted in Greco-Roman philosophy and Judeo-Christian cosmology. As such, it partakes of a tradition based on a human-centered world view reflecting a unique Western idea of human nature and rights. As it is so often unquestionably accepted by Western countries as an expression of universal applicability, it would appear that cultural traditions have not been examined nor understood.

It is natural, however, that peoples with underlying different cultural traditions may oppose Western concepts of human rights being imposed and enforced on their societies. For instance, an Indian philosopher regards human beings as included in the eternal rotation of the universe (Panikkar 1992); an African ontologist asserts the holistic human maku-up of the physical, mental, and metaphysical (Akbar 1992). An Oceanic lawyer appeals for legal protection of the cultural fabric of a people (Narokobi 1886), while Latin American experts declare the inalienable right of indigenous groups (Crawford 1988: 202–204), and Islamic lawyers give priority over individual rights to rights of the Islamic community (Khaddduri 1984: 233–239; cf. Conference 1976?).

In the face of severely opposing opinions, many who support peace through law complain of rare hope for a solution of the above issue. In fact, a UN report states that, "no universal recipe exists" (UN 1992: 20). It would appear, accordingly, that the issue could be reasonably understood by distinguishing between two different but related concepts of human rights. This is particularly important as the prevailing idea of human rights is prejudiced when viewing the problems from a perspective different from Western law universalism and state law monism.

Of truly universal applicability across differing cultures is the new perception of the *ideal concept of human rights* which may be evolved by reformulating the prevailing West-originated concept. Supporting and working with this ideal must be the *intermediate concept of human rights*, which is especially useful to non-Western peoples and is based on existing indigenous laws reflective of particular basic cultural postulates.

Reformulated by these two ideas, the prevailing concept of human rights may be found situated on a point nearer to the ideal extreme with the many intermediate concepts at differing points. While there is an apparent difference among the ideal and intermediate concepts and much more existing concepts, it never forms an unbridgeable gulf but creates an approachable distance, for they are both a variation of another collective concept, *intermediate variables of human rights* (see chap. 13 for details).

The following is a set of suggestions concluding the above discussion.

First, the search for realistic world peace cannot be the complete extermination of social conflicts. It must, however, reflect the wise coexistence of law with conflicts by intrusive management of those of violent and enduring nature. The accommodation of minor conflicts must be guided through sensitive perception of the cultural factors which may form their cause and may also offer their solution.

Second, the legal standards to manage and accommodate conflicts for peace in society should not be limited to those of the prevailing law, that is to West-originated modern state law. They should embrace a pluralistic view including unofficial, indigenous law of the peoples concerned and reflective of their own cultural identity postulates.

Third, the people concerned must be given the opportunity to choose their own legal standards for individual cases. This should be reguired even if the choice by non-Western peoples of their indigenous laws is not reflective of prevailing Western modern law. While this may ultimately create difficult conflicts between parties, all people should have the freedom to choose their own cultural portulates.

Fourth, in the face of conflict each party must refrain from ethnocentrically insisting upon its own standards and should be required to consider all efforts to accommodae the conflict.

Fifth, non-Western peoples are each required to make a best effort to refine their own legal culture striving to create an ideal common to human society. This requirement will certainly prove difficult adaptation to both internal and external cultural change. However, it forms the fundamental prerequisite to ensure peaceful communication and exchange between all peoples in the world.

Part IV

EXPLORING METHODOLOGY

Chapter 13. The Intermediate Variable of Human Rights*

No one would deny the essential value and universal applicability of human rights. At the same time, no one would doubt the difficult circumstances surrounding the implimentation of human rights, especially in non-Western countries. Many of the difficulties are too often said to be caused by plain lack of respect for the essential value of human rights among so-called underdeveloped peoples.

In contrast, there is another opinion to find the real cause in their traditional cultures. Two cases among many will suffice to show the seriousness of the problem. One is the debate on the Tienanmen case in Beijing in 1989, in which the Chinese socialist government justified their use of military power to oppress the people gathering at the gate plaza to appeal for popular freedom. The other is the right of indigenous peoples to retain traditional cultures, which the United Nations is eagerly trying to protect against their disregarded status under modern national govemments.

The core of those problems may be approached from various perspectives. I find them first to be grouped into two: practical ones and theoretical ones. Then, as the main one of the former was argued elsewhere(chap. 12 of this book), I would try here to advance an important one of the latter: a theoretical, or rather methodological issue underlying the concept 'human right.'

1. The Chinese government did not make clear any further legal ground for its assertion. However, Chinese leaders must be convinced of their own notion of human nature and rights founded on the traditional culture, which I call the identity postulate[1] of the Chinese legal culture (cf. Chiba 1989: 180), that is, the principle of Tien, meaning Heaven.

Similarly, in fact, some different notions of human nature and rights are found being convincedly advocated from many other cultural regions based on so tenaciously maintained traditional cultures as to rival the Western Christian culture which fostered the modern notion of human rights.

Panikkar is a noted advocate for Indian notion of human rights. He accepts the term 'human rights' as a universal symbol, but never in their prevailing notion. Because the notion, says he, "clearly was articulated along the lines of the historical trends of the Western world during the last three centuries, and in tune with a certain philosophical anthropology or individualistic humanism which helped justify them." He emphasizes the Indian notion of human nature and rights based on the principle of Dahrma, enumerating its six features (1992: 410-412).

Other cultural regions have also voiced their identity postulates. For instance, the "African ontological conception of man as a model of humanity in general" was advanced in 1984 with its five features by Akbar as an alternative to, but not excluding, the Western notion characterized by individualism, rationalism and materialism (1992: 376-384).

From the Oceanic culture, a homicide case joins them. Judge Narokobi ordered the accused to pay compensation to the victim instead of prescribed criminal punishment, in accordance with underlying law in the Melanesian Way which is declared as an official legal source in the Papua New Guinean Constitution. It was a reasonable outcome of his assertion that "law is not quantifiable as an autonomous institution, but is an aspect of the total way of the people" when seen "from our own perspective" (1992: 425, 434), like the Indian and African cosmology.

A similar cosmology is found among Latin American people. According to the Declaration of San Jose at the UNESCO Latin-American Conference, 1981, the experts attached the basic importance to the "ethnocide, that is, cultural genocide" deemed to have violated "an inalienable right of the Indian groups." They claimed "a right to acess and use" the "entire cultural heritage of these peoples," including "their philosophy of life and their experience" on their land which "is the foundation and source of their relationship with the universe and the mainstay of their view of the world." (Crawford 1988: 202-204)

The Islamic notion of human nature and rights contrasts most drastically with the modern Western. Khadduri truly admits that the belief in the "(r)eligion as the symbol of identity in the Muslim brotherhood is now being superseded by national identity on the national plane," but insists that "Islam did not deal with 'human rights' merely as individual rights, but as rights of the community of believers as a whole", and explicated main human rights as derived from "God's Will" not from human nature (1984: 233-239).

The above advocators are convinced of their own notion of human rights in their established ideational systems, although the systems are varied in the advancement of theoretical and institutional elaboration. In other words, each of them is provided, though in a variety of ways, with the identity postulate of their legal culture and a related notion of human rights.

2. Then, the problem on the right of indigenous people is clearly seen in the unending discussions at the United Nations.

The contemporary interest of the United Nations in indigenous peoples appears to be manifested by the two events in 1993 of the International Year of the World's Indigenous Peoples and the Vienna Declaration and Programme of Action at the World Congress of Human Rights. Because the Declaration affirmed "to ensure (indigenous peoples') enjoyment of all human rights and fundamental freedoms and to respect the value and diversity of their cultures and identities."

Such an appearance must prove a remarkable advancement in respecting the legal standing of indigenous peoples which had been unduly disregarded or rather suppressed by dominant nations or cultures. Their rights should be effectuated, for this reason, into valid moral and legal systems by human efforts. Still, we have to recognize an insurmountable difficulty in the efforts. Succeeding discussions presented in many UN reports seem never to have gone an effective step to resolve the basic difficulty, as a progress report in 1992 confessed, "No universal recipe exists to guide States on this difficult road" (UN 1992: 20).

The conclusion of the report was to question about approaches "best suited to establish peaceful and constructive relations between the groups" maintaining "some distinguishable separate modes of behavior or ways of life" (ibid.: 26). The essence of the problem is just the same as one of the Tienanmen case above. I would attempt to search for a solution to the question by investigating the concept of human rights.

3. Obviously, the prevailing concept of human rights is accepted as valid by every discussant above, but different notions form an apparently unbridgeable gulf between the Western and non-Western. Still both sides are eager for establishing its truly universal concept. If the gulf is bridged over first in the terminology, the door to the common goal across the human kind will be opend.

The gulf may truly appear unbridgeable, when comparing the opposing features of both sides exemplified above. However, I find some suggestions on a formula having been advanced by Panikkar and Renteln.

The first suggestion is the adoption of "cross-cultural" approach (Panikkar 1992: 413; Renteln 1990: 78-79), for the approach to human rights must facilitate recognition of the "need for human pluralism" (Panikkar) and scientifically to uncover "empirical universals" (Renteln).

Then, methodological questions may arise as to how to conceptually categorize cross-cultural data. Panikkar makes a useful suggestion in this that the term human rights should be not a definite concept but "a symbol which … is by its nature polyvalent and polysemic" (ibid.: 404). The words disclose the prevailing terminological misuse of the term but accepts its terminological utility as a universal symbol.

Furthermore, the two scholars advance a proposal to invent a device to intermediate the both sides of the gulf. Panikkar mentions an idea to afford an "intermediary space" for mutual dialogue (ibid.: 413), and Renteln took a step forward by suggesting "an intermediate standard" to resolve cultural conflict in law (1994a). The proposals urge us to realize an intermediate device between the opposing notions of human rights.

4. A basic device to scientifically tackle this difficult conflict would be to devide the meaning of human rights into two: the only ideal concept and many

intermediate concepts.

Main elements of the ideal concept may have been given by the prevailing concept as represented by the Universal Declaration of Human Rights, which is a respectable product of Western wisdom. However, not all its elements are ideal, because some of them are culturally characterized by particular Western philosophies which are mainly colored by Christian ethics and European traditions based on Greek-Roman cosmology, and which are, for this reason, not necessarily compatible with other cultural traditions. The ideal concept of human rights may be obtained by reforming those imcompatible elements.

The intermediate concept may be scientifically elaborated on different working notions of numerous non-Western peoples. Because most of those notions remain diffuse and far from scientific usefulness, the operation will first demand to accurately identify the elements constiuting the notion of those human rights, which may be filled by careful empirical investigation and insightful philosophical understanding. It will then demand to select admittable and useful elements out of the diffuse notions in order to formulate a scientific concept, which must fulfil two criteria: respect for the cultural traits of the people concerned and relevancy to the ideal concept across various peoples in the world.

To be noticed of the terminological nature of the intermediate concept is that the concept is never definite as it is but variable with the progress of scientific inquiry, thus being in operational definition. It may be, for this reason, more adequately called an *intermediate variable of human rights*, which, in fact, includes the prevailing Western concept in so far as it is still not ideal. Then, the concepts of human rights varienty discoverd in the world may be found, roughly summarizing, to form a continuum as a whole, ranging from numerous working non-Western ones, through intermediate variables among both Western and non-Western peoples, and to the final ideal one.

My suggestion above of the ideal concept and intermediate variable of human rights may be used, as I believe, as a preparatory step toward the demanded recipe to help us devise a practical policy of the difficult problem. I feel, however, to have to make some warnings to discourage possible misuse of the intermediate variable.

First, each people, among others, non-Western, who have cherished their own notions of human rights in their traditional cultures is qualified to maintain it for themselves and require to respect it to surrounding others. However, the qualification is very likely to be accompanied by pitfalls. It is self-destructing if they are either too persistant in their traditional culture to duly respect fellow cultures or too conservative to stick to outdated elements in it[2]. Each people is destined to continually strive to prevent against such self-destruction by eliminating the negative eliments from their traditional culture and developing the positive ones in a reformulated concept.

Second, although Western peoples may be proud of their advanced concepts of human rights, they should not be so bold as ethnocentrically force their particularly colored notions up on so-called less advanced ones, being aware of the character of their concepts as still one of intermediate variables.

Finally, supposing that it is required to establish the ideal concept of human rights by reformulating the existing varient, or even opposing, notions, every people is requested to work within their capacities to meet the demand. Roughly speaking, the non-Western may contribute by accurately formulating their own notions of human rights into scientific intermediate variables, and the Western may in response contribute by providing their advanced one and scientific methodology with the readiness to revise theirs to be adequate for the non-Western reality[3].

Notes

(*) A revised, abridged version of my presentation at the Annual Meeting of the International Sociologocal Association Research Committee on Sociology of Law, Tokyo, August, 1995. Its another version is preceding Chapter 12,
(1) Defined as "basic legal postulate for the people's cultural identity in law." It guides a people in choosing how to formulate and reformulate the whole structure of their law, including the combination of official law and unofficial law, indigenous law and transplanted law, and legal rules and legal postulates, in order

Chapter 13. The Intermediate Variable of Human Rights *215*

to maintain their accommodation to changing circumstances."
(2) See the warning argument by Baxi (1986a) against the negative function of legal pluralism for minor laws. That is as much persuading as he is a noted advocate for people's law.
(3) I know that the last point related to the Western methodology is a most serious issue of my argument to be further discussed. But, it is beyond the scope of the present topic.

Chapter 14. The Intermediate Variable of Legal Concept*

The conflict of legal conceptions from different cultures

It is obvious that legal concepts or conceptions expressed in official discourse differ from ordinary legal notions or conceptions in daily usage in a society, whether Western or non-Western. There is a contrast, however, between the tendency of Western people to take those differences for granted, and the frequent feeling of non-Western people to take them for an infringement upon their human identity.

Recent studies in legal pluralism or legal culture have reported many conflicts of this kind. These contemporary studies have been concerned not only to confirm or document such cases, but also to examine whether any device can be used to manage such conflicts. I wish here to suggest a step toward finding such a device by reformulating the cultural system of legal concepts. Some representative examples will first be reviewed briefly to underline the vital importance of this issue.

One is the concept of so-called 'witchcraft' among a tribe in Zimbabwe (Howman 1994). When a native midwife was charged with violating the Witchcraft Suppression Act, the Magistrate in charge, who was also native, was confronted with the difficult task "striving to fit the sharp-edged, narrow and relevant instrument of a legal mind to the intangible, vast and impenetrable maze of African life" (ibid.: 639). The problem was how to apply the officially prescribed definition of witchcraft, namely "the use of non-natural means in causing any disease in any other person", to her allegation that another woman was a 'witch'. Investigating the native word *muroyi*, which had been equated with the English 'witchcraft', he found that it had twelve different meanings in the native usage, both natural and unnatural. He concluded that the effect of one of those definitions was that "until a definite series of rites have been observed which concentrate or inject this non-natural influence into the word *muroyi*, it remains a mere word", as distinct from some others which were characterized as official or unofficial crimes (ibid.: 651). Adopting this definition, he declared her not guilty and dischaged her.

Similar differences in the conceptions of legal terms are well known in the area of property, one of the most fundamental concepts in modern legal systems. Historical evidences relating to the Latin American Indians, North American Indians, Canadian Inuits, and Australian Aborigines demonstrate that the modern concept of 'ownership' or 'fee simple', the absolute, inheritable title in property empowering its holders to exclude every encroachment onto the object, was not known among non-Westen peoples (cf. Kludze 1998), and that, when imposed upon them, it eventually worked to deprive them of the lands they had peacefullly appropriated. A great variety of conceptions of property different from modern ownership have recently been revealed by a Japanese legal scholar, Masanobu Kato, who collected anthropological data from around the world, as having operated among or been employed by various non-Western peoples (Kato 1995).

The concept of 'contract,' which, together with that of ownership, forms one of the two fundamental components of modern legal system, has also been found to differ from non-Western conceptions. A recent report from Trinidad revealed a typical example (Haraksingh 1993). Nearly half of the population of that country derives from the offspring of Indian laborers who came to work in sugar plantations in the period 1845–1917. The legal ground for thier agreement to undertake the long voyage and hard labor was a formal contract of 'indenture' settled in a document allegedly on the basis of the individual will and decision of both parties, the validity of which was never doubted by the recruiters who acted as the planters' agents. The other party to the contract, the laborers, could never grasp the legal meaning of the document they signed, since the kinds of contract they had been accustomed to were valid if made orally, the parties being "bound together by a course of dealings of the kind on which village and caste networks were sustained" (ibid.: 63). The laborers were destined legally to be at the mercy of planters backed by an official legal system of Western origin.

Chapter 14. The Intermediate Variable of Legal Concept *219*

Such differences in legal conceptions may provoke mortal conflicts between opposite meanings when concerned with human life. A few decades ago, a young girl in a village in North India was reported to have died of cholera just before her marriage and after the the performance of the preceding traditional ceremonies. Astonishingly, she had in fact been murdered by her father with the full knowledge and approval of all his family, lineage, caste and village. Even the police would not arrest him to mete out criminal punishment. The reason was clear. The girl had been found by her fiancé to be pregnant by "inllicit adultery" violating "both clan and village exogamy and caste endogamy". The father, a leading Brahman, had no choice but to give her "merciful" death for her "rebirth in future lives" in accordance with Hindu law. So the opposing concepts of human life and murder were in conflict here. (Freed 1994)

This case may have resulted from the overwhelming influence of established Hinduism. However, a similar case provoked by a secular legal conception has been reported from Papua New Guinea. When five men were accused of having murdered an alleged sorceress in a village soon after the independence of the country in 1975, a native judge sentenced four of the accused to pay compensation and acquitted the fifth, a son of the murdered woman. In doing this he acted in accordance with the indigenous law in place of the official criminal law. The judge's reason was that the accused had acted in fulfilment of their duty to the village to put an end to a vicious course of sorcery, that they had preformed the required procedures immediately after the deed in faithful compliance with their own law, and that such indigenous law was officially sanctioned by the Constitution as the 'underlying law'. The judges of the Supreme Court reversed the decision on appeal and imposed criminal punishment upon the four as prescribed by the official law (Narokobi 1986, 1993).

It is true that most reports of conflicts between legal conceptions come from non-Western societies, and specifically relate to the cultural definitions of lawful acts under the indigenous laws of native socio-legal entities such as tribes, castes and villages. However, similar conflicts take place even in Western society where different cultures coexist. The United States may be the most prone to such conflicts for her social structure is a melting pot of races of different cultures, and her legal structure respects individual freedom to the untmost under the rule of law principle. American judges are often challenged by cases that involve culturally different legal conceptions. For instance, is it just for them to punish a Japanese wife in accordance with American offical law for the murder of her children, when she has attempted to commit suicide with them, an act which is punished less severely in Japan according to their tradition ? Or, is a Hmong youth to be punished for the kidnap and rape of his Americanized lover, when he has forcibly performed the procedure of 'marriage by capture' in accordance with the practice of his homeland ? (Renteln 1992. These questions will be answered later.)

Management of the conflicts

We are thus presented with the serious problem of how to deal with such conflicts. There are many "jurists opposed to the use of the concept of folk law" (Woodman 1993a: 263). That attitude has recently been criticized, however, as indicating a tendency to ethnocentrism or imperialism by the established Western concept towards non-Western conceptions. The contemporary trend is not to disregard the conceptions of one of the conflicting parties, but rather to admit the cultural value of both on their merits.

A few sensitive scholars have warned Western scholars and practitioners to be prudent and careful in dealing with conflicts of this kind. In 1927 Cornelis van Vollenhoven, who was sympathetic toward the practices of native people, praised two officials of the British colonial government of India for their defence of the people against many others who had "promoted simple, uniform laws after good European models" (van Vollenhoven 1994: 259). They were Mountstuart Elphinstone, who was convinced that one should be "careful to avoid forcing [one's] own views upon existing conditions", and Henry S. Maine, who "fought aginst the 'insularity' of the English attitude towards jurisprudence" (ibid.: 252, 260).

The most systematic study in history of conflicting conceptions must surely been the British efforts to restate African indigenous law. Antony N. Allott, who is regarded as having been the most "influential and prolific" scholar in the study of African law (Renteln & Dundes 1994: 285), was well aware of the pitfalls in

Chapter 14. The Intermediate Variable of Legal Concept *221*

the way of the task of restatement, and enumerated brief but useful practical warnings. He did not forget to advise against wrong interpretation "distorted by the introduction of English legal concepts", and concluded that "one must regret the frequent attempts to force customary legal systems into alien frameworks" (Allott 1994: 291, 293). His warnings were fully justified with respect to the restatement then in progress.

Today, some decades after Allott's warnings, the prevalence of conflicting conceptions appears to have been more widely and deeply disclosed through the use of the concept of legal pluralism. At the same time, some leading scholars in this area remain critical of the lack of develpment in the scientific treatment of these conflicting conceptions. For instance, Robert L. Kidder has criticized the general tendency to go not further than simply regarding non-Western legal culture as a 'black-box' (1993) and Gordon R. Woodman has warned of the "non-state, unbounded, unsystematic" nature of African law (1993b).

This theoretical maze is sometimes noticed as practically important to modern legal systems and contemporary world peace as exemplified by the field of human rights. Human rights are declared in the Constitution of every nation and in the Universal Declaration of Human Rights, and their universality has never been doubted. It is also recognized that the implementatin of human rights as declared in these documents is so difficult as to appear impossible to achieve in the near future on account of the irreconcilable conflict between the established concept of human rights and the opposing conceptions based mainly on non-Western cultures. The conflict may be symbolized in practice by the debate on the Tienanmen Square incident in Beijing on June 3-4, 1989 between the American Government manifestly supported by other Western governments, and the Chinese Government latently backed by the other non-Western.

Human reason and intellect have begun to work overtly through the activities of the United Nations to resolve similar conflicts concerning indigenous peoples. These are expected to be managed through the adoption of appropriate policies by sovereign states, avoiding political confrontation of the type likely to develop between the governments of states. UN bodies have suggested two requirements to be accepted by sovereign states: namely, "to ensure respect for equal enjoyment of human rights" and "to accept and to respect the diversity inherent in any plural society". But they have also had to profess the conclusion that the "pursuit of each of these tasks ··· is practically difficult. *No universal recipe exists* to guide States on this difficult road" (UN 1992: 20, emphasis added). Despite their best efforts to promote their proposal, there has yet to be progress beyond the stage on "no universal recipe".

This issue will be never resolved in the absence of appropriate political and economic policies. At the same time, such policies will never be formulated without accurate conceptualization of conflicting notions of human rights. From a theoretical viewpoint, Raimundo Panikkar was the first scholar, as far as I know, to advance a proposal to admit a different idea of human rights and another scheme for conceptualizing them (Panikkar 1992, originally 1982). His arguments were based on the premise that the term 'human rights' should be used not to refer to any specific notion but as a 'symbol' which could connote various notions. To illustrate his argument he showed that Indian culture had long cherished its own notion of human nature and human rights just as Western culture had exhibited the prevailing concept of human rights (ibid.: 404). This was an attempt to correct the misuse of the Western term. He suggested further the formation of a "*cross-cultural intermediary space*" for mutual dialogue between conflicting notions (ibid.: 413, emphasis added). This was in effect a step towards the required recipe.

This step was advanced further by two scholars nearly a decade later. One was Peter Sack, who rejected in principle the advocacy of either the Western or the non-Western perspective and demanded "a *third criterion* which can deal with the plurality of the world" to remedy the lack of neutral perspective (Sack 1998: 52, emphasis added). The other was Alison D. Renteln, who suggested that "an *intermediate standard*" might offer a cross-cultural solution (Renteln 1994a: 28, emphasis added). These suggestions clearly lead to the conclusion that another standard of human rights should be formulated as a third criterion in a cross-cultural space.

Chapter 14. The Intermediate Variable of Legal Concept **223**

Renteln proposed specifically as part of her general scheme for tackling the issue that a "cultural defense as a partial excuse" be recognized to assist the reasonable management of cultural conflicts in the law of the United States (Renteln 1994a: 69; 1994b: 505). This she substituted for her earlier assertion that there was "no need for a cultural defense because mechanisms already exist which can take culture into account" (Renteln 1992: 487-489, 497). Her new idea may have been devised as an intermediate standard for those cases.

Encouraged by these advances, I have recently proposed that the intermediate variable on human rights be employed as a tool concept (Chapter 13). In brief, the concept of human rights should not be limited only to that established by Western jurisprudence, but rather divided into *ideal concept* which should be a further elaboration of the established concept to be designed to render it compatible with otherwise conflicting non-Western conceptions, and *intermediate concept* which may be reformulated on the basis of varying non-Western conceptions in the light of steady advances toward the achievement of the ideal. Thus reformulated, the various particular intermediate concepts of human rights will form a group of variations of the ideal concept, namely, the *intermediate variable*. The established Western concept and apparently conflicting non-Western conceptions belong together to this intermediate variable of the ideal, that is, a truly universal, concept of human rights. Both the established concept and conflicting conceptions thus work to implement the ideal concept in cooperation, although the former may be assessed to be more or less advanced.

The intermediate variable of the legal term

It was when I dealt specifically with human rights that I developed the idea of the intermediate variable. My basic objective was, however, to advance some methodological device of applicability to manage conflicts between modern legal concepts established in jurisprudence and the legal conceptions prevailing among non-Western peoples. This is, from a cultural point of view, an issue of vital importance not only to the non-Western laws I have long pursued, but to the Western social norms which interact in practice with official law. I felt compelled to make an attempt to formulate the device in concrete terms when I came across the reprinted report on witchcraft from Zimbabwe introduced at the outset.

The witchcraft case provides a typical example of indigenous legal conceptions liable to be "force[d]… into alien frameworks". Similar remarkable situations must occur frequently whenever established legal concepts are applied one-sidedly to non-Western situations. Several of the reports introduced in the first section must have concerned one or another fundamental human right. The device of the intermediate variable may be applied more widely to the concepts of other legal terms, and need not be limited to that of human rights alone.

For instance, the twelve indigenous notions of witchcraft found in daily usage among the people in Zimbabwe could be scientifically formulated into some intermediate concepts vis-à-vis the universal concept of witchcraft, collectively forming its intermediate variable. This intermediate variable may be elaborated further with others to form another intermediate variable in a supra-system, which, when logically inferred, may ultimately attain the cross-culturally universal concept of witchcraft.

Similarly, intermediate concepts and variables may be reformulated vis-à-vis the established concepts of ownership, contract, murder, and many other legal terms. So treated, the culturally different notions among non-Western peoples may work, from a scientific point of view, in the form of the intermediate variable rather than remain a "black-box" or retain a "non-state, unbounded, unsystematic" nature. The *intermediate variable of the legal concept* thus forms a tool concept which is indispensable to the accurate observation and analysis of legal conceptions prevailing among non-Western peoples when these are culturally different from modern legal concepts.

The serious question may then be raised as to the significance of the intermediate variable of the legal concept to the established modern legal system, which is alleged to be armed with intolerably rigid concepts and relentlessly normative logic, as symbolized by the pure theory of law by Kelsen. That is, would the prevailing legal system allow such a group of apparently heterogeneous concepts to coexist with its own concepts in the name of the intermediate variable ? I believe this question can be answered in the affirmative for two reasons, although I am well aware that the assistance of other interested scholars will be necessary to supplement the deficiencies of my proposal.

First, the modern legal system presumes in fact the existence of innumerable sets of both universal and intermediate concepts of socio-cultural terms. Moreover, the modern legal system in fact includes similar sets in its system. I have little specialized knowledge of Anglo-American law, and consequently I feel difficulty in offering sufficient examples. But I can suggest that the legal concept of witchcraft presupposes some other definitions of related cultural terms, for instance, magic as the universal concept and sorcery and witchcraft as intermediate concepts. Ownership forms an intermediate concept of the universal concept of property, together with possession and others. Contract is an intermediate concept of the universal concept of agreement, together with others. Murder is an intermediate concept of the universal concept of homicide, together with variations such as manslaughter. Those who are well acquainted with Anglo-American law will easily enumerate better and more examples. Thus, the intermediate variable must never be heterogeneous, but rather homogeneous, to the established legal system.

Second, the science of modern law is required in practice to theorize indigenous legal conceptions which coexist plurally with transplanted modern concepts, if this science is to treat non-Western law. Gordon R. Woodman believes this to be possible when he maintains that "other [legal] norms could be precisely specified in terms of strict duties" among African peoples (Woodman 1992: 147). My earlier suggestion of 'functional complements' (See Appendix 2 of this book), which was in effect an attempt to devise a conceptual scheme adequate to non-Western law, was accepted as "useful", though perhaps needing "some amendment" by Woodman (1992: 146). The intermediate variable proposed here is devised from a viewpoint which is similar to but different from that of the functional complement.

The idea of functional complements was devised over twenty years ago to compare the African and Japanese conceptions of individual rights with that of the West. Initially the African conception was characterised as elastic and the

Japanese as indefinite, with the result that neither appeared able to work as an effective legal standard, rigidly specifying the behavioral patten the law required to be observed. It was argued, however, that in reality they were complemented by specific indigenous legal conceptions which enabled the people concerned to identify their legal standards as rigidly as Westerners did. The African and Japanese functional complements found were respectively the "social status of the parties" and "the particular relationships between the parties". It was suggested that fnctional complements were to be found not only among Africans and Japanese, but among other peoples including Westerners.

That argument concerning functional complements may be reformulated by use of the intermediate concept or variable. That is, African and Japanese conceptions of individual rights may each be seen as composed of both an intermediate variable of their own concept and the alleged universal concept of transplanted law. Such a function of the intermediate variable as the functional complement must hold true with respect to peoples other than Africans and Japanese as well as to rights other than individual rights.

The intermediate variable truly seems to play a most positive role in respect of the legal concepts of official law. It may play however also a negative role against it. Viewed structurally, intermediate variables, cherished in the indigenous law of a people, tend to be unofficially maintained irrespective of what the official law may provide, while some features of the indigenous law are often officialized, subject to varying degrees of modification. Viewed functionally, however, it is possible for indigenous law to bring unintended or even opposing influences to bear upon the official law. When the people concerned prefer their indigenous patterns of behavior to those enjoined in official legal concepts, the negative result may be to lay the official concepts aside and to invite evasive, unlawful, or even resistant behavioral patterns (cf. Rosen 1992). A detailed investigation would disclose even more complicated relations between intermediate variables and functional complements. It may however be safely asserted that the intermediate variable has a wider coverage in its application than the functional complement on account of the possiblitity that it may have a negative function against official concepts. In sum, I would like to conclude that the intermediate variable of the legal concept

Chapter 14. The Intermediate Variable of Legal Concept *227*

is a useful tool concept, and is more inclusive than the functional complement.

Concluding comments on the intermediate variable

The conclusion is subject to some comments on possible problems and some warnings about the proper use of the intermediate variable.

First, in the contemporary circumstances of law and legal science, the intermediate variable may initially be formulated vis-à-vis legal concepts of the modern law which has been established in Western countries and transplanted to non-Western contries. This will cast scientific illumination upon the allegedly strange non-Western legal notions or conceptions from the viewpoint of the modern legal system and authentic jurisprudence. Then, in order to construct a truly scientific theory of law, the intermediate variable should be reformulated vis-à-vis the ideal, truly universal legal concept. The status of modern legal concepts will in consequence change from being regarded as if they were universal concepts to being one of the intermediate variables vis-à-vis a truly universal 'third criterion', though they may be assessed as more or less advanced than the non-Western.

Second, I am well aware that such a procedure might be viewed by some radical critics as still bearing some ethnocentric inclination. For instance, one such critic has pointed out that the "cultural relativivism" advocated by most anthropologists is still inclined to ethnocentrism in so far as their arguments tend to "focus on enculturation" rather than "true relativism" on the basis of "cross-cultural universals" (Renteln 1990: 86-87). Another has rejected "superfluous translations [of non-Western terms into Western languages]" for the reason that "readers would easily miss the point" (Sack 1993: 409; see also Arnaud 1993: XXIX). And in fact, my theory concerning the concept of functional complements was criticized for giving "undue preeminence to the state" (Woodman 1992: 147).

My fear of such criticisms in presumption and reality may have arisen from the fact that the intermediate variable was first devised in opposition to the established modern legal concepts of Western orgin, in order to recognize the function of non-Western indigenous law. In other words, the critical approach could perhaps be nothing but a variation of the Western perspective in observing non-Westrn facts. In my former theory the standard to identify the functional complement was truly based on established Western concepts, for non-Western indigenous law was recognized as far as it functioned to complement the former. Still, I am not convinced of any bias to the theory of the intermediate variable, but convinced of its usefulness and necessity in the advancement of the contemporary scientific study of law.

Why do I say so ? First, because methodologically the intermediate variable is to be formulated as a tool concept to provide an adequate scietific classification for existing legal conceptions with no biased preconceptions as to their substantial nature as law. The term used in a particular case might sound, to some critics, as if it depends to some extent on the Western concept. This is, however, no more than a matter of terminology. As a proof, one might replace the terms used by obviously unbiased terms. For example, if one expresses the established concepts of ownership, contract, and human rights as A2, B2, and C2 respectively, and the intermediate variables of them as A3, B3, and C3, then this criticism would lose its significance. In addition, the final goal in formulating the intermediate variables is not simply to find the characteristics of non-Western law, but also to establish a scientific system of legal concepts including both Western and non-Western conceptions.

Second, because substantially it cannot be denied that the modern legal concepts and systems of Western origin have prevailed overwhelmingly throughout the world to an extent unrivalled by any other system. It must therefore be justified to use their concepts as a tentative standard for recognizing the different conceptions of non-Western indigenous law at a heuristic stage of the scientific procedure, supposing that other steps will follow to advance ultimately into a perfect system of legal concepts of truly universal applicability. Such a procedural step is also admitted by the above critics as far as they "use the Western perspective of law as a starting point" (Sack 1993: 409) or advocate true "cross-cultural relativism" (Renteln 1990).

For these reasons, the intermediate variable is expected through its essential neutrality to contribute to expose the Western bias of established legal concepts.

It will thereby promote a proper appreciation of non-Western indigenous law as it works in reality, and to take a firm step towards the ultimate establishment of a system of truly universal legal concepts. At the same time it must be recognised that, however neutral a symbol may be, none can be immune from the potential danger that it may be misused through bias in practice, whether overt or covert. Here it is necessary, as a third comment, to add a set of warnings against the positive and negative misuse of the intermediate variable.

First, as a specialist in African law has observed, "recent signs of 'traditional' norms and practices" are coming to be "the proud reminders of a pre-colonial past, sysmbols of cohesion in an uncertain contemporary world" (Roberts 1993: 143). Certainly, it is admitted that each non-Western people which has cherished its own cultural system of law may be qualified to maintain its unique systematical concepts by reformulating them into a system of intermediate variables and to demand that others may respect these. At the same time, they must be most prudent to avoid the accompanying pitfalls. If they are too attached to their own culture to pay due respect to fellow cultures, or too conservative to adapt their outdated practices to changing circumstances (cf. Baxi 1986a), thier strategy will be self-destructive. Each people is destined to strive incessantly to avoid such pitfalls by eliminating the negative features of their indigenous culture and developing the positive features which are compatible with other peoples, by making the best use of the intermediate variable of the universal concept.

In contrast, Western peoples may not only be qualified to maintain their own concepts of the modern legal system, but also be proud of the progress they have aehieved. At the same time, they must realize that even their advanced concepts still leave some way to go before they reach the ideal of truly universal concepts, and that they must also strive to achieve the ideal by reformulating their intermediate variables in cooperation with non-Western peoples, respecting and assisting the latter to advance by themselves.

Notes

(*) This article is an extended development of the basic idea of Chapters 12 and 13.

Chapter 15. An Operational Definition of Legal Culture*

The three distributed papers present essential issues for us to endeavor to resolve. Nelken demands that "the concept of legal culture" be altered from "the taken-for-granted assumptions of their own legal — and academic — culture" to "cross-cultural categories" by "operationalizing" it, since law exists and works in the midst of "the various aspects of legal life as a whole" (1995: 437, 443, 439, 444). Blankenburg attempts to opeationalize the concept of legal culture through the use of "sociological indicators" (in Blankenburg & Bruinsma 1994), and Gessner proposes a new perspective of "actor's levels" of legal culture (1996). Thus is suggested to us the task of *operationalizing the concept of legal culture* to be adequate for general application.

I hope to present my own idea from a different perspective. Frankly speaking, all of the three seem to have not fully escaped from the taken-for-granted concept of law and legal culture that may be applicable to the Western world alone. I would like to advance an efficient step toward our common goal to formulate an operational definition of legal culture in a holistic view, that is, adequate for applying to non-Western legal culture along with the Western. In reality, the main factors of my idea are not new as have already been presented, albeit separately, in my theories of law, legal pluralism, and legal culture (Chiba 1989: esp. chap. 12). Here, I wish to integrate all of them synthetically into one for your examination. My presentation will, therefore, not only discuss legal culture, but also to include law and legal pluralism.

1 The nature of the scientific definiition

One shortcoming of numerous discussions on law and legal culture has been their general indifference to the nature of the scientific definition of the concepts used.

I recall, among others, the classic argument by Kant dividing the nature of the definition into two: "theological definition" presupposing a truth to be verified by deductive reasoning as in theology and aesthetics, and "philosophical definition" delineating the extension of the objective to be verified by inductive reasoning on the basis of more information to be added as in philosophy and other learnings. Roughly dividing contemporary fields of law in accordance with Kant's division, jurisprudence belongs to the theological definition insofar as it presupposes a legitimate authority of state law, while sociology/anthropolgy of law does to the philosophical definition insofar as it aims to develop scientific truth on the basis of empirical data.

No one would deny that every modern social science stands on the foundation of the latter type, as seen by its featuring methodology, dependent upon the operational definition that is the contemporary version of the Kant's philosophical definition. In contrast, there is a methodological lag in the study of law as an empirical science, that it is far behind those of other social sciences in recognizing the operational definition. I wish for this reason to make an effort to advance one step further. Before arguing the operational definition, I feel the suggestive importance of another division of definition by Kant. The reason is as follows.

Scientific procedure demands that the *delineative definition* of the concept, which distinctly delineates of a cereain objective, be formulated at the start of a scientific research as a modern version of the Kant's two kind definitions. Of course, an established science may not need to delineatie its odjective at each start by reason of the satisfactory sharing of a common starting point among interested scholars. Jurisprudence may be thought to belong to such a one, insofar as it undoubtedly limits law to that of a sovereing state. In contrast, all who wish to search for unshared objectives, such as various forms of law other than state law, must clearly delineate their objectives. In actual fact, there have been many attempts to define different forms of law such as natureal law, customay law, folk law, tribal law, and the like, and those of legal culture such as values or attitudes with respect to law or litigation. However, effective definitions of the issues have been not necessarily established to be operationally verified, thus causing a general confusion of the different issues and concepts of our objectives.

Chapter 15. An Operational Definition of Legal Culture **233**

There may be two reasons for this confusion. One may be the excessive inclination, not manifest but latent, toward the established jurisprudence, which has made scholars indifferent to the singnificance of the delineative definition. The other, vital to us, is the lack of intentional efforts to formulate the operational definition, which is to clearly define the intension of the term to repeatedly reformulate as the scientific research proceeds with the final goal ahead. Among the many scholars who have attempted delineative definitions of legal culture, only a few are seen to have been interested in formulating operational definitions (the Blankenburg's is one of them together with similar statistical attempts by Bierbrauer 1994; Gibson & Caldeira 1996). Their contribution is appreciated, but they still leave much for us to do before reaching our common goal. Of course, the delineative definition of a concept may not particularly be needed when the operational definition can satisfactorily delineate the objective clearly and distinctly.

The main reason for my negative appreciation of the prevailing definitions of legsl culture, whether delineative or operational, is that they have paid rare correct attention to the non-Western legal culture. The difference in legal cultures between Western and non-Western has no room to doubt for their socio-cultural nature, while compatibility and commonness between them should be also accurately explored. Their differences in law and litigation are well known (cf. Sack 1998a; Abel 1974). The difference in legal culture has been recently remarked even among Wesetrn countries. For instance, in USA, called a melting pot of races, Renteln, who found some Western bias in apparently objective conception of 'cultural relativism' (1990: chap. 3), began to argue to officialize the "cultural defense as partial excuse" for "immigrants, refugees, and indigenous people based on their customs or customary law" (1994a: 439). In Germany where foreign immigrants and refugees are increasing, Bierbrauer found a clear contrast of the attitudes toward legal authority between German monism on state law and Kurdish/Lebanese pluralism on different traditions and religions (1994). The operational definition of legal culture is demanded to be adequately applied to the home countries of those immigrants and refugees.

I attempt below to formulate the operational definition of law and legal culture, together with their delineative definitions.

2 Law

Law may be, as a delineative definition, a particular type of social norms. It is, as an operational definition, the whole system or its constituent factors of a social norm, whose mechanism positively and negatively sanctions the specified qualification for a certain entitled behavior pattern as *right* and the corresponding responsibility for the obliged behavior pattern as *duty*, being supported by a particular set of *values and ideas*, on the one hand, and by the legitimate *authority/power* of a certain *sociological unit* on the other. This definition of mine may be not satisfactory, but I am convinced of its probability to be verified thanks to the achievements of some forerunning scholars, for instance, the empirical correlation between rights and duties by Hoebel (1954: chap. 4), legal values and ideas by many legal philosophers (see their discussions on justice or natural law) and legal sociologists (see Galanter 1981; Abel 1981), and the coercing mechanism of law by Weber (1967).

The 'sociological unit' of law is not limited to a national country or sovereign state, but extends broadly to a variety of social organizations that maintain their own law as defined above, which are duly called a *socio-legal entity*. The law of a sovereign nation as a socio-legal entity is *state law*. The socio-legal entities in society, and accordingly their laws, may be classified roughly into three levels, though multifarious in reality: say *minor law*, working within the jurisdiction of a state, *state law*, and *world law*, crossing the boundaries of state law and including both *universal law* and *regional law*. State law appears, at present, to be trusted with the formal role of integrating the discrete legal systems of various socio-legal entities coexisting within its jurisdiction into a single whole, but is, by nature, one of numerous legal systems in human society.

Law never presents a simple form, but rather various forms. The forms are first divided on the basis of different sources of its authority/validity into two dichotomic forms. One is *official law*, which includes state law and the other legal systems officially authorized by state law. The other is *unofficial law*, which validly prevails among the people of a socio-legal entity without being officially authorized by state law. Its legal relevance is essential when it functions clearly and distinctly to supplement or else conflict with or even undermine the official law, especially state law. This function forms the criterion by which unofficial law is differentiated from custom.

Law may also be divided into two on the basis of differences in its cultural origins. One is *indigenous law*, which originates in the native culture of a socio-legal entity. The other is *transplanted law*, which is transplanted from foreign cultures. Transplanted law may be voluntarily *received law* or forcibly *imposed law* (cf. Burman & Harrell-Bond 1979) at the time of initial transplantation. It is important to note the function of *acculturation* during a long history, for initially imposed law may, as its usual outcomes, be indigenized to the transplanting law, or initially received law may be modified or replaced by the acculturating indigenous law. The contemporary importance of this division appears to lie mainly in the transplantation of modern Western law by non-Western countries, but transplantation of foreign law has often taken place in both Western and non-Western worlds. This is why I dismiss the customary usage of 'reception' as a general term since it tends to regard Western law as the only model.

Law is further divided into two on the basis of differences in formality. One is *legal rules*, which are formalized verbal expressions designating particular behavior patterns to the persons concerned. The other is *legal postulates*, which are particular values and ideas to ideationally support, supplement, or revise the legal rules. The legal postulate of state law have been established as 'justice, equity, natural law, or others,' but their role seems modest compared with the overwhelming function of so magnificiently systematized legal rules. In contrast, legal postulates of various unofficial laws are generally broader in their role vis-à-vis legal rules, because the legal rules tend not to be well formalized or systematized, and their vacuums need to be supplemented by the profound function of legal postulates.

Law in society is thus found to exist and work at three levels of mimor, state, and world law and in three dichotomies of law stated above. How then can each socio-legal entity integrate all the correlated but different legal systems coexisting within its boundaries into a larger system ? For, even the simplest socio-legal entity, such as the extended family or village community, must maintain its integration of coexisting familial, religious, local, state, and some other types of law, let alone much more complex socio-legal entities like national countries. A basic postulate of law must have worked to enable a socio-legal entity to make the vital decision as to what legal systems should be adopted, rejected or utilized with more or less modification in order to maintain their social individuality and cultural identity among fellow entities. I call the basic postulate the *identity postulate* of a legal culture, defined delineatively as the basic legal postulate for the people's cultural identity in law, which guides the people in choosing how to form and reform the whole structure of their law.

In sum, the working structure of the law of a socio-legal entity, whether tribal, local, religious, national, or regional, is the legal systems plurally coexisting or correlated in the entity and integrated into a whole by the identity postulate.

3 Legl pluralism and legal culture

Legal pluralism seems generally to be regarded as the coexistence of a state legal system with different legal systems under its jurisdiction, among othres, in non-Western countries (cf. Hooker 1975: 1). The legal pluralism thus implies dual structure of law: state law transplanted from the Western model and indigenous minor law of non-Western origin. The implication proves that most legal pluralists have not fully escaped from the traditional state law monism and Western law universlism, though they should have wanted to overcome them. The literal meaning of legal pluralism and its realities in the world demand that we catch sight of more forms than the dual structure. For example, we non-Westerners regret the general indifference of Western scholars to their own legal pluralism except recently growing interest in their legal cultures (cf. Varga 1992; Gessner et al. 1996; Gibson & Caldeira 1996); the triple structure, added by world law to the dual structure, may be caught in their singht; the combination of the three dichotomies of law should be investigated alongside/in addition to the simple dichotomy of indigenous law and transplanted law; the data regarding legal pluralism may be collected much more from all the world, especially those regions, information of which have rarely been afforded, such as Latin America, Oceania, Northern region; and the pluralism of regional legal cultures should be reexamined such as South East Asian region as the meeting place of the representative human legal cultures or Central Asia as the crossroads of surrounding legal cultures.

However, the vital significance of legal pluralism lies in yet another perspective. For instance, try asking an Indian or a Papua New Guinean native living on the spot, "Which is your law among the plural many ? " The Indian would answer, "The primary one is Indian law based on Dharma, while state, tribal, and other lews are secondary" (cf. Panikkar 1992), and the PNG native, who killed his mother suspected to be a sorceress in accordance with his duty as a village member, must answer, "It is village or tribal law, while state, Christian, and other laws supplement it according to different circumstances" (cf. Narokobi 1986). The native "actor" (cf. Gessner 1996) of a legal system qualified to select a legal standard among the plural systems, more naturally and easily than the cases of immigrants or refugees in Western countries as found by Renteln or Bierbrauer. These examples present a new perspective of legal pluralism: observing *law in subjectivity* against the jarisprudential one of *law in obiectivity* (cf. Chapters 10, 11).

The whole working structure of the law of each socio-legal entity is a form of legal pluralism, with different traits from entity to entity. The differences between various entities are nothing but the presentaion of cultural traits in the law of individual entities, comparable among one another as legal culture. *Legal culture* may thus delineatively be defined as the 'cultural traits of the legal pluralism of a socio-legal entity, or among a certain circle of socio-legal entities'. As a result, the identity postulate of the legal culture of a socio-legal entity forms a most striking trait to represent the legal culture concerned, comparable with neighboring or coexisting others. Thus, this definition of legal culture has already been operationalized, for the concept of legal pluralism, the key term of the definition, has been operationalized beforehand. Of course, still further refinement may be required with the cooperation of interested scholars as is usual of the operational definition.

As the above idea represents a new attempt of mine, some comments may be helpful for readers to understand, and critically improve, my scheme. I appreciate the various attempts already made to formulate the delineative definition of legal culture, including Friedman (1975). However, I also acknowledge their failure in three essential requisites. Two of them are general lackings in their interest in operational definition of legal culture and its non-Western realities. The other one is that of the perspective from anthropology. I wonder why they have paid no attention to the concept and achievements of culture by anthropologists, who are undoubted specialists in the study of culture. The only recent example I have noticed was Macaulay (1989), but his interest in Geertz (1983) ultimately failed to grasp correctly, in my view, the non-Western anthropological essentials of law, which aspired the Geertz's interest in law. Without efficient cooperation with the anthropological studies, the disussion of legal culture by legal scholars alone will fail in grasping legal *culture* in reality.

I have presented the "cultural configuration in law" as my delineative definition of legal culture, adopting one of anthropological concepts, 'cultural configuration', meaning "a more or less consistent pattern" of thought and action of a "significant sociological unit," by Ruth Benedict (1934: 42-43, 225-227). This was intended to elicit the cooperation of anthropologists to our attempt, without which the study of legal culture could not be effectively advanced. It has yet to be achieved. My scheme in this paper is to proceed a step further to an operational definition communicable with anthropologists, by rephrasing the cultural configuration in law into the cultural trait of the legal pluralism of a socio-legal entity.

I feel the operational definitions above require further elaboration. At the same time, I think it more useful for me to give some practical examples, in which I apply the above operational definitions, than to attempt further explanation at the abstract level of methodology.

4 Some examples of my own

First, I will provide an analytical observation of the historical development of

Chapter 15. An Operational Definition of Legal Culture 239

Japanese law (see Chapter 2 for details). The original Japanese law was, of course, indigenous law with no clear diversion into pluralism. It is known, however, that a primitive legal pluralism developed in the second to third centuries of ruler's and clan laws, which was composed of overwhelming indigenous law and partially transplanted Korean law. In the seventh century, the central government, under the growing authority of the Tenno (Emperor), tnspsplanted Chinese law systematically as the official state law. However, indigenous factors remained in two ways. A set of highest legal postulates was first declared by a leading Prince, mixing transplanted Confucian and Buddhist ideas into the indigenous Shinto/Tenno philosophy. Then, unofficial law was left to be developed freely by the people, as had been the case with their Chinese model. Soon later, as a resalt, the official state legal system was almost wholly replaced by an indigenous system produced earlier by ruling nobles and later by the rising warrior class as well as by people in localities.

The process of replacement was completed in a few centuries, and thereafter warrior rule by the Shogunate for the Tenno continued from 1192 until 1868. During this long period, indigenous law was developed in a complex manner: official state law was administered by the central *Bakuhu* Law coexisting with limited Court Law administered by the Tenno and the local *Han* law for the lords' estates and people; unofficial law was diversified into many different systems among farmers, fishermen, villagers, city dwellers, adherents at Shinto Shrines and Buddhism temples, classes, professions, and the like; and legal postulates of wider application were developed, such as *wa* (harmony), *nakama* (soildary community), *ie* (familial ties), and *mibun* (status hierarchy).

The modern codification, which took place after the Meiji Restoration of Tenno authoriry in 1868, was modeled on Western law, among others, Prussian law. Even in this transplanted system, the leading postulates were founded on indigenous ones, albeit somewhat reorganized, such as Tenno authority assisted by the *ie* system, *mura* spirit, and staus hierarchy, and they were wholly embodied in the Imperial Rescript on Education in 1890 as the highest 'legal postulate outside of the law,' This legal system was wholly reformed, following Japan's defeat in World War II, by the present system mainly modeled on American law. The

240   Chapter 15. An Operational Definition of Legal Culture

effects of the official reformation of the state law has been so dramatic that people speak of 'the firmly rooted democratic constitution.' However, Tenno still occupies a constitutional position with a symbolic nature that is nothing but a restoration to his older status. The social *ie* sysytem and status hierarchy may be revived to some degree through official legal measures as far as the people wish to realize them. Various unofficial laws seem truly to have been transformed. However, the transformation never means total disappearing, but rather partial disguises in symbolic or fictitious form, leaving the essences of the original forms as they were, 'Legal postulates outside of the law' are working rather unchangedlly, as seen from the tactful use of 'true intention or formal excuse', 'principle or exception', '*wa* principle', and the like.

The whole working structure of Japanese law has always been a legal pluralism of official law and unofficial law, and of indigenous law and transplanted law. The cultural traits underlying it must surely be a phase of Japanese legal culture, the striking feature of which is represented by its identity postulate, *amoeba-like situationism* as I name it. It features the Japanese behavior pattern in their legal culture to behave flexibly so as to adapt themselves to changing circumstances insofar as it is possible to maintain their individuality/identity. With this feature, the Japanese legal culture is unique among the countries in this cultural region of Chinese character or Confucian philosophy.

A neighboring country, Karea, has developed its own legal pluralism. The entire Korean history reveals the coexistence of indigenous law and various legal systems transplanted from China, whether Buddhistic or Confucian, as well as the mutually indifferent coexistence of official sub-state legal systems and unofficial ones. Such traits still remain in the whole structure of their contemporary law, as expressed by "alegalness among people" (see p. 188, Chapter 11). An identity postulate of their legal culture is found in their eagerness for the only legitmacy as derived from their mythical Creator, Hanunim, but their disappointment at actual struggles between competing legitimacies, as typically seen in the present separation into north and south. I wish to name it *hanunim legitimism*.

China, the largest among the three examples, presents another unique legal pluralism in human history. Their pluralism had long developed in their indigenous systems, composed of various levels of official law, on the one hand: typically of central governments and by such powerful socio-legal entities with quasi-independent power as Tibet and Inner Mongolia, and vast areas of private law as unofficial law produced by people outside of the official law which limited itself to public law, on the other. Their pluralism with transplanted law began only after their encounter with Western law in modern times and the later adoption of socialist law added by recent partial adoption of modern law. Their cultural traits are clear in this form of legal pluralism. Its identity postulate may be named *Tien* (Heaven) *pluralism* by reason of its far-reaching capacity to include the apparently heterogeneous systems, as today seen by the examples of mainland and Taiwan in opposition.

I am not in a position to assert the cultural traits and identity postulates of other socio-legal entities, which should be clearly disclosed by specialists in the study of each socio-legal entitiy. If I may, however, mention some of them to induce critical discussions on the identity postulate, they may be: *Dharma pluralism* for Indian law including Hindu and Theravada Buddhist law, *Umma pluralism* for Islamic law, each *religious doctrine* for the religious law of each denomination, *gentlemanly reasonableness* for British common law, *rule-of-law first* for American common law, *Germanic systemism* for German civil law, *esprit symbolism* for French civil law, *utmost fair* for sports law, *inward rhythm of local knowledge* for local law, and *informal justice* for various indigenous laws.

Note

(*) This chapter was originally my presentation before the workshop on "Changing Legal Cultures" sponsored by and held at the International Institute for the Sociology of Law, ISA Research Committee on Sociology of Law, Oñati in Spain, on June 13-14, 1996.

Being written in a last year of my academic activity, it aimed to synthetically conclude my preceding ideas to devise a theoretical scheme adequate to observe and analyze non-Western law. Rereading it to include in this collection, I realized it to be both successful and failed. It may have succeeded in presenting the

Chapter 15. An Operational Definition of Legal Culture

points of my ideas ever published, while it failed in synthesizing the ideas into a consistent system so as to be understandable and applicable by other scholars. In sum, my aim was found unattained. The reson for I dare to put this in the last Chapter in spite of its failure is that I eagerly hope the aim to be attained by endeavors of interested scholars, especially those from non-Western cultures, through verifying or nullifying the ideas.

I find a hope to advance the aim further to know some friends advocating them. Poh-Ling Tan, of Malaysia origin working at an Australian university, appreciated my idea as one of useful conceptual schemes to be applicable to the study of Asian legal systems (1997). Werner Menski examined my theoretical scheme in details to re-phrase its three basic concepts of official law, unofficial law and legal postulate into the 'tripartite model of law' to apply it to non-Western law in a global context (2000). Two young scholars let me know by E-mail in 2000 that they found my ideas effective to accurately discern conflicting or cooperating various laws of their home countries; they are Turkish Ihsan Yilmaz at Centre for Islamic Studies, University of Oxford, and Tahitian Tamatoa Bambridge at CERSO, University of Paris-IX-Dauphine.

APPENDIX

Appendix 1. Survey Research on Crime, Criminal Law and Criminal Justice in Japan (1973)*

Introduction

A considerable body of data relating to public attitudes toward the law has been acquired by legal sociologists from various countries. It is significant enough to convince us of the prospect of a successful comparative study of the topic by means of public opinion research. However, it would be premature to draw conclusions on the ground of statistical figures so far presented. We are required on the results obtained until now only to specify issues that can fruitfully be pursued further and to develop methods that can be effectively applied. To fulfil these requirements, this paper aims to advance suggestions on the results of various surveys on crime, criminal law and criminal justice in Japan.

As stated in my previous paper, various reliable public surveys have been conducted on the knowledge and opinions of the law in Japan (Chiba 1972). "Crime, criminal law and criminal justice" has been the topic treated most repeatedly, as in other countries. A few important results of the topic are included in my earlier work[1]. I present here some others that, I hope, will be valuable for our purpose. The sources, from which the data in this paper have been selected, are:

GOVERNMENT[2] 1956B on the death penalty (Sorifu 1956b).

GOVERNMENT 1967A on the death penalty (Sorifu 1967a).

SANKEI[3] 1971A on increasing fines for criminal offences (Sankei 1972: 274).

SANKEI 1972A on death penalty (Sankei 1973: 251), 1972B on increasing fines for criminal offences (ibid.: 257), 1972C on public morality (ibid.: 45), 1972D on lowering the age limit of the juvenile (ibid.: 252), 1972E on killing one's lineal ancestor (ibid.: 90), and 1972F on euthanasia (ibid.: 113).

J.C.C. 1971 on Japanese consciousness of the law (N.B.K. 1973). A special committee was organized in Nihon Bunka Kaigi, the Japan Culture Council, by two members of the government-established Institute of Statistical Mathematics and three law professors. Their opinion research is methodologically the most elaborate one on the topic. From among many questions surveyed, three concerning criminal justice have been chosen for presentation here. The respondents numbered 1053 of both sexes among 1500 samples over 20 years old selected from the metropolitan area of Tokyo and Yokohama by a stratified two stage probability sampling method.

The data adopted here are listed in six tables. The questions and answers, figures and comments in the tables are cited or abridged from those in the original sources. Unspecified figures represent percentages. 20-24, 25-29, etc. refer to age brackets; p.s., m.s., h.s. and u.c. to primary school, middle school, high school, and university and college education levels, respectively. A few questions marked with asterisks in the tables are cited again for comparison from my previous paper.

Findings

The death penalty. With reference to Q. 1 in Table 1, it comes as no surprise to find that the answers are, as usual, against- than pro-abolition, that limited abolition is slightly favored over total abolition, and that the simple surveys such as MAINICHI 1956, comprising one question, and SANKEI 1972A, comprising four questions, recorded more pro-abolition answers than the other surveys which were complicated with additional relevant questions. However, the most remarkable correlation to be made from the five surveys in Tables 1 and 2 is that they establish a trend: the younger and more highly educated the respondents, the more they are in favor of abolition. The main reasons given in support of abolition are shown in the answers to Q. 2. It is clear, however, that the answers of the respondents are affected by how 'choice questions' are framed. The relative significance of the reasons given for or against abolition is not always definite.

The answers to Q. 3 in Table 2 shows that life imprisonment is greatly preferred to the more lenient punishment as an alternative to the death penalty. It is to be noticed, however, that each of both opinions carries various implications. This would support previous tentative conclusion with respect to the death pen-

Appendix 1. Survey Research on Crime, Criminal Law and Criminal Justice in Japan (1973)

Table 1. THE DEATH PENALTY I

1. Pro-abolition of the death penalty, or contra-abolition.
   QUESTONS.
   (MAINICHI 1956)* "Are you in favor of abolishing it, or not?"
   (GOVERNMENT 1956B: i) "Do you think there are certain major crimes that justify it?"
   (ditto: ii)* "Are you in favor of its total abolition?"[1]
   (GOVERNMENT 1967A: i) "Are you in favor of maintaining the possibility of it?"
   (ditto: ii)* "Are you in favor of its total abolition?"
   (J.C.C. 1971) "Are you more in favor of its total abolition, or of maintaining the possibility of it?"
   (SANKEI 1972A) "Would you like it to be abolished, or not?"
   ANSWERS.[2]

		M. 1956 N = 2904	G. 1956B N = 2536		G. 1967A N = 2500		J.C.C. 1971 N = 1053	S. 1972A N = 995
			i	ii	i	ii		
a	Pro	24	20	18	17	16	15	30
b	Contra	59	63	65	70	71	84	54
c	Others	17	17	17	14	13	1	16

2. Reasns for opinions in Q. 1.
   ANSWERS.

		G. 1956B		G. 1967A*	S. 1972A
		N = 502	N = 445	N = 399	N = 301
		i	ii	ii	
A. Pro-abolition					
a	It is inhuman, barbarous	45	61	34[3]	7
b	Crimes. may be rehabilitated	30	—	20	45
c	They should atone alive	—	—	14	—
d	It will not prevent crime	5	—	14	20
e	It is irrevocable in case of misjudgement	5	22	12	23
f	Others	15	17	7	4
B. Contra-abolition		N = 1602	N = 1658	N = 1763	N = 533
a	Crimes will increase without it	17	49	43[4]	57
b	Crims. should atone with life	40	17	24	18
c	They will commit crimes again	29	23	21	14
d	The injured would not be satisfied without it	2	6	7	7
e	Others	11	5	5	4

NOTE. 1. Previously the question was wrongly translated as "Are you in favor of abolishing the death penalty or not?" (Chiba 1972: 13). 2. The wording of the following answers was not the same in each survey. The same shall apply hereinafter. 3. The figures in this column have been recalculated, based on a denominator of 100 (previously 156). 4. As above (previously 144).

Table 2. THE DEATH PENALTY II (GOVERNMENT 1967A)

QUESTONS.
3. "What punishment should replace the death penalty when it is abolished?"
4. "Are you in favor of having laymen participate in awarding the death sentence, or leaving it to the professional judge as is now the case?"
5. "Do you think a unanimous decision would be preferable in sentencing death to the present majority of three judges?"

ANSWERS, N = 2500

				Tot.	Noticeable trends
3.	a	Life imprisonment		74	Of a: Among younger women and the higher-educated, and those with more intellectual occupations and a higher atandard of living, the more.
		with release on parole		30	
		without it		33	
		D.K.		11	
	b	Impt. for a limited term		12	
	c	Others and D.K.		14	
4.	a	Laymen should participate		32	Of b: The higher-educated, and those with a higher standard of living, the more.
	b	The professional only		50	
	c	Not sure		2	
	d	D.K.		16	
5.	a	Yes, it is preferable		44	Of a: The younger, the more.
	b	No, majority is preferable		42	
	c	Can't say whether		1	
	d	D.K.		13	

CROSS TAVBULATIONS.

				Total abolition of death penalty	
				pro, N = 399	con, N = 1763
3.	a	Life imprisonment	with release on parole	38	30
			without it	23	39
			D.K.	11	11
	b	Imprisonment for a limited term		16	11
4.	a	Laymen should participate		37	33
	b	The professional only		48	54
5.	a	Unanimous decision is preferable		65	40
	b	Majority is preferable		24	50
Q. 1 in Table 3.	a	The main cause in the society		44	40
	b	In the criminal		29	33

alty, that many respondents, both for and against abolition, were found to be inconsistent in their opinions when questioned with various examples and suggestions of the possibility of gradual and experimental abolition (Chiba 1972: 17). I would further conclude from the data that the opinions regarding the death penalty showed a small but not negligible difference according to the nature of the crime.

What the criminal is. In the answers to Q. 1 in Table 3 no significant trend can be found except that those who think the cause of major crime lies in the society seem to have decreased in number over the years and finally to have become fewer than those who think it lying in the criminal himself. Another apparent trend in GOVERNMENT 1956B, that the younger- and lower-educated the respondents, the fewer found the cause of major crime to lie in the criminal, is not supported by the other two surveys. It cannot therefore be affirmed before reexamination.

The questions may be thought roughly to discriminate the two opposing types of criminal theorists: those who support the theory of corrective punishment and those who support the theory of retributive punishment. As far as the four questions other than Q. 2 are concerned, this holds true because the former group (1*a*, 2*b*, 3*b*, 4*b*, and 5*a*) returned a higher percentage than the other (1*b*, 2*a*, 3*a*, 4*a*, and 5*b*) in each of the four questions. The cross tabulations might suggest any correlations between some factors. They are not farreaching, however, enough to make us affirm any definite correlations. It would be required to reexamine how the questions should be framed.

Sense of guilt and fines. The answers to the questions in Table 4 suggest that the respondents, especially the middle-aged, favored more severe punishment, but that not all who complained of a generally blunted sense of guilt supported an increase in fines for criminal offences. Also, it can be seen that the percentage of those who thought it effective in combatting crime to increase fines in Q. 3 and Q. 4 was much lower than that of those who favored to increase fines in Q. 2. Nevertheless, these trends are inconsistent with the data previously reported (Chiba 1972: 11).

Purpose and object of criminal punishment. In the answers to the two questions included in Q. 1 in Table 5, the high percentage of those in favor of rehabilitation was almost the same (70% and 71%), but the clear trend in age and education in GOVERNMENT 19576B was somewhat negated by J.C.C. 1971. Also, a

Table 3. WHAT THE CRIMINAL IS

QUESTIONS.
1. The cause of major crimes.
   (GOVERNMENT 1956B) "Which do you think is the cause?"
   (GOVERNMENT 1967A) "Which is the main cause?"
   (SANKEI 1972A) "Which is the main cause?"
2. (GOVERNMENT 1956B) "Do you think most murderers are quite different from normal men, or not?"
3. (ditto) "Do you think any way may be found to rehabilitate the major criminal, or not?"
4. (ditto) "Do you think it is desirable for the major criminal to be excluded from society due to the possibility of his committing a second offence, or not?"
5. (ditto) "Do you think the human rights of the major criminal should be respected, or not?"

ANSWERS.

			Tot.			Noticeable trends
			G. 1956B N=2904	G. 1967A N=2500	S. 1972A N=995	
1.	a	The society	44	39	26	
	b	The criminal	18	31	41	
	c	Others and D.K.	38	30	31	
2.	a	I think they are different			48	Of a: The older- and higher-educated, the more.
	b	I don't think so			42	
	c	D.K.			10	
3.	a	I don't think so			12	
	b	I think so			54	
	c	Others and D.K.			34	
4.	a	I think it is desirable			36	
	b	I don't think so			45	
	c	D.K.			19	
5.	a	They should be respected			58	
	b	It is not necessary			19	
	c	D.K.			23	

CROSS TABULATIONS.

			Death penalty for			
			major criminals		any criminals	
			pro(%-N)	con(%-N)	pro	con
1.	a	The society[1]	73-327	14- 64	71-322	13- 58
	b	The criminal	63-701	25-283	67-750	22-241
2.	a	Murderers different	71-864	16-195	82-877	13-162
	b	Not different	58-607	26-276	62-648	24-253
3.	a	Rehabilitation likely	80-247	10- 32	78-241	8- 24
	b	Not likely	60-819	26-364	65-893	22-295
4.	a	He is to be excluded	79-720	12-105	77-649	10- 95
	b	Not to be excluded	54-621	30-244	60-687	26-300

NOTE. 1. Cf. the last cross tabulation in Table 2.

Table 4. SENSE OF GUILT AND THE AMOUNT OF THE FINE
(SANKEI 1971A, 1972B, 1972C)

QUESTIONS.
1. (S. 1971A) "Do you agree with the opinion that the sense of guilt has in general been blunted?"
2. (ditto) "What do you think about increasing fines for criminal offences?"
3. (ditto) "Do you think increasing fines would be effective in lessening crimes?"
4. (S. 1972B) "Do you think it would be effective to increase fines, as the government is planning?"
5. (S. 1972C) "Are you in favor of imposing fines for offences against public morals such as spitting in the street or feeding animals in the zoo, as in Europe and America?"

ANSWERS, N = 1046

			Tot.	Noticeable trends
1.	a	I think it blunted	79	More among the middle-aged.
	b	I do not think so	14	Men 20%, women 10%.
	c	D.K.	7	
2.	a	They should be increased	76	More among the middle-aged.
	b	They are resonable and should not be increased	14	More among the younger and students.
	c	They are already very high and should not be increased	6	
	d	D.K.	5	
3.	a	Yes, very effective	17	More among those over 30.
	b	Yes, rather effective	33	
	c	No, for money would rule the world	18	More among those under 30.
	d	No, never, for it would not lessen crimes	27	
	e	D.K.	4	
4.	N = 1074			
	a	Yes, very } as in Q. 3	14	More among those in their 30s and 40s
	b	Yes, rather	32	
	c	No	24	More among students.
	d	No, never	27	
	e	D.K.	3	
5.	N = 998			
	a	Yes, in favor	65	The older, the more.
	b	No, not in favor	26	More among men and younger people.
	c	Not sure	8	
	d	D.K.	1	

COMMENTS. 79% of *a* in Q. 1 is included in *a* in Q. 2, while 56% of *b* in Q. 1 in the same. More than 30% of *a* in Q. 2 answered *c* or *d* in Q. 3.

Appendix 1. Survey Research on Crime, Criminal Law and Criminal Justice in Japan (1973)

Table 5. PURPOSE OF CRIMINAL PUNISHMWNAT

QUESTIONS.
1. The purpose of criminal punishment.
    (GOVERNMENT 1956B)* "What do you think is the main purpose?"
    (J.C.C. 1971) "Which of the two do you agree with?"
2. The age limit of the juvenile.
    (J.C.C. 1971) "Major criminals under 20 are treated more leniently than adults on account of their legal minority, while they have a higher crime rate. Do you agree with the opinion that they should be punished more severely?"
    (SANKEI 1972D) "What do you think of the idea to lower the age limit in the Japanese Juvenile Law from 20 to 18?"
3. Punishment of the ancestor killer.
    (SANKEI 1972E) "Do you think it necessary to punish the killer of his lineal ancestor more severely than other killers, as is provided in the Japanese Penal Code?"[1]

ANSWERS.

	Tot.	Noticeable trends
1. G. 1956B, N = 2536		
a Retribution	2	
b Doterrment of criminals	14	The younger, the more (20–29 = 79%, 60 and over = 50%).
c Deterrment, unspecified	8	
d Corrective training	70	The higher educated, the more (u.c. = 84%, p.s. = 55%).
e Others and D.K.	6	
1. J. 1971, N = 1053		
a Retribution	25	20–24 = 76%, 40–44 = 70% p.s. ⎫
b Rehabilitation	71	25–29 = 69%, 45–49 = 67% m.s. ⎬ 72%
c D.K. and N.A.	4	30–34 = 69%, 50–59 = 71% h.s. = 70%
		35–39 = 73%, 60– = 70% u.c. = 71%
2. J. 1971, N = 1053		
a Yes, more severely	83	20–24 = 77%, 40–44 = 88% p.s. ⎫
b No change	14	25–29 = 83%, 45–49 = 83% m.s. ⎬ 85%
c No, more leniently	1	30–34 = 88%, 50–59 = 81% h.s. = 82%
d D.K. and N.A.	3	35–39 = 86%, 60– = 79% u.c. = 81%
2. J. 1972D, N = 901		
a Should be lowered	71	15–19 = 60%, 49–49 = 67%
b Should remain as it is	20	20–29 = 70%, 50–59 = 68%
c Not sure	8	30–39 = 81%, 60– = 73%
d D.K.	1	
3. S. 1972E, N = 962		
a Yes, necessary	36	The older, the more.
b No, unnecessary	54	More among men and students.
c Not sure	7	
d D.K.	3	

NOTE. 1. The Japanese Supreme Court ruled the present provision as unconstitutional in April, 1973, because of its excessively severe punishment.

certain tendency for respondents to want juvenile delinquents to be more severely punished is found in the answers to Q. 2. It is to be noticed that of these respondents the youngest showed the least enthusiasm for severer punishment, while the middle-aged were the most in favor. The more severe punishment meeted to the ancestor killer derives from an aspect of traditional Japanese morality. The answers to Q. 3 show, however, that this has been invalidated as a re-

Table 6. EUTHANASIA (SANKEI 1972F)

QUESTIONS,
1. "If you were suffering from the pain of an incurable disease, which would you prefer?"
2. "What would you think, if a member of your family, suffering painfully from a fatal disease, begged you to bring him a gentle and easy death?"
3. "What do you think of the aged wife who, at his request, kills her aged husband who is suffering from painful heart disease?"
4. "What do you think of the idea of sanctioning conditional euthanasia by law?"

ANSWERS, N = 1033

			Tot.	Noticeable trends
1.	a	Easy death to pain	50	The older, the more.
	b	Bearing pain to death	35	Men 40%, women 29%.
	c	Not sure	13	
	d	D.K.	2	
2.	a	It is human to meet his wish	38	More among the younger.
	b	I would do nothing like killing	47	The older, the more. / More among the less-educated.
	c	Not sure	13	
	d	D.K.	2	
3.	a	She should not be blamed	58	More among the highly educated.
	b	Killing is never justified	30	The older, the more.
	c	Not sure	12	
	d	D.K.	1	
4.	a	I agree with it	36	More among the highly educated.
	b	I disagree with it	48	More among the older.
	c	Not sure	14	
	d	D.K.	2	

CROSS TAMBULATIONS.

(1)

	Q. 2.		Q. 3.		Q. 4.	
	a	b	a	b	a	b
Q. 1. a	49%	37%	48%	35%	65%	21%

(2)

	Q. 4.	
	a	b
Q. 2. a	49%	39%

sult of the democratization of the country following World War II.

Euthanasia. It can be seen that a majority of the respondents to each question in Table 6 were in favor of euthanasia, and, according to the cross tabulations, that many of them maintained a consistent attitude in all their answers. Notice, however, that the bias in favor of euthanasia was most marked when the question referred to the respondent himself (Q. 1), less so when it referred to members of his family, and least of all when it applied to others. Excepting when the question referred to themselves, those most in favor were the younger and more highly educated. It may therefore be concluded that the attitude of the respondent varied not only with age and education but according as the question referred more or less directly to himself.

Conclusion

The above data and findings are thought to support the tendency in the opinion previously found of the law in general:

"Relative sex patterns are generally constant: men almost invariably showing more concern for the law than women. With few exceptions, also, a pattern can be discerned with respect to age and education: the younger and the more highly educated likewise showing more concern for the law. The middle-aged and the highly educated, however, often tend to show greater concern for public interest and order than for individual rights...."[4] (Chiba 1972: 22)

They may suggest several issues to be fruitfully pursued, for example, 1. the tendency that the younger and more highly educated, the more in favor of abolishing the death penalty; 2. main reasons given for and against abolition of the death penalty; 3. factors correlative with opinions favoring the theory of corrective or retributive punishment; 4. correlations among opinions concerning the severity of punishment; 5. the possibility of the rehabilitation of the criminal, and the increasing of punishment; 6. the distance of the question from the personal experience of the respondent; 7. reexamination of how to formulate a questionnaire.

I doubt, however, that the simple or cross tabulation of the figures acquired of the answers to the questions about particular problems may be effective to disclose some comparative characteristics of the Japanese people as well as the other peoples. What is more effective would be quantification and comparison of the systematic correlation among various interrelated factors included in particular problems. New methods such as factor analysis[5] or the theory of quantification[6] may be called for this purpose. And the issues may be selected in consideration of the legal system of each country. More specialists in statistics, criminal law and culture are expected to coperate in this direction of study.

Notes

(*) Originally, a paper presented before a session of the XXVI ESOMAR/WAPOR Congress-Budapest, September 9–13, 1973. Both the data and conclusion contained may be outdated from the usual point of view. From my point of view, however, the conclusion approved partial utility of the prevalent statistical method but doubted its holistic utility and expected another appropriate method to be devised in order to accurately observe and analyze legal culture in the contemporary usage. (This point was furthered by Appendix 2.) In this meaning, the paper formed a ground, I am convinced, for the advanced study today of legal culture I tried in the Chapters.

(1) Some of the data presented already in my previous paper are cited here in tables or referred to in the text for their significance.

(2) GOVERNMENT refers to the government-sponsored public opinion survey usually conducted of adults sampled from all over the country. Cf. Chiba 1972: 3 for its details.

(3) SANKEI refers to the periodically conducted opinion survey of current topics by the newspaper publisher called Sankei. The designated samples are 1200 persons aged between 15 and 64 living within 70 kilometers of the centers of Tokyo and Osaka, periodically reselected after a number of consecutive surveys.

(4) The mistyped words in the original have been corrected.

(5) Results of research by factor analysis will be reported soon by specialists in criminal law.

(6) Being developed by a statistician, Chikio Hayashi at the Institute of Statistical Mathematics, the theory of quantification (Hayashi 1959 and 1961) is efficiently applied in N.B.K. 1973 and Hayashi 1972.

Supplementary Note to the Chapter on the Data from Japan

First, some trends mentioned in Chiba 1972 are briefly represented here because of their relevance to the topics in question.

Severity of criminal punishment for such crimes as blackmail, extortion, assault, intimidation, etc. in GOVERNMENT 1961. (1) The answers 'too lenient' showed a remarked increase over those in GOVERNMENT 1957. (The 1961 survey was carried out when such crimes as exemplified above were particularly discussed among people, while the 1957 survey was done, on the contrary, of criminal punishment in general). (2) Among the answers 'too lenient': Men were more in favor of severity than women; the higher educated, the more men favored severity, but women not; the younger, the more women favored severity, but men not; commerce, industry and service, and white collar workers favored severity. (3) Among the answers 'too severe', no trend was found. But among those 'about adequate', a meaningful trend of decreasing according to age was found.

The will to help rehabilitation of ex-convicts in GOVERNMENT 1956A. (1) The higher educated and with the higher standard of living, the more positive will to help ex-convicts. (2) Among various ways to help ex-convicts, to be the consultant for ex-convicts was most favored. To contribute financially to the activities for their rehabilitation was next to it. Those living in more urbanised areas and engaged in more urban occupations preferred the latter way more than those not.

The same topic in GOVERNMENT 1960. The samples were among heads of block associations in cities and towns. (1) As to the respondents' willingness to hire ex-convcts, manufactures and constructors stood in marked contrast to farmers. (2) The longer the respondents kept their post and the higher educated they were, the more they tended to favor ex-convicts.

Next are added some relevant facts found among various surveys in Japan. First, several surveys were carried out of juvenile delinquency, violation of election and trafic laws, and some other particular offenses, by specialists in psychology and criminology. Such problems are, however, left untouched here because of particularity of their interest except a survey of euthanasia. Second, we can collect some results of surveys showing a remarkable discrepancy between crimes by the law and public opinion. But the results can not be straightforwardly generalized, because they were carried out of crimes such as kidnaping, violation of election and trafic laws, blackmail and intimidation, and so on when a case or some of each crime aroused much discussion among people. Third, no meaningful survey is found which had interest in religious affiliation of the samples as their background factor. This is a resonable reflection of the Japanese socio-cultural characteristics. Fourth, no general survey of the opinion would be possible of judges and convicts, because the authorities would not allow such a survey. This is also a reflection of the Japanese plitico-social climate. Fifth, two suggestions mentioned in Chiba 1972 are worth while repeating here: the significance of cultural tradition in Japan and a tendency to be reluctant to respond opinion surveys among Japanese people. Finally, the surveys from among which the data in the present paper were collected were indeed planned and carried out with sufficient statistical techniques as are appreciated. But they seem to have been satisfied with obtaining some figures of particular objectives under particular situations, leaving it undone to formulate or validate hypotheses by operationalizing the figures. (The survey in N.B.K. 1973 presided by Chikio Hayashi forms an exception.)

To sum up, some suggestions are found to further our study. Comparison of the Japanese data with those from other countries may be done in two levels: the *figures* of the public opinion and the *original* opinion. The figures can be compared as far as obtained by strict statistical techniques. But what is to be finally compared must be not symbols such as the figures but the meaning of the symbols for the original public opinion. For this purpose, two requirements should be meeted. One is to furnish hypotheses of the value system of a people symbolized in crime and punishment. This is especially difficult concerning Japanese people, because they are permeated by a traditional and peculiar value system as shown, though fragmentarily, by some data and facts stated above. It is to overcome this difficulty that both Japanese scholars in discursive orientation in the study of the 'consciousness of the law' and specialists in criminal law and criminology are requested to cooperate with us for their suggestive findings. The other requirement is to elaborate further statistical methods enough to quantify the value system. Factor analysis, theory of quantification, or any other may be useful for the attempt to develop such methods. It is for this reason that specialists in statistics are alike requested to cooperate with us.

REFERENCES

Chiba, Masaji 1972 "Results and Problems of K.O.L. Research in Japan: A Preliminary Report," mimeo., presented at the Symposium of the International Research Committee on Sociology of Law, Noordwijk, The Netherlands, September 20, 1972

Hayashi, Chikio 1959 "Fundamental Concepts of the Theory of Quantification and Prediction," *Proceedings of the Institute of Statistical Mathematics*, 7 (1), pp. 43–64

—— 1961 "Sample Surveys and Theory of Quantification," *Bulletin of the International Statistical Institute*, 38 (4), pp. 505–514

—— 1972 "Supplement: Japanese National Character," mimeo., presented at the XXth International Congress of Psychology, Tokyo, August 14, 1972

N.B.K. 1973 = Nihon Bunka Kaigi (The Japan Culture Council), ed., *Nihonjin no Hoishiki* (Japanese Consciousness of the Law), Tokyo, Shiseido, 243 pp.

Sankei 1972 = Sankei, The. *Iken to Ishiki no Hyakkajiten* (An Encyclopedia of Opinions and Consciousness), Tokyo: Sankei Shinbunsha, 306 pp.

—— 1973 *73nen Iken to Ishiki no Hyakkajiten* ('73 Encyclopedia of Opinions and Consciousness), Tokyo: Sankei Shinbunsha, 314 pp.

Sorifu 1956b = Sorifu (Prime Minister's Office), ed., *Shikei Mondai ni kansuru Seron-chosa* (An Opinion Survey on the Problem of the Death Penalty), mimeo., 50 pp.
―― 1967a = *Shikei ni kansuru Seron-chosa* (An Opinion Survey on the Death Penalty), mimeo., 153 pp.

Appendix 2. A Comparative Analysis of Attitudes toward Individual Rights among Westerners, Africans and Japanese (1975) *

1. Promoted by European scholars of the International Research Group on Knowledge and Opinion about Law,[1] a working sub-group of the ISA Research Committee on Sociology of Law has considerably advanced the comparative study of attitudes toward the law. This assertion is supported by a collection of the results of their study (Podgorecki et al. 1973).

Their studies are characterized by methodical, quantitative statistical opinion surveys designed to collect pertinent data and oriented to cross-national comparison. The studies have been successful in so far as the collected quantitative figures have indicated some differences in attitudes toward the law among some countries. Also they have indicated that there were problems with the factors which define the meaning of the quantitative figures, such as socio-economic system, judicial subculture and psychosocial determinants of a personality in Adam Podgorecki's scheme (ibid.: 82) or cultural, sociological and psychological factors in Berl Kutchinsky's (ibid.: 133). On the other hand the studies have not been successful in that they have failed to make a true comparison of the cultural patterns of the attitudes underlying the quantitative figures. Their contribution may be said by and large to have been heuristic. In order to validate their focus upon knowledge and opinion about law, which prevails in culturally diverse societies, we need to identify and explore further a vast field of problems.

It seems to have been an unfortunate choice that the attitudes toward crimes, criminal law and related topic have almost wholly occupied the scholars interested in the study of attitudes toward the law.

Of course their choice was not groundless. There are good reasons for it. For example, more or less specified variables, such as the rules of law as an independent variable and the attitudes of people toward them as a dependent variable, can be identified on these topics by one measure or other. Furthermore such topics are in reality serious enough to have people show certain attitudes toward criminal law more explicitly than other topics of law. Judging from the voluminous results accomplished by American scholars (cf. Biderman et al. 1972) in addition to those by the Europeans, their choice of these topics would have been reasonable for some purposes. However, even when some correlations between the rules of the law and the attitudes toward them within each society are analyzed, there still remains undisclosed in their studies the comparative correlations among these same societies between those attitudes as a dependent variable and the cultural patterns as an independent variable. In sum, as far as the present accomplishments are concerned, the study of attitudes toward crimes, criminal justice and related topics has been successful in disclosing differences in attitudes among culturally diverse societies, but unsuccessful in comparing the cultural patterns underlying the attitudes. A further in-depth study of the attitudes toward the law among various cultures is required.[2]

Instead of topics treating criminality, the author would suggest that individual rights in general can be another fruitful topic in the comparative exploration of cultural patterns among various societies. This topic is not without its disadvantages. Certainly the results of an attitude survey on such a general topic are often reversed by those on more specific topics. It has a good possibility for fruitfulness for our purpose, however, since the general conception of individual rights is really prevalent among people in each society. It has two further advantages in that general conceptions are reasonably believed to be correlated more closely with the cultural pattern of the society in question, and that reliable, though not always quantitative, data on this topic concerning Westerners, Africans and Japanese have been presented.[3]

2. It may sound curious that the Western conception of individual rights has been rarely discussed by Western scholars themselves. This would be reasonable, for people do not tend to think of their own cultural matters unless they are put into a position which forces them to compare themselves with other peoples. The topic in question more often has been discussed by non-Western scholars for purposes of comparison.

By way of continuation, Japanese scholars have emphasized *conceptual definity* as a distinguishing characteristic of the Western conception of individual rights. Western people are said to have a tendency to accept individual rights as so definitively conceptualized as to reject the least arbitrariness of the interested persons, whether private or official. It thus suffices for the judge in court to declare the substantials of the individual rights with its universally valid conceptual clarity and rigidity. In this system the primary objective of jurisprudence is to interpret the conceptual framework and the system of various rights irrespective of their possible variations and functions in practice. This conception, which is characteristic of Westerners, is an idealized pattern which may be properly called 'modern.' No one would deny that this type of conception prevails in Western societies, whether it is called Western or modern. It is this type of conception that is discussed here under the rubric of Western.

In contrast with the Western, the African conception of individual rights may be characterized by *conceptual elasticity*. Of course, African peoples and cultures are too diversified among multiple tribes for us to speak of their universal nature. As far as they are compared with the Western and other continental, however, some distinctive traits common to them can be spoken of as has been written and ascertained by many scholars.

Seeing that the Western definition of law is too narrowly conceptualized to embrace African legal ideas of law, T. Olawale Elias suggested another definition, viz., that " 'The law of a given community is the body of rules which are recognized as obligatory by its members.' This recognition must be in accordance with the principles cf their social imperative, because operating in every community is a dynamic of social conduct, an accepted norm of behavior which the vast majority of its members regard as absolutely necessitated for the common weal. This determinant of the ethos of the community is its social imperative" (1975: 55). Almost at the same time Max Gluckman used "elastic generality" to express an essential characteristic of important key concepts in the Lozi legal system. It was the summary term for "general, unspecific, multiple, permeable and absorbent" characteristics "of all concepts of law and ethics" (1955: 293–294). He argued this primarily about the Lozi legal system, but he is understood as not limiting the use of this term to the Lozi alone but extending it to other African legal systems. We can safely regard 'conceptual elasticity' as an essential African idea of law, including their conception of individual rights.

In comparison with the Western and African, the distinctive feature of the Japanese conception of individual rights has been unanimously discussed in its character of 'conceptual indefiniteness' or 'weak consciousness.' As a result of his opinion survey in 1952, the auther concluded that "people's consciousness of individual rights and the law was likely to be weak, uncertain or even non-existent, in view of their attachment to traditional feelings toward the unity of the family," while "there were nevertheless a few fields in which a consciousness of individual rights was clearly found" (Chiba 1972). This was to substantiate the points upon which agreement among Japanese scholars had been found.[4] Later in his book in 1967 which treated Japanese conciousness of law, Takeyoshi Kawashima argued "that the Japanese had evolved unique traditional views of right and duty, law and legal procedure which in their indefiniteness, diffuseness, authoritarian proclivities, general aversion to the law and so on, contrasted distinctively with idealized modern concepts prevailing in European and American society" (cited by Chiba 1972). No one would challenge this view. *Conceptual indefiniteness* can be said thus to be the distinguishing characteristic of the Japanese conception of individual rights.

In summation we can comparatively denote the characteristics of Western, African and Japanese conception of individual rights by 'conceptual definity,' 'conceptual elasticity' and 'conceptual indefiniteness' respectively. The aim of this paper is to formulate a sufficient analytical scheme of these characteristics to compare the cultural patterns underlying them. Before starting a discussion of the subject, however, some comments may be helpful for delimiting the scope of the subject.

First, the words used to characterize the three types of conceptual structures lack the necessary elaboration sufficient enough to encompass the existing variations already knowm within each area. They are worthy of operational use for our purpose, however, for they are adopted not to define analytical terms to be applied to observed facts but to denote comparative differences among three cultural areas.

Second, some people might reject the primitive law of the African native as law. Primitive law has been long treated as custom or a quite different kind of law, which lies far beyond the range of Western or modern law. But several decades have passed since primitive law could be vitalized as law by virtue of such data and arguments as presented by Malinowski and Evans-Pritchard.[5] Their data and arguments were so wellgrounded as to convince us that the difference between law and custom is not one in quality but in quantity. Essential to our scientific work here is not only to demarcate the boundary between law and custom but rather to make clear the comparative characteristics of primitive and modern law grouped within a single continuum of the concept of law.

Finally, such expressions as "uncertain or even non-existent" by the author (1972) and "people traditionally lack in the consciousness of individual rights" by Kawashima (1967: 15) are found concerning the Japanese conception of individual rights. They might seem to discredit the existence of the conception altogether. However, they can not be understood literally. Judging from the whole context both writers evolved, the significance of the expressions must be that Japanese people are often found to have a peculiar kind of conception different from the Western type. This difference often has prompted observers to conclude that the Japanese people has no concept of law. Instead, the writers should have noted that the Japanese people has a peculiar conception of law.

3. When seen from the Western conception of individual rights characterized by 'conceptual definity' with a rigid alternative of law and custom, the African conception probably appears so uncertain and ambiguous as to allow arbitrary interpretations to creep in undisturbedly to such an extent that it appears to be completely foreign to a concept of law. However, such a view is untenable. As Siegfried Nadel justfiably stated, "This rigid alternative must be modified. For within 'costom' a distinction analogus to that between custom and law reappears" (1947: 500). Assuming that this distinction is reasonable, some kinds of custom must function as law in the Western sense which can be clearly discerned from other kinds of custom. Westerners, however, may doubt their nature as law. As far as they function as law with the objective criteria of justice involved, the statement of Elias, that "African judges in judging a case do not make use of their personal knowledge to any greater extent than do English

judges," (1957: 251) is tenable. Quoting P.A. Talbot, "it is probable that the right decision is given with as much certainty as in an European Court" (ibid.: 260), and that "the ultimate purpose of law in a society, be it African or European, is to secure order and regularity in the conduct of human affairs and to ensure the stability of the body politic" (ibid.: 218). These statements assure us of the existence of law, that is differentiated from custom to define certain patterns of behavior as distinctively legal. To validate this assurance, however, any factor or other must function to determine the meaning in practice of the apparently uncertain and ambiguous conception certainly and clearly enough to define legal patterns of behavior. Without such a factor, Gluckman's so appealing assertion, "the paradox of the 'uncertainty' of legal concepts and the 'certainty' of law" (1955: 291-320) would be groundless too.

The decisive determinant of this kind is said to be the *social status of the parties* to a legal relationship. The ties originated in social status establish, said Gluckman, "the most important sets of obligations between persons, and hence transactions between persons are determined by their status (in Maine's sense) relative to one another. The relations involved stand in sharp contrast with the relations... in which we nowadays become associated with other persons through the many contracts into which we enter throughout our daily lives" (1972: 5). Elias recognized the bargaining powers of the individual increasing among African people, but he could not help saying that "these individual rights and duties vary with the type of social organization and the degree of cohesion already achieved. Thus, kinship as a bond of social cohesion is more powerful in any society that lacks a developed political organization than it is in one less heterogeneous or atomistic" (1957: 84). As a conclusion, Gluckman maintained that "all disputes take place between people each of whom occupies several social positions, and the judges determine first in what roles the litigants are disputing.... Hence law operates in a framework of social positions, and in the judicial process these must first be settled. They set the limits within which a particular judgment has to be given: hence they tend to have *a high degree of precise definition*" (1955: 296-297; emphasis by the quoter). Gluckman did not limit social position to status in the kinship system, but extended it to social relationships and interactions in localities. Nevertheless this can not be understood as denying that

Appendix 2. A Comparative Analysis of Attitudes toward Individual Rights (1975) **265**

status in the kinship system is the most typical social position not only among the Lozi he surveyed but also in other African peoples. Therefore we can safely ascertain that 'social status of the parties' chiefly originated in the kinship system is the decisive determinant in the practice of the African conception of individual rights apparently so uncertain and ambiguous.

When he argued on the Japanese conception of individual rights, Kawashima set forth the Western concept as a standard to evaluate the Japanese one. As far as the present topic is concerned, he emphasized that both parties to a right-and-duty relationship in the Western conception are treated equally and conflicts between them are managed by a clear-cut decision according to the specific and fixed substantials of right and duty prescribed under certain objective criteria beyond all individual particularities (1967: 24-28). He maintained that in sharp contrast with the Western the Japanese conception is characterized by unfixedness and diffuseness of individual rights with their detailed substantials varying with different situations and by duty-centeredness rather than right-centeredness resulting in an unequal relationship between the parties (ibid.: 28-33). At the same time, he pointed out a traditional tendency among Japanese people to give priority to compromise between the parties in conflict. According to him, they "not only hesitate to resort to a law suit but are also quite ready to settle an action already instituted through conciliatory processes even during the course of litigation" and Japanese courts, contrary to expectation, "prefer to accept the fait accompli and try to reconcile the litigants through extrajudicial negotiations" (1963: 47-49). The preference for compromise led him to conclude that "right as a legal norm is not so rigidly differentiated from the state of affairs in facts as to allow the parties to confuse the facts with the norms, in brief, a continuity of fact onto norm" (1967: 85). This is what Japanese writers have called the indefinite conception of individual rights. A reliable statistical survey led by Chikio Hayashi proved this tendency to be supported.[6]

This characterization of the Japanese conception is by and large to be approved. Then how is it different from 'conceptual elasticity' among Africans? What is the decisive determinant in practice, if any, of the apparently indefinite conception, which is equivalent to 'social status of the parties' in African societies? Some ideas of Kawashima are suggestive of the determinant, though he did not distinctively set them forth. He argued that there are two characteristics of the traditional social groups in Japan; "hierarchically differentiated social status in terms of deference and authority" on the one hand and "particularistic and functionally diffuse relationships between people of equal status" on the other (1963: 43-44). These relationships were typically found in village communities and in the prewar patriarchal type of families.

In a later book in 1967, he noted that there is a vast circle of people, who were not confined to the relationships in terms of deference and authority, and concluded the 'conceptual indefiniteness' among Japanese people, for whom it still held true that their "social roles are defined by general and flexible terms so that they may be modified *whenever circumstances dictate*" (Kawashima 1963: 44; emphasis by the quoter). In some cases, "circumstances" in Japan may be more or less similar to 'social status' in Africa. But they may be not in other cases. Any social relationships which can be patternized in relation to the "circumstances" will throw light on finding the differences in the conception between Africans and Japanese.

Among the various examples and generalizations Kawashima presented, some are especially worth noticing for patternizing the "circumstances" in the Japanese conception. First, the detailed substantials in the practice of rights and duties, which are to be defined by a contract, depend not only upon the contents of the agreement between the parties, as is the case of Westerners, but also on both "*a paid earnest or written deed*" and "*close relationships*" underlying between them as "cohabitants in a village community or relatives of a family" (1967: 93; emphasis by the quoter). Second, the parties to a contract tend to prefer literally uncertain expressions to prescribed certain clauses in order to determine specific obligations "*according to existing circumstances*" or through "*occasional arrangements* on the intervention of a third party as a mediator who gives not more than advices of compromise, not as an arbitrator or judge who makes a clear-cut decision of right or not" (ibid.: 110-117; emphasis by the quoter). Third, the parties to a contract also tend not to prescribe contractual clauses certainly nor fixedly "when they perceive *the relationship between themselves as connected by certain interests other than legal* such as protection and dependence or certain feelings of continuity as in a family or between close friends" (ibid.: 120; emphasis by the quoter). Finally, as clearly seen of the traditional idea of ownership among Japanese, "the detailed substantials of an individual right are *determined by state of affairs at all occasions*" rather than the prescribed normative clauses (ibid.: 85; emphasis by the quoter). For these reasons, Kawashima adopted the concepts of "functional diffuseness" and "particularistic" in contrast with "functional specificity" and "universalistic" according to the Parsonian scheme of action (ibid.: 120-121). However, the Parsonian scheme is too general and diffuse to specify the particular difference between Africans and Japanese. A middle-ranged scheme is required to patternize certain social circumstances. The auther would suggest the *particular relationship between the parties* as such a middle-ranged pattern of behavior for Japanese people.

4. As a result of the above discussion, we can draw the following conclusions regarding the comparison of the Western, African and Japanese conceptions of individual rights. First, the Western conception is characterized in general by 'conceptual definity,' while the African is characterized by 'conceptual elasticity' and the Japanese by 'conceptual indefiniteness.' This does not mean, however, that African and Japanese people do not have clear and distinct conception of individual rights. On the contrary, they have another kind of conceptual scheme which works on all occasions to complement their apparently elastic and indefinite conceptions of individual rights so that the conception may function clearly and distinctively enough to specify particular detailed substantials in the practice of each right and duty. For Africans and Japanese, this kind of conceptual scheme forms a *functional complement* to the elastic and indefinite conception of individual rights in order to have them perceive on all occasions definite patterns of behavior prescribed by the law just as the Western definitive concept of individual rights does without any help from other types of conceptual schemes. The African conception and the Japanese are in this sense common to each other and different from the Western.

Nevertheless, the African and the Japanese are not one and the same. The African functional complement to their 'conceptual elasticity' of individual rights is the 'social status of the parties' which chiefly originates in kinship organization.

Among Africans, the social role of each person is definitely prescribed in accordance with one's social status in one's own social system. The social system may be of clansman, tribal citizen, local resident or national member. But the most fundamental is that of kinsman. The social status of each African may be difficult or impossible to perceive and discern correctly for people not belonging to African societies. However, people belonging to his society are well acquainted with it and aware of its normative validity. So on all occasions the Africans are in the position of being limited by their own social status. Nevertheless when they choose specified patterns of behavior, their individual rights may appear to the outsider to be elastic and to allow them other possibilities. Both the social status of each party and the responsibility of the parties to be faithful to it are self-evidently known not only by the parties but also normatively expected by the whole community. In sum, complemented by the specific patterns of behavior in accordance with the "social status of the parties," the apparently elastic African conception works in practice clearly and effectively just as the definite Western conception does.

In Japan, however, the influence of kinship organization upon the social position of each person has been modified remarkably and much earlier than in Africa. In Japanese society, kinship organization is rather ficticious than real, be it the peculiar family system which had been legalized before World War II or the boss-gang system which is still found among gamblers. Generally speaking, social status with its origin in the kinship organization has lost its gravity in Japanese society, as has the hierarchical system of social stratification. It has been considerably conventionalized in Sumner's meaning. To speak of it from the reverse, the social position among Japanese has been too much personalized to be defined by social status as in Africa. Yet, the personalization is not quite similar to that in Western society. The individual right of a person is not always defined by the clauses prescribed on a contract or by the law. There still remains room for being complemented by certain kinds of social relationships which should be non-legal from the Western conception. Whether the parties are employee and employer, tanant and landowner, citizen and government, or some others, whether they are connected by particular common goals or by close relationships, and whether they are negotiating each other directly or through mediation, they are apt to be compelled, as well as allowed, to accept some factors of their particular relationships on all occasions as specifying the detailed substantials of their rights and duties. 'Particular relationships' on all occasions can be said to form the functional complement to the Japanese conceptual indefiniteness of individual rights and to help the Japanese indefinite conception function as a legal frame of reference equivalently to the Western definitive concept of individual rights.

In conclusion, the African conception of individual rights, characterized by 'conceptual elasticity,' and the Japanese, characterized by 'conceptual indefiniteness,' may first appear to be ambiguous. But, when they function in practice as a legal frame of reference to specify clearly and distinctively certain patterns of behavior, they are usually coupled with functional complements, the 'social status of the parties' and the 'particular relationships between the parties' respectively. In comparison with the African and the Japanese conceptions, the Western concept of individual rights appears to function as self-sufficient legal frame of reference without any other conceptual complements.

The last view of the Western conception is what the above-cited writers assumed and many other supported. Yet this author has doubts about its validity. Methodologically, on the one hand, the writers made their comparative discussions on two levels, although they seem to have little consciousness of this. First is to discuss 'ideal norms,' one of three roads which Karl Llewellyn and E. Adamson Hoebel pointed out to seek for the law in a society (1941: 20–21). The findings of 'couceptual definity, elasticity and indefiniteness' were discussed chiefly on this ideal level. The 'social status of the parties' in Africa and the 'particular relationships between the parties' in Japan were chiefly found as functional complements on another, practical level, which Llewellyn and Hobel classified into 'practices' and 'trouble cases.' On this practical level, any functional complements to the Western concept of individual rights should be sought therefore as corresponding to those in Africa and Japan. Substantially, on the other, conceptions of individual rights, on a practical level different with Western societies are not non-existent. Certainly the KOL researchers who focussed "upon the knowledge and opinion of law prevailing *in their culturally diverse societies*" (Podgorecki et al. 1973: 8; emphasis by the quoter) assumed that they exist. Following the conclusion summarized above, we are confronted with a question of how to identify the Western functional complement to their definitive concept of individual rights, which may be characterized as common to the culturally diverse Western societies.

Unfortunately, no reliable results have been presented before on this problem. The author would suggest a hypothetical concept as a step toward further elaboration. It would be that each party is free to resort to the definitive concept of individual rights. In Western culture, each party to a legal relationship is priviledged to resort to fixedly prescribed substantials of individual rights, rejecting any personal interpretation of them, whether coming from their social status or particular relationships between the parties. He is priviledged furthermore to waive his individual rights according to his preference. This means that the 'freedom of each party' includes not only his free choice to resort to his individual right protected by the law but also his preference for social pressures on the other party which he can apply in place of legal measures. When he chooses his legal rights, the legal system can be said function selfsufficiently as a whole. When not, on the contrary, any other social system functions in place of the legal system. The function of the social system may in some cases support the legal system, thus resulting in maintaining the latter. The function may in other cases contradict or even undermine the legal system. For this reason, it is incorrect to say that the Western concept of individual rights necessarily serves to promote legal security by virtue of its definitive character. The efficiency of the Western definitive concept should be assessed by the results, that is, how it functions complementarily to the conceps of 'freedom of each party.'

In final conclusion, the Western, African and Japanese conception of individual rights were first formulated comparatively in reference to ideal norms as 'conceptual definity,' 'conceptual elasticity' and 'conceptual indefiniteness' respectively. Each of them is found to be complemented in practice by another cultural concept which function as valid legal frames of reference: 'freedom of each party,' 'social status of the parties' and 'particular relationships between the parties' again respectively. Finally, therefore, people's attitudes toward individual rights are not simply a result of their concepts of rights on an ideal level, but they are also a function of the conceptions complemented by the cultural concepts on a practical level.

Notes

(*) Originally, presentation before a session of the Annual Meeting of the ISA Research Committee on Sociology of Law, Hakone, Japan, September 1-4, 1975. The reason for adding this one as an appendix is similar to the preceding Appendix 1 (cf, its note *) but more or less advanced in clearly designating the essential factor of the problem: culture.

(1) These scholars coined the word KOL to abbreviate 'Knowledge and Opinion about Law'.

(2) Scholars engaging in the KOL research are understood to have been aware of this task to be pursued, as shown by Kutchinsky's doubts about prospects of the method of attitude survey (Kutchinsky 1973: 133).

(3) The author would not necessarily hold that the individual rights really exist in its general form in each of Western, African and Japanese societies. It might be more accurate to suggest that more specific forms of various individual rights really exist within each cultural unit. It can not be denied, however, that certain concepts or conceptions of individual rights in their general form are *assumed* to really exist in each culture.

(4) Urged by a critical reflection of prewar society and culture of Japan after her defeat in World War II, a hot discussion of Japanese consciousness of law exploded among Japanese scholars. And it was not limited to specialists in law. What the author states in the text is the view shared by most of them irrespective of their differences in ideological standpoints.

(5) Because of his lucid explanation, we need not paraphrase Malinowski's arguments which were advanced at the outset of his book and which were supported by sufficient evidence (1926). We wish on the contrary to comment on Evans-Pritchard's arguments for he once refused to admit the existence of law among the Nuer saying that "In a strict sense Nuer has no law." Nevertheless, he admitted that "there are conventional compensations for damages, adultery, loss of limb, and so forth, but there is no authority with power to adjudicate on such matters or to enforce a verdict" (1940: 162). Taking various practices and the role of the leopard-skin chief, a functioning mediator, into consideration, he concludingly declared that "The Nuer has *a keen sense of personal dignity and rights. The notion of right, wrong, is strong*. It is recognized that a man ought to obtain redress for certain wrong" (ibid.: 171; emphasis by the quoter). Without dout, problem is not that the Nuer did not have law at all but that Evans-Pritchard had a limited concept of law which could not embrace the African conception.

(6) An opinion survey on the Japanese consciousness of law (Nihon Bunks Kaigi 1973), made in 1971 by a group of scholars led by Chikio Hayashi, statistical

mathematician, is distinguished among not a few others of similar aim for its advanced methods. "The orientation to adaptability of the law to circumstances" was one of its main results, employing the data gained from 1,053 respodents out of 1,500 assigned samples aged 20 and over living in the metropolitan area of Tokyo. The above result was based on an analysis of the answers given to eight questions below.

a. The judge who died from malnutrition as a result of rejecting opportunities to obtain black-market rice in the years of short subsistences following Japan's defeat in World War II:

He was literal-minded, foolish.	84%
He was admirable.	15%

b. To obey or disobey the law:

It is inevitable to disobey the law when a just aim should be given priority.	56%
The law should be obeyed under any circumstances.	43%

c. Two types pf public servants:

I like better ones tending to apply the law resorting to the requirements of the moment.	66%
I like better ones tending to apply the law in strict conformity with its literal sense.	29%

d. The purpose of the law:

To have people get along easily together.	55%
To have justice be done in the world.	42%

e. Application of the law:

The law should be enforced as elastically as adoptable to circumstances.	62%
The law should be strictly enforced against violation.	34%

f. Trespass in an unused private land:

Children may play free on the land.	54%
Permission of the owner is needed.	43%

g. Tresspass in a state land to collect wild grasses popular for food against a bulletin board to prohibit trespass:

It was not matter, for there is no actual damage.	42%
One must not trespass, for it is a steal.	55%

h. A contract made several years ago which has proved unsuitable for the present state of affairs:

I will negotiate for its revision to immunize the obligations.	64%
I will observe it; contract is contract.	32%

REFERENCES

Biderman, Albert, et al. 1972. *An Inventory of Survey of the Public on Crime, Justice and Related Topics*, Washington, D.C.: Government Printing Office

Chiba, Masaji 1972. "Results and Problems of K.O.L. Research in Japan: A Preliminary Report," presented at the Symposium of ISA Research Committee on Sociology of Law, Noordwijk, The Netherlands.

Elias, T. Olawale 1957. *The Nature of African Customany Law*, Manchester: Manchester University Press

Evans-Pritchard, E.E. 1940. *The Nuer*, Oxford: Claredon Press

Gluckman, Max 1955. *The Judicial Process among the Barotse of Northern Rhodesia*, Manchester: Manchester University Press

—— 1972. *The Ideas in Barotse Jurisprudence*, 2nd ed., Manchester: Manchester University Press

Kawashima, Takeyoshi 1963. "Dispute Resolution in Contemporary Japan," in *Law in Japan*, ed. by Arthur T. von Mehren, Cambridge, Mass.: Harvard University Press, pp. 41–72

—— 1967. *Nihonjin no Ho-Ishiki* (The Japanese Consciousness of Law), Tokyo: Iwanami Shoten

Llewellyn, Karl N., & E. Adamson Hoebel 1941. *The Cheyenne Way*, Norman: University of Oklahoma Press

Malinowski, Bronislaw K. 1926. *Crime and Custom in Savage Society*, London: Routledge and Kegan Paul

Nadel, Siegfried F. 1947. *The Nuba*, London: Oxford University Press

Nihon Bunka Kaigi (The Japan Culture Congress), ed. 1973. *Nihonjin no Ho-Ishiki* (The Japanese Consciousness of Law), Tokyo: Shiseido

Podgorecki, Adam, et al. 1973. *Knowledge and Opinion about Law*, London: Martin Robertson

References

(Those of two Appendixes are listed not here but in each of the two)

Abel, R. 1974. "A Comparative Theory of Dispute Institutions in Society," *Law & Society Rev.* 8 (2)
———, ed. 1982. *The Politics of Informal Justice*, 2 vols., New York: Academic Pr.
Afchar, H. 1975. "The Musulim Conception of Law," in David 1975
Akbar, N. 1992. "Africentric Social Sciences for Human Liberation," in Sack & Aleck 1992
Alaphilippe, F., & J.-P. Karaquillo 1985. *L'activité sportive dans les balances de la justice*, Collection *Droit et economie du sport* 5, Paris: Dalloz
Allott, A.N. 1994. "Methods of Legal Research into Customary Law," repr. in Renteln & Dundes 1994
——— & G. Woodman, eds. 1985. *People's Law and State Law: The Bellagio Papers*, Dordrecht: Foris Pub.
Appelbaum, R. P. et al. 2001. *Rules and Networks: The legal Culture of Global Business Transactions*, Oxford: Hart Pub.
Arnaud, A.-J. 1995. "Legal Pluralism and the Building of Europe," in Petersen & Zahle 1995
——— 1998. "We are All E.T.s," *Jour. of Leg. Plur.* (41)
———, ed. 1988. *Dictionnaire encyclopédique de théorie et de sociologie du droit*, Paris: LGDJ
———, ed. 1993. Ibid., 2nd ed.
Arbena, J.T., ed. 1988. *Sport and Society in Latin America: Diffusion, Dependency, and the Rise of Mass Culture*, New York: Greenwood Pr.
Baker, W.J., & A. Mangan, eds. 1987. *Sport in Africa: Essays in Social History*, New York: Africa Pub.
Barnes, U. 1983. *Sports and the Law in Canada*, Toronto: Butterworths
Baxi, U. 1986a. "Discipline, Represssion and Legal Pluralism," in Sack & Minchin 1986
——— 1986b. "Peple's Law in India: The Hindu Society," in Chiba 1986
Benedict, R. 1934. *Patterns of Culture*, Boston: Houghton Mifflin
——— 1946. *The Chrysanthemum and Sword: Patterns of Japanese Culture*, Boston: Houghton Mifflin
Berman, H.J. 1983. *Law and Revolution: The Formation of the Western Legal Tradition*, Cambridge: Harvard U.P.
——— 1993. "Tradition juridique occidentale," in Arnaud 1993
Berry, R.C. 1984. *Common Concern in Professional and Amateur Sports*, Chicago: American Bar Assn.
——— & G. Wong 1985. *Law and Business of the Sports Industries*, Dover. Mass.: Auburn

House

Bierbrauer, G. 1994. "Toward an Understanding of Legal Culture: Variations in Individualism and Collectivism between Kurds, Lebanese, and Germans," *Law & Society Rev.* 28 (2)

Blankenburg, E. 1994. "The Infrastructure for Avoiding Civil Litigation: Comparing Cultures of Legal Behavior in the Netherlands and West Germany," *Law & Society Rev.* 28 (4)

—— & J.R.A. Verwoerd 1988. "The Courts as a Final Resort ? : Some Comparisons between the Legal Cultures of the Netherlands and the Federal Republic of Germany," *Netherlands International Law Rev*. 35 (1)

—— & F. Bruinsma 1994. *Dutch Legal Culture*, 2nd ed., Deventer: Kluwer; 1st ed. 1991

Blanpain, R., ed. 1997. *Law in Motion*, The Hague: Kluwer

Botiveau, B. 1998. "Le droit islamique comme ensemble de normes et valeurs, comme savoir et techniques, comme modes de réalization d'une exigence sociale de justice," in Capeller & Kitamura 1998; orig. in Arnaud 1993

Boudahrain, A. 1997. "In Support of an Informal Symbiosis of Islam and the Law," in Blanpain 1997

Brailsford, D. 1991. *Sport, Time, and Society: The British at Play*, London: Routledge

Britt, R.R., & M. Strouse 1995. *Japanese Law in English: An Index to the EHS Law Bulletin Series*, Seattle: U. of Washington Gallaher Law-Library

Burman, S.B., & B.E. Harrell-Bond, eds. 1979. *The Imposition of Law*, London: Academic Pr.

Capeller, W. 1995. *L'engrenage de la répression: stratégies securitaires et politiques criminelles*, Paris: LGDJ

—— & T. Kitamura, eds. 1998. *Une introduction aux cultures jutidiques non occidentales: autour de Masaji Chiba*, Brussels: Bruylant

Carbonnier, J. 1978. *Sociologie juridique*, 3rd ed., Paris: Universitaires de France

Care, J.C. et al., eds. 1999. *Introduction to South Pacific Law*, Sydney: Cavendish Pub.

CFDC = Centre Français de Droit Comparé 1989. *Etudes de Droit Japonais*, Paris: Société de Législation Comparé

Champion, W.T., Jr. 1990. *Fundamentals of Sports Law*, San Fransisco: Bancroft-Witney

Chang, R.T. 1984. *The Justice of Western Consular Courts in Nineteenth Century Japan*, Westport: Greenwood Pr.

Chehata, Ch. 1975. "Islamic Law," in David 1975

Chiba, M. 1962. (in Jap.) *A Socio-Legal Study of School District System: State Power vs Village Community*, Tokyo: Keiso Shobo

—— 1969. (in Jap.) *Modern Anthropology of Law*, Tokyo: Hokubosha

—— 1970. (in Jap.) *A Socio-Legal Study of Shinto Shrine and Its Festival*, Tokyo: Kobundo

—— 1976. "The Search for a Theory of Law: Report of the Symposium on Theory in the Sociology of Law, Hakone, 1975," *Sociologia del diritto* 1976 (1)

—— 1980. (in Jap.) *Law and Conflict*, Tokyo: Sanseido
—— 1989. *Legal Pluralism: Toward a General Theory through Japanese Legal Culture*, Tokyo: Tokai U.P.
—— 1991. (in Jap.) *Frontiers of Legal Culture*, Tokyo: Seibundo
——, ed. 1986. *Asian Indigenous Law: Interaction with Received Law*, London: KPI
——, ed. 1993. *Sociology of Law in Non-Western Countries*, Oñati, Spain: IISL
Coghlan, J.F. 1990. *Sport and British Politics since 1960*, London: The Farmer Pr.
Coing, H., et al. 1990. *Die Japanisierung des Westlichen Rechts*, Tübingen: J.C.B. Moor
Coleman, R., & J.O. Haley, eds. 1975. *An Index to Japanese Law: A Bibliography of Western Language Materials 1867–1973*, Tokyo: U. of Tokyo Pr.
Collomb, P., ed. 1988. *Sport et Décentralisation*, Paris: Economica
Conference = Conference on Moslem Doctrine and Human Right in Islam 1976(?). Riyad: Ministry of Justice
Cooray, J.A.L. 1971. *An Introduction to the Legal System of Ceylon*, Colombo: Lake House Bookshop
Coser, L.A. 1956. *The Function of Social Conflict*, Glencoe, Ill.: The U. of Chicago Pr.
Cottran, E. 1975. "African Law," in David 1975
Crawford, J., ed. 1988. *The Rights of Peoples*, Oxford: Clarendon Pr.
Creemers, W. 1968. *Shinto Shrines after World War II*, Leiden: E.J. Brill
David, R., ed. 1975. *The Legal System of the World: Their Comparison and Unification*, IECL II
—— & J.E. Brierley 1985. *Major Legal Systems in the World Today*, 3rd ed., London: Stevens
Derrett, V.J.D.M., & T.K.K. Iyer 1974. "The Hindu Conception of Law," in David 1975
De Vos, G., & H. Wagatsuma 1966. *Japan's Invisible Race Caste: In Culture and Personality*, Los Angels: U. of California Pr.
Droit et Sport 1984. *Actualité legislative Dalloz: Loi N°s 84–610 du 16 Juillet 1984 et commentaires*, Paris: Dalloz
Dupret, B., et al., eds. 1999. *Legal Pluralism in the Arab World*, The Hague: Kluwer Law Intl.
Ehrmann, H.W. 1976. *Comparative Legal Culture*, Englewood Cliffs, NJ: Prentice-Hall
Ellul, J. 1993. "Culture juridique protestante," in Arnaud 1993
Engel, D. 1984. "The Oven Bird's Songs: Insiders, Outsiders, and Personal Injuries in an American Community," *Law & Society Rev.* 18: 551
Feiermann, J.V. 1994. "The Meiji Reception of Western Law," in V.W. Müller-Freienfels, Herg., *Nomos*, Heft 9
Feest, J., ed. 1999. *Globaization and Legal Cultures: Oñati Summer Course 1997*, Oñati, Spain: IISL
——, & E. Blankenburg, eds. 1997. *Changing Legal Cultures*, Oñati, Spain: IISL
Freed, R.S. 1994. "The Legal Process in a Village in North India: The Case of Maya," repr. in Renteln & Dundes 1994

French, R.R. 1995. *Golden Yoke: The Legal Cosmology of Buddhist Tibet*, Ithaca: Cornell U.P.

Fridell, W. 1073. *Japanese Shrine Merger 1906–1912*, Tokyo: Sophia U.

Friedman, L.M. 1975. *The Legal System: A Social Science Perspective*, New York: Russell Sage Foundation

—— 1989. "Law, Lawyers, and Popular Culture," *The Yale Law Journal* 98: 1579

Galanter, M. 1981. "Justice in Many Rooms," *Jl. of Leg. Plur.* (19)

Gaudemet, J. 1993. "Culture juridique catholique," in Arnaud 1993

Geertz, C. 1983. *Local Knowledge: Further Essays in Interpretive Anthropology*, New York: Basic Books

Gessner, V. 1997. "Teaching Legal Culture," in Feest & Blankenburg 1997.

—— et al., eds. 1996. *European Legal Cultures*, Aldershot: Dartmouth

Gibson, J.L., & G.A. Caldeira 1996. "The Legal Cultures of Europe," *Law & Society Rev.* 30 (1)

Gilissen, J., ed. 1972. *Le pluralisme juridique*, Bruxelles: l' Université de Bruxelles

Gluckman, M. 1955. *The Judicial Process among the Barotse of Northern Rohdesia*, Manchester: Manchester U.P.

—— 1965a. *Politics, Law and Ritual in Tribal Society*, Chicago: Aldine

—— 1965b. *The Ideas in Barotse Jurisprudence*, Manchester: Manchester U.P.; 2nd ed., 1972

Goodman, R., & K. Refsing, eds. 1992. *Ideology and Practice in Modern Japan*, London: Routledge

Grahl-Madsen, A., & J. Tomen, eds. 1984. *The Spirit of Uppsala*, Berlin: Walter de Gruyter

Grayson, E. 1988. *Sports and the Law*, London: Butterworths

Greenhouse, C. 1989. "Temporal and Spatial Dimensions of Legal Pluralism," *Anthropologie et Société* 13

Griffiths, J. 1986. "What is Legal Pluralism," *Jour. of Leg. Plur.* (24)

Gusfield, J.R. 1967. *Symbolic Crusade: Status Politics and the American Temperance Movement*, Urbana: U. of Illinois P.

—— 1981. *The Culture of Public Problems: Drinking-Driving and the Symbolic Order*, Chicago: The U. of Chicago P.

Hahm, P.C. 1969. "The Decision Process in Korea," in G. Schubert & D. Danelski, eds., *Comparative Judicial Behavior: Cross-Cultural Studies of Political Decision Making in the East and West*, New York: Oxford U.P.

Haley, J.O. 1991. *Authority without Power: Law and the Japanese Paradox*, Oxford: Oxford U.P.

Hall, J.C. 1979. *Japanese Feudal Law*: Washington: U. Publications of America

Hamada, T. 1992. "Under the Silk Banner: The Japanese Company and its Overseas Managers," in Lebra 1992

Haraksingh, K. 1993. "English Law and Indians in Trinidad," in Chiba 1993

Hargreaves, J. 1986. *Sport, Power and Culture: A Social and Historical Analysis of Popular Sports in Britain,* Cambridge: Polity Pr.
Harvey, J., & H. Cantelon, eds. 1988. *Not Just a Game: Essays in Canadian Sport Sociology,* Ottawa: U. of Ottawa P.
Hashimoto, K. 1963. "The Role of Law: Some Aspects of Judicial Review of Administrative Action," in von Mehren 1963
Hellum, A. 1995. "Actor Perspective on Gender and Legal Pluralism," in Petersen & Zahle 1995
Henderson, G.F. 1965. *Conciliation and Japanese Law,* Seattle: U. of Washington Pr.
Hladczuk, J., et al., eds. 1991. *Sports Law and Legislation: An Annotated Bibliography,* New York: Greenwood Pr.
Hoebel, E.A. 1954. *The Law of Primitive Man: A Study in Comparative Legal Dynamics,* Cambridge: Harvard U.P.
―― 1972. *Anthropology: The Study of Man,* New York: McGraw-Hill
Hooker, M.B. 1975. *Legal Pluralism: An Introduction to Colonial and Neo-Colonial Laws,* Oxford: Clarendon Pr.
Howell, R.C. 1994. "The Otieno Case: African Customary Law Versus Western Jurisprudence," repr. in Renteln & Dundes 1994
Howman, R. 1994. "Witchcraft and the Law," repr. in Renteln & Dundes 1994
Hsu, F.L.K. 1975. *Iemoto: The Heart of Japan,* Cambridge: Schenkman
Igarashi, K. 1990. *Einfürung in das japanischen Recht,* Darmstadt: Wissenschaftliche Buchgesellschaft
IECL = International Encyclopedia of Camparative Law 1975–. Tübingen: J.C.B. Moor & The Hague: Mouton
IISL = International Institute for the Sociology of Law 1991. *30 Years for the Sociology of Law,* Oñati: IISL
International Legal Center 1974. *Law and Development: The Future of Law and Development,* New York: ILC
Ishii, R. 1980. *A History of Political Institution in Japan,* Tokyo: U. of Tokyo Pr.
Ishii, Y. 1998. "Tradition juridique bouddhique," in Capeller & Kitamura 1998; orig. in Arnaud 1993,
Ji, W. 1993. "The Chinese Experience: A Great Treasure House for the Sociology of Law," in Chiba 1993
Johnson, A.T., & J.H. Frey, eds. 1985. *Government and Sport: The Public Policy Issues,* Tonowa, NJ: Borman & Allanhead
Johnston, F.A. 1993. *Dependency and Japanese Socialization: Psychoanalytic and Anthropological Investigation into Amae,* New York: New York U.P.
Jones, S.G. 1988. *Sport, Politics and the Working Class,* Manchester: Manchester U.P.
Jørgensen, S. 1982. "Pluralis Juris: Toward a Realistic Theory of Law," *Acta Jutlandica* 96, Soc. Sci. Ser. 14
Kato, M. 1995. (in Jap.) "Development of the Conception of Property," *Jurist* (1069–

1078)

Kawashima, T. 1963. "Dispute Resolution in Contemporary Japan," in von Mehren 1963

―― 1967. (in Jap.) *Japanese Consciousness of Law*, Tokyo: Iwanami Shoten

Khadduri, M. 1984. "Human Rights in Islam," in id., *The Islamic Conception of Justice*, Baltimore: Johns Hopkins U.P.

―― 1998. "Le droit islamique dans la culture: la structure du style de vie islamique," in Capellr & Kitamura 1998; orig. in Arnaud 1993

Kidder, R. 1993. "Ideological Functions of Culture in the Study of Asian Legal System," in Chiba 1993

Kludze, A.K.P. 1998. "La proprieté dans les sociétés africaines," in Capeller & Kitamura 1998: orig. in Arnaud 1993

Krähe, Ch., Herg. 1987. *Wassersport auf Binnengewässern und Bodensee, Recht und Sport* 8, Heidelberg: C.F. Müller

Lebra, T.S. 1976. *Japanese Patterns of Behavior*, Honolulu: U. of Hawaii Pr.

――, ed. 1992. *Japanese Social Organization*, Honolulu: U. of Hawaii Pr.

Lu, D.J. 1974. *Sources of Japanese History*, 2 vols., New York: McGraw-Hill

Luhmann, N. 1987. Rechtssoziologie, 3rd ed., Opladen: Westdeutscher Verlag

Macaulay, S. 1989. "Popular Legal Culture: An Introduction." *Yale Law Jour*. 98: 1545

Maine, H.S. 1954. *Ancient Law*, Everyman's Library, orig. 1861

Maison du Japon 1991. *Boissonade et la Reception du Droit Français au japon*; Paris: Société de Législation Comparé

Malatos, A. 1988. *Berufsfussball in europäischen Rechtsvergleich*, Kehl: N.P. Engel

Malinowski, B.K. 1926. *Crime and Custom in Savage Society*, London: Routledge & Kegan Paul

Mandell, R.D. 1984. *Sport: A Cultural History*, New York: Colombia U.P.

Marasinghe, M.L. 1993. "Law, Custom, and Society," in Chiba 1993

―― & W.E. Conklin, eds. 1984. *Essays on Third World Perspectives in Jurisprudence*, Singapore: Malayan Law Jour.

Matsukawa, H. 1991. *La famille et droit au japon*, Paris: Economica

M'baye, K. 1975. "The African Conception of Law," in David 1975

Menkhaus, H., ed. 1994. *Das Japanische in Japanischen Recht*, München: Indicium

Menski, W.F. 2000. *Comparative Law in a Global Context: The Legal Systems of Asia and Africa*, London: Platinium

Merry, S.E. 1988. "Legal Pluralism," *Law & Society Rev*. 22 (5)

Mommsen, W.J., & J.A. de Moore, eds. 1992. *European Expansion and Law*, Cambridge: Harvard U.P.

Moore, S.F. 1978. *Law as Process: An Anthropological Approach*, London: Routledge & Kegan Paul

Morioka, K. 1970. "The Impact of Suburbanization on Shinto Belief and Behavior," *Social Compass* 17

Morse, R.W., & G.R. Woodman, eds. 1988. *Indigenous Law and the State*, Dordrecht: Foris Pub.

Murakami, J. 1974. *Einführung in die Grundlagen des Japanischen Recht*, Darmstadt Wissenschaftliche Buchgesellschaft

Nadaraja, T. 1972. *The Legal System of Ceylon in Its Historical Setting*, Leiden: E.J. Brill

Nafziger, L.A.R. 1988. *International Sports Law*, Dobbs Ferry: Transactional Publishers

Narokobi, B. 1986. "In Search of a Melanesian Jurisprudence," in Sack & Minchin 1986

Nelken, D. 1995. "Disclosing/Invoking Legal Culture: An Introduction," *Social & Legal Studies* 4

——, ed. 1997. *Comparing Legal Cultures*, Aldershot: Dartmouth

—— & J. Feest, eds. 2001. *Adapting Legal Cultures*, Oxford: Hart Pub.

Nezami Talesh, M.A. 1986. "Modern Law and Judiciary Reform in Iran," in Chiba 1986

Noda, Y. 1975. "The Far Eastern Conception of Law," in David 1975

—— 1976. *Introduction to Japanese Law*, Tokyo: U. of Tokyo Pr.

Oda, Y. 1992. *Japanese Law*, London: Butterworths

Ohnuki-Tienney, E. 1984. *Illness and Culture in Contemporary Japan: An Anthropological View*, Cambridge: Cambridge U.P.

Panikkar, R. 1992. "Is the Notion of Human Rights a Western Concept?," repr. in Sack & Aleck 1992

Pérez Perdomo, R. 1993. "Western and Non-Western: Themes of Latin American Sociology of Law," in Chiba 1993

Petersen, H. 1996. *Knitted Law: Norms and Values in Gendered Rule-Making*, Aldershot: Dartmouth

—— & H. Zahle, eds. 1995. *Legal Polycentricity: Consequences of Pluralism in Law*, Aldershot: Dartmouth

Podgorecki, A. 1974. *Law and Society*, London: Routledge & Kegan Paul

—— et al. 1973. *Knowledge and Opinion about Law*, London: Martin Robertson

Port, K.L. 1996. *Comparative Law: Law and the Legal Process in Japan*, Durham: Varolina Academic Pr.

Recht und Sport 1984–. Bde. 1–, Heidelberg: C.F. Müller, later Stuttgart: Borberg

Renteln, A.D. 1988. "Relativism and the Search for Human Rights," *American Anthropologist* 90 (1)

—— 1990. *International Human Rights: Universal Versus Relativism*, Newbury Park, CA: Sage Pub.

—— 1992. "Culture and Culpability: A Study of Contrasts," repr. in Sack & Aleck 1992; orig. 1989

—— 1994a. "Is the Cultural Defense Detrimental to the Health of Children?", *Law and Anthroplogy* 7

—— 1994b. "A Justification of the Cultural Defense as Partial Excuse," *Rev. of Law and Women's Studies* 2

—— & A. Dundes, eds. 1994. *Folk Law: Essays in the Theory and Practice of Lex Non Scripta*, 2 vols., New York: Garland

Rheinstein, M. 1967. *Max Weber on Law in Economy and Society*, New York: Simon & Schuster

Riles, A., ed. 2001. *Rethinking the Masters of Comparative Law*, Oxford & Portland, Oregon: Hart Publishing

Roberts, S. 1998. "Nature de l'ordre juridique en Afrique," in Capeller & Kitamura 1998: orig. in Arnaud 1993

Röhl, W. 1994. "Rechtsgeschichtliches zu Jori," in Menkhaus 1994

Rosen, K. 1992. "The Jeito: Brasil's Institutional Bypass of the Formal System and Its Developmental Implications," repr. in Varga 1992

Rouland, N. 1988. *Anthropologie juridique*, Paris: PUF

—— 1990. *L'anthropologie juridique*, Que sais-ji?, No. 2528, Paris: PUF

—— et al. 1996. *Droit des minorites des peuples autochtones*, Paris: PUF

Sack. P. 1998a. "Perspectives occidentales et non-occidentales du droit" in Capeller & Kitamura 1998; orig. in Arnaud 1993

—— 1998b. "Culture juridique en Océanie," in Capeller & Kitamura 1998; orig. in Arnaud 1993

—— 2001. *Phantom History, the Rule of Law, and the Colonial State: The Case of German New Guinea* Canberra: Div. of Pac. and Asian His., RSSS, Aust. Nat. U.

——, ed. 1982. *Pacific Constitutions: Proceedings of the Canberra Law Workshop VI*, Law Dept., RSSS, Aust. Nat. U.

—— & E. Minchin, eds. 1986. *Legal Pluralism: Proceedings of the Canberra Law Workshop VII*, Law Dept., RSSS, Aust. Nat. U.

—— & J. Aleck, eds. 1992. *Law and Anthropology*, Aldrshot: Dartmouth

Sheer, M.K. 1993. *Japanese Law in Western Languages 1974–1989: A Bibliography*, Hamburg: Deutsch-Japanischen Juristenvereiniung

Scholler, H., Herg. 1993. *Die Entwicklung der Rezeption westlichen Rechts auf die sozialen Verhältnisse in der fernostlichen Rechtskultur*, Baden-Baden: Nomos

Snyder, F.E. 1985. *Latin American Society and Culture: A Bibliography*, Westport: Greenwood Pr.

Sonoda, M. 1975. "The Traditional Festival in Urban Society," *Transactions of the Institute for Japanese Culture and Classics of Kokugakuin University* (35)

Sports and the Courts: Physical Education and Sports Law Newsletter 1980–. Winston-Salem, NJ: Sports and the Courts, Inc.

Steenstrup, C. 1991. *A History of Law in Japan until 1868*, Leiden: E.J. Brill

Takayanagi, K. 1963. "A Century of Innovation: The Development of Japanese Law, 1868–1961," in von Mehren 1963

Tamanaha, B. 1993. *Understanding Law in Micronesia: An Interpretive Approach to Transplanted Law*, Leiden: E.J. Brill

Tambiah, F.W. 1950. *The Laws and Customs of the Tamils of Jaffna*, Colombo: Times of Ceylon

—— 1968. *Sinhala Laws and Customs*, Colombo: Lake House Investment

―― 1972. *Principles of Ceylon Law*, Colombo: F.W. Cave
Tan, P.-L., ed. 1997. *East Asian Legal Systems: Law, Society and Pluralism in East Asia*, Sydney: Butterworths
Tanaka, H. 1976. *The Japanese Legal System: Introductory Cases and Materials*, Tokyo: U. of Tokyo Pr.
Tay, A.E.-S. 1998. "Culture juridique chinoise," in Capellre & Kitamura 1998; orig. in Arnaud 1993
Tie, W. 1999. *Legal Pluralism: Toward a Multicultural Conception of Law*, Aldershot: Ashgate
Tiruchelvam, N. 1986. "Comparing Ideologies of Conflict Resolution in Sri Lanka," in Chiba 1986
―― & R. Coomaraswami, eds. 1987. *The Role of the Judiciary in Plural Societies*, London: Francis Printer
Uberstine, G.A. 1985. *Covering All the Bases: A Complihensive Research Guide to Sports Law*, Buffalo: William S. Helm
UN 1992 = E/CN. 4/Sub. 2/1992/37. "Protection of Minorities: Possible Ways and Means of Facilitating the Peaceful and Constructive Solution of Problems involving Minorities," Comn. of Human Rights of ECOSOC
Upham, F.K. 1987. *Law and Social Change in Postwar Japan*, Cambridge: Harvard U.P.
Van den Bergh, G.C.J.J. 1993. "Réception du droit," in Arnaud 1993
Vanderlinden, J. 1972. "Le pluralisme juridique: essay de synthése," in Gilissen 1972
――1989. "Return to Legal Pluralism: Twenty Years Later," *Jour. of Leg. Plur*. (28)
van Vollenhoven, C. 1994. "Aspect of the Controversy on Customary Law in India," repr. in Renteln & Dundes 1994.
Varga, C., ed. 1992. *Comparative Legal Cultures*, Aldershot: Dartmouth
Verma, A. 1997. "The Experience in India," in Blanpain 1997
Vinokur, M.B. 1988. *More than a Game: Sports and Politics*, Westport: Greenwood Pr.
von Benda-Beckmann, F. 1992, "Symbiosis of Indigenous and Western Law in Africa and Asia: An Essay in Legal Pluralism," in Mommsen & de Moore 1992
―― et al., eds. 1988. *Between Kinship and the State: Social Security and Law in Developing Countries*, Dordrecht: Foris Pub.
von Mehren, A.T., ed. 1963. *Law in Japan: The Legal Order in a Changing Society*, Cambridge: Harvard U.P.
Watanabe, Y. 1963. "The Family and the Law: The Individualistic Premise and Modern Japanese Family Law," in von Mehren 1963
Weisemann, U. 1983. *Sport, Spiel und Recht*, München: C.H. Beck
Weistart, J.C., & C.H. Lowell 1979. *The Law of Sports*, Charlottesville, Va: Bobbs-Merrill
Wigmore, J.H., ed. 1967-86. *Law and Justice in Tokugawa Japan*, 10 Parts in 21 books, repr. by U. of Tokyo Pr., Tokyo.
Will, M.R., Herg. 1988. *Sport und Recht in Europa: Kolloquium*, Saarbrücken: Europa-Institut der Universität des Saarbrücken

―, Herg. 1993. *Sportrecht in Europa, Recht und Sport* 11, Heidellberg: C.F. Müller
Williams, R.F. 1997. "Comparative State Constitutional Law: A Research Agenda on Subnational Constitutions in Federal Systems," in Blanpain 1997
Woodman, G.R. 1992. "Book Review: Masaji Chiba, *Legal Pluralism,*" *Jour. of Leg. Plur.* (32)
―― 1993a. "Folk Law," in Arnaud 1993
―― 1993b. "Non-State, Ubounded, Unsystematic, Non-western Law," in Chiba 1993
―― 1994. "Some Realism About Customary Law: The West African Experience,"repr. in Renteln & Dundes 1994
Yasuda, N. 1995. "The Evolution of the East Asian Law Region," in K. Kroeschell & A. Cordes, Herg., *Vom nationalen zum transnationalen Recht*, Heidelberg: C.F. Müller

Subject Index

A

acculturation	18, 235
adat law	142, 143
Afganistan	84–5
Africa	79–80, 142, 151, 162, 173, 210, 310
agricultural law	74
amoeba-like situationism	54–5, 240
Anglo-American law	225
Anglo-Muhammadan law	83
anthropology (of law)	99–102, 112, 141, 145, 238
anticipation complex	167
attitudes toward the law	245, 254–60
Australia	101, 118
Aztéques	120

B

Bakufu Law	29
Balkan	143
Bangladesh	83–4
Bedouin	143
Berber	143
biblical and cuneiform law	143
Brésil	120
Britain	150, 158–9
British colonies	144
Buddhist law	70–3
Buke Law	29–30

C

Cambodge	118
Canada	101, 151
Central Asia	237
China	33–4, 80–1, 162, 189–90
Chinese law	24–5, 240–1
challenge-absorbing mechanism	167
challenge-rejecting mechanism	167–8
clan law	21–2
Code of Manu	70, 124, 125
common law	70, 142
community solidarity	31–2, 49–50
communal law	30, 42, 49, 241
conceptual definity	261
conceptual elasficity	261–2
conceptual indefiniteness	262
Conciliation Board	71
conflict	199–200, 219–22
conflict theory	108–9, 168–9
contract	218
court law	21–3
Court Law	23, 40, 45
crime	245–6
criminal	249
criminal justice	245–6
criminal Law	259–60
criminal punishment	249, 256
culture juridique (régionale)	107–13, 114–26, 128, 131–5
— africain	114, 122
— buddhist	125
— chinois	115–6, 125–6
— de l' Asie centrale	121, 128–9, 133
— de l' Asie du sud-est	119, 133
— d' Extréme-Orient	115–7
— du buddisme Theravada	118–9, 125
— du Nord	121, 128
— hindu	114
— indienne	123–5
— islamique	117, 122–3
— latin-americain	120–1
— non-occidental	128–30
— occidental	130–2
— océanique	117–8, 126
custom	263–4
customary law	142

D

death penalty	246–7
deliniative definition	232–3
Dharma	123–4
dozoku	59
droi	112, 135
— dans la objectivité	127

Subject Index

— dans la subjectivité 127
— étatique 128–9
— indigène 128
— non-occidental 91–7, 104–6, 110–1
— non-officiel 128–9
— occidental 105, 110
— officiel 128–9
— socialiste 137
— transplanté 127
dual structure 12–4, 185

E

English law 142, 143–4
entité socio-juridique 127–8
Ethiopia 114, 160, 162
Ethnological jurisprudence 142
Europe 142, 143, 151
euthanasia 253–4
exception to general principle 60

F

famille juridique 114
folk law 7, 73, 141–7
France 144, 151, 159, 241
freedom of each party 270
functional complement
 173, 178, 225–6, 227–8, 267–70

G

Genroku era 35–6
Germany 151, 159
German-speaking people 142, 143
Ghana 142
Greek 143
guilt and fines 249

H

Han Law 29
Hindu law 70, 72
Holland 144
human rights 202–4, 209–14, 271–2

I

identity postulate 19–20, 77, 221, 236, 241
iemoto law 52, 177
immigrants 140, 144, 145, 237

immunity doctrine 156–7
Imperial Rescript on Education 43–4
imposed law 18, 235
imposition 18, 134
Inca 120
India
 33, 83, 100, 142, 144, 210, 219, 237, 240–1
indigenous law
 15, 18, 76–7, 51–2, 211, 235, 241
individual rights 260
 African conception of —
 261–2, 263–5, 267–8
 Japanese conception of —
 262, 265–7, 268–9
 Western conception of — 260–1, 269–70
Indo-China 80
Indonesia 81–2, 119
intermediate concept 213, 223
intermediate variable 213–4, 223–9
International custom 145
International Institute for the Sociology
 of Law 1, 8, 241
International Third World Legal Studies
 Association 93
ISA Research Committee on Sociology
 of Law 1, 4, 8, 77, 165, 214, 259, 271
Islamic law 70, 72, 79–87, 101, 184, 211, 241
 — in Africa 80
 — in Asia 80
 home of — 79–80
Italy 138
IUAES Commission on Folk Law and
 Legal Pluralism 93, 108, 199

J, K

Japan 80, 99, 100, 151, 113, 158, 165
 172–3, 178, 187–8, 238–40
kami 22, 54
Kandyan law 70
Kebiishi 28
Kenya 143, 144, 160, 162
KOL 269, 271
Korea 22, 26, 34, 80, 124, 188–90, 240
Kuge Law 28–9

L

Laos	118
Latin America	51, 151, 159, 162, 210
law	17–20, 181–2, 193–5, 200–2, 234–7
— in objectivity	175, 191
— in subjectivity	175–7, 191–3
legal ambivalence	175–7
legal culture	15–6, 20, 169, 196, 237
legal education in Japan	38
legal pluralism	6–8, 12–5, 26, 63
	170–2, 175–7, 179–81, 196, 236–7
— in conflict	173–4, 181–2, 186–90
analytical variables of —	174–5
normative ambivalence under —	175–6
legal postulate	19, 23, 27, 49, 235
— outside of the law	25, 33, 43–4, 239–40
legal rule	18–9, 235
legal symbolism	143, 145
legal tradition	15
life imprisonment	246

M

Malaysia	82, 143
marriage by capture	220
Meiji Legal System	39, 44
merciful death	219
Mexico	101
Middle and Eastern Europe	101
minor law	12–4
modern law	149–50, 227–8
murder	225
Myanmar (Burma)	100, 118

N

national isolation	34–5
Near and Middle East	74
Népal	125
New Zealand	118
Nigeria	142–3
non-occidental	91, 104–5, 113
non-Western law	25–8, 63–6

O

occidental	104–5
Oceania	210
official law	17–8, 230
Olympic Games	151, 158, 161, 162
operational definition	16–7, 231–5
oral ordeal	143
Otieno case	144

P

Pakistan	83–4
Panchayat	71
Papua New Guinea	100, 210, 219, 237
particular relationships between the parties	269
patriarchal family	41–2, 45–6
Philippines	81, 100, 119, 144
pluralisme juridique	108–9
postulat de identité	112, 128–9
postulat juridique	113, 128, 136
pre-Hammurapi code	143
primitive law	64, 262–3
Prince Shotoku	23
property	218, 225
public opiniun research	245

R

received law	18, 235
reception	18
recéption	134
refugees	145, 237
régles juridiqes	128
rehabilitation of ex-convicts	256
religious law	157, 164, 237
restatement	142, 221
ritsuryo	24
Ritsuryo System	24–5, 28
Roman customary iaw	142
Roman-Dutch law	70
Russia	142
Ryoge-no-kan	28

S

Saudi Arabia	197
Seventeen Articles of Constitution	23, 25
Shah Bano case	83
Shaji Law	28
Shoen Law	28
Showa Legal System	44–9

shrine law 41, 45, 501
soual status of the parties 264-5, 267-8
socialist countries 159, 162
socio-legal entity 13-4, 188, 234
sociology of law 3-8
sorcery 214
South Africa 143
South East Asia 237
Spain 165
sports law 150-4
  international — 161-5
  specific — 153-4, 155-7, 160-4
  state — 152-5
Sri Lanka 69-77, 84, 100, 118
state law 13, 17, 234
  — monism 6, 13, 168, 200-1
statistical opinin survey 259
status hierarchy 30, 32, 42
suicide 220

T

tank irrigation 73-4
tatemae and/or *honnne* 33-4, 46, 55
Tesavalamai 70
Thiland 73, 82, 100, 118, 143
Third World countries 160
three dichotoies of law 17-20, 75-7, 193-5
three-level structure of law 68-9
Tibet 124-5, 137, 143
transplantation (of law)
  18, 53-4, 70-2, 116-7, 133-5, 164-5, 235
transplanted law 18, 76-7, 255
trans-state law 185-6, 197
tribal law 64
Trinidad 146, 218
tripartite model of law 242
triple structure of law 14, 186
troits dichotomies de droit 113, 128-9
true intention or formal excuse 48
Tswana 142
Turkey 85

U, V

Uganda 100
United Nations 211-2
University of Tokyo 38

unofficial law 17-8, 75-7, 235
unwritten law in Europe 142
USA 101, 140, 144, 145, 150, 159, 190, 219-20
Vietnam 100

W, Z

wa 23, 30, 41, 54
Western jurisprudence 63
Western law 33, 36-7
  — universalism 200-1
witchcraft 144, 217, 224, 225
women 45, 74
world law 14, 234
Zimbabwe 144, 217

Name Index

A

Aikyou	100
Akbar	210
Ali	142
Allott	142, 220–1
Arnaud	1–3, 8, 86, 135, 186
Austin	93

B

Bailey	143
Baltl	143
Bambridge	242
Barton	144
Baxi	215
Benedict	16, 112, 238
Benson	145
Bernhardt	145
Bierbrauer	233
Blankenburg	15, 111, 231, 233
Bock	143
Boisonade	37, 38, 41
Botiveau	122, 135
Brewster	143

C

Carbonnier	3
Chamberlain	143
Conklin	193
Cotran	143

D

Danilenko	145
Danquah	142
Dumber	145

E

Ehrlich	1, 7
Elias	142, 261, 263, 264
Elphinstone	220
Epstein	144
Erickson	145

Evan	3
Evans-Prtchard	95, 263, 271

F

Farnsworth	144
Freed	144
Friedman	235, 238
Friedrich	154

G

Geertz	54, 177, 238
Gény	145
Gessner	231
Gierke	59
Glastra van Loon	2
Gluckman	75, 96, 99, 261, 264
Goetz	143
Gordon	143
Green	144
Griffiths	193
Gusfield	146

H

Hagiwara	86
Hasegawa	101
Hartog	144
Hayashi	255, 257, 265, 271
Hazard	143
Hoebel	58, 95, 99, 112, 136, 234, 269
Holleman	144
Howell	144
Howman	144

I

Iida	86, 100
Ishii	86, 125

J

Jain	142
Jørgensen	196
Josselan de Jong	142

K

Kaneshiro	101
Kant	16–7, 232
Kato	218
Kawashima	262–3, 265–7
Kelsen	93, 224
Khadduri	122, 211
Kidder	29, 221
Kitakamae	99, 100
Kitamura	99
Kludze	122
Kobayashi, M.	87
Kobayashi, Y.	86
Kohler	95
Koike	143
Kojder	101
Kojima	86
Kollewijn	144
Kotani	138
Krstic	143
Kurcherov	142
Kutchinsky	259, 271

L

Levy	143
Llewellyn	269
Luhmann	167, 177

M

Macaulay	238
Maeda	99
Maine	95, 167, 177, 220, 264
Malinowski	95, 99, 263, 271
Marasinghe	193
Markovitz	191
Menski	242
Merry	191, 193
Messinger, Jr.	143
Mill	37
Minattur	140
Miyamoto	100
Miyazawa	99
Morgan	95
Mori, M.	86
Mori, T.	99

N

Nadel	263
Nafziger	161–4
Nagarathan	145
Nakamura	78
Narita	100
Narokobi	210
Ndulo	142
Nelken	231

O

Ohashi	101
Okudaira	100
Okuyama	78, 87, 99, 100
Ollennu	142
Omori	76, 100
Otsuka	99

P

Panikkar	210–2, 222
Petersen	191–2
Podgorecki	3, 154, 259
Post	95

R

Radcliffe-Brown	99
Reik	143
Renteln	144, 212, 222–3, 233
Roberts	122, 142
Rösler	37
Rouland	97, 102
Rousseau	37, 38
Rosas	145

S

Sack	126, 127, 182, 186, 222
Samuels	144
Sarbah	142
Schiller	142
Schneebaum	145
Schott	142
Seidman	144
Simpson	142
Sinitsina	142
Strijbosch	142

Sugimoto	78, 100
Sugita	101
Sumner	268
Suzuki, K.	86
Suzuki, Y.	78, 99, 101

T

Talbot	264
Tan	196, 197, 242
Tanaka	87
Tárkány-Szücs	142, 146
Taniguchi	78
Tay	125, 196
Thurnwald	95
Tönnies	78
Tiruchelvam	77
Treves	3

U

Ueda	101
Unsworth	144

V

Van den Bergh	141
van Houtte	2
Vanderlinden	173, 182, 191, 193
van Vollenhoven	142, 226
Vereschetin	145

W

Watson	142
Wazaki	99
Weber	142, 234
Westbrook	143
Westermarck	143
Woodman	142, 221, 225

Y

Yamada	78
Yasuda	78, 87
Yilmaz	242
Yuasa	78, 86, 87, 100, 101
Yü Li	143

信山社

記念論文集の一部
執筆は総目録参照

大木雅夫先生古稀記念 滝沢正編集代表 14,800円
比較法学の課題と展望
西原道雄先生古稀記念 佐藤進・齋藤修編集代表
上巻16,000円 下巻予価16,000円 近刊
現代民事法学の理論
品川孝次先生古稀記念 須田晟雄・辻伸行編
民法解釈学の展開 17,800円
中澤巷一先生還暦 京都大学日本法史研究会 8,240円
法と国制の史的考察
栗城壽夫先生古稀記念 樋口陽一・上村貞美・戸波江二編
新日独憲法学の展開（仮題）続刊
田島裕教授記念 矢崎幸生編集代表 15,000円
現代先端法学の展開
菅野喜八郎先生古稀記念
新正幸・早坂禮子・赤坂正浩編 13,000円
公法の思想と制度
清水睦先生古稀記念 植野妙実子編 12,000円
現代国家の憲法的考
石村善治先生 **法と情報** 15,000円
古稀記念
山村恒年先生古稀記念 13,000円
環境法学の生成と未来
林良平・甲斐道太郎編集代表（全3巻）58,058円
谷口知平先生追悼論文集 I II III
五十嵐清・山畠正男・藪重夫先生記念 39,300円
民法学と比較法学の諸相 上中下
高祥龍先生還暦記念 近刊
21世紀の日韓民事法学
広瀬健二・多田辰也編 上巻12,000円下巻予価15,000円続刊
田宮裕博士追悼論集
筑波大学企業法学創設10周年記念 18,000円
現代企業法学の研究
菅原菊志先生古稀記念 平出慶道・小島康裕・庄子良男編 20,000円
現代企業法の理論

五十嵐清著 8,600円
現代比較法学の諸相
石黒一憲著 2,800円
国際摩擦と法
重松一義著 3,200円
少年法の思想と発展

平出慶道先生・髙窪利一先生古稀記念 上下各5,000円
現代企業・金融法の課題
小島康裕教授退官記念泉田栄一・関英昭・藤田勝利編12,000円
現代企業法の新展開
酒巻俊雄・志村治美編 中村真澄古稀 15,000円
現代会社法の理論
佐々木吉男先生追悼論集 22,000円
民事紛争の解決と手続
白川和雄先生古稀記念 15,000円
民事紛争をめぐる法的諸問題
内田久司先生古稀記念 栁原正治編 14,000円
国際社会の組織化と法
山口浩一郎・渡辺章・菅野和夫・中嶋士元也編
花見忠先生古稀記念 15,000円
労働関係法の国際的潮流
本間崇先生還暦記念中山信弘・小島武司編 8,544円
知的財産権の現代的課題
牧野利明判事退官記念 中山信弘編 18,000円
知的財産法と現代社会
成城学園100年・法学部10周年記念 16,000円
21世紀を展望する法学と政治学
塙浩著作集
（全19巻）1,161,000円 第20巻編集中
小山昇著作集
（全13巻+別巻2冊）257,282円
小室直人著
民事訴訟法論集
上9,800円・中12,000円・下9,800円
外尾健一著作集
（全8巻）刊行中
蓼沼謙一著作集（全5巻）近刊
佐藤進著作集（全13巻）刊行中
内田力蔵著作集（全11巻）
来栖三郎著作集（全3巻）続刊
椿寿夫著作集（全11巻）続刊
民法研究3号／国際人権13号／国際私法年報3号／民事訴訟法研究 *創刊*

梅本吉彦著 5,800円
民事訴訟法
板寺一太郎著 12,000円
外国法文献の調べ方
梅謙次郎著 50,000円
[DE LA TRANSACTION]（仏文）
和 解 論